Dancing Bahia

Dancing Bahia

Essays on Afro-Brazilian Dance, Education, Memory, and Race

Edited by
Lucía M. Suárez, Amélia Conrado, and Yvonne Daniel

intellect Bristol, UK / Chicago, USA

First published in the UK in 2018 by
Intellect, The Mill, Parnall Road, Fishponds, Bristol, BS16 3JG, UK

First published in the USA in 2018 by
Intellect, The University of Chicago Press, 1427 E. 60th Street,
Chicago, IL 60637, USA

A catalogue record for this book is available from the
British Library.

Cover image: Photograph by and courtesy of Leonardo Pastor;
from "Encruzilhada" performed by Igor Costa, in *Maria Meia Noite*,
choreographed by Amélia Conrado, Bahia, Brazil, 2014.

Inside front cover image: Photograph by and courtesy of Leonardo
Pastor; dancer, Lucimar Cerqueira Souza, in *Maria Meia Noite*,
choreographed by Amélia Conrado, Bahia, Brazil, 2014.

Inside back cover image: Photograph by Ivan Kashinsky, courtesy of
Viver Brasil; *Revealed*, choreographed by Shelby Williams-Gonzalez,
dancer, Rachel Hernandez.

Copy-editor: MPS Technologies
Cover designer: Aleksandra Szumlas
Production manager: Naomi Curston
Typesetting: Contentra Technologies

Print ISBN: 978-1-78320-880-7
ePDF ISBN: 978-1-78320-882-1
ePUB ISBN: 978-1-78320-881-4

Printed and bound by TJ International, UK

Contents

List of Illustrations

Foreword

I could barely contain the thrill and excitement, but also a niggling apprehension, as I waited for the bus that would take me to my first *bloco afro* rehearsal, this time not as a spectator as I had been previously, but as an actual participant! My dear friend and gifted dancer Sel Guanaes was already inside the bus waving smilingly at me through the window as it halted making its usual hissing sound. We had agreed to catch the same *buzu* (the Bahian slang for buses) since Sel lived in Brotas and thus several stops before Luis Anselmo, where I would hop on and join her. It was about 6 p.m. on a January weekday and the streets were packed with people making their way home from work as the day's heat gave way to the evening breeze. Enjoying our break from college, we could indulge in making that summer of our lives revolve around the preparation for *carnaval*. We had "jumped *carnaval*" many times before in our home city of Salvador, always as "*foliãs pipocas*," the "popcorn revelers" that hop freely from *trio* to *trio* and from *bloco* to *bloco*, no strings attached, no rehearsals needed. The year of 1992 would be different, though, as we were given the opportunity to participate as dancers in none other than the *bloco afro* Muzenza, attending the rehearsals led by none greater than the revered choreographer Augusto de Omolú!

Located in the neighborhood of Liberdade, Muzenza is one of the several *blocos afro* that emerged in Salvador in the 1970s with the goal of carving out spaces for the recognition and acceptance of blackness in the racist and classist sphere of Bahian *carnaval*. Muzenza itself was founded in 1981, strongly inspired by the philosophy and aesthetics of Rastafarianism, and contributing, in turn, to reinventing Bahia's blackness by exploring diasporic routes while revisiting African roots. This resignification of blackness as positive and beautiful, which promoted, among other processes, the blackening of the body through movement and aesthetics, relied on Afro-Bahian dance as one of its central pillars. Dance and music have powerfully produced pleasure, pride, dignity, and the sense of belongingness to something bigger. During those rehearsal evenings, as our sweaty bodies swayed in unison responding to the call of the drums, my initial unease as to whether I would be able to follow the dance movements that I so deeply appreciated morphed into a collective exhilaration that set in motion all the senses of our bodies and souls.

Yet, Afro-Bahian dance makes itself present way beyond the time period or designated spaces of *carnaval*. And although in some locations of Salvador it might be more markedly visible in specific seasons of the year, in other parts of the city it is practiced all year round, and by people of different ages, genders, and racial and class backgrounds. Like other dance forms, Afro-Bahian dance defies containment within rigid boundaries as it is constantly taking on new forms and redefining itself, but without letting go of its links to its multiple African origins, the transatlantic slave past and the contemporary Brazilian present. And whether it is danced in Bahia or elsewhere around the globe, Afro-Bahian dance is necessarily associated with some version of *baianidade*, or *Bahianness*. This might mean the stereotypical images of the joyful, colorful, and tropical location, so often disseminated by the tourism industry. But it may also entail a means of expressing black pride, love for one's body, support for one's community, and the still necessary claim that "Black Lives Matter" in this city whose public image paradoxically revolves around black bodies dancing, performing, and playing *capoeira*. Bahia is, after all, Brazil's most African state. Not only does it "export" black culture to other regions of the country; it is globally recognized as one of the centers of the Black Atlantic.

Afro-Bahian dance is a central component of the lives of many people in Bahia and beyond, thus my enthusiasm for this beautifully organized and well thought out book. This is the first edited volume to focus on Afro-Bahian dance. The authors represent a multiplicity of voices: they are scholars, dancers, activists, and educators from across the Americas, including the United States, Canada, Colombia, and different cities of Brazil. The essays enmesh theory and practical and personal experience in a finely balanced dose, while also including historical overviews and proposing new paradigms for the study of dance. This collection engages with the multifaceted meanings and dimensions of Afro-Bahian dance, examining it as a source of history, memory, and tradition, but also assessing its dynamic role in creating social and cultural change. Afro-Bahian dance has increasingly been deployed as an educational resource and political tool, and it has been a central element in processes of self-esteem elevation and racial consciousness raising. This book shows that, while grounded on a past that it is constantly reinventing, Afro-Bahian dance transforms the present and creates new possibilities for the future.

The topics examined in this book cover a wide range of important issues, including the deployment of Afro-Bahian dance in black activism; the uses of old and new technologies for the teaching of dance, from the more conventional classes in studios to the use of YouTube videos; the establishment of *samba de roda* as intangible heritage; the complex relations between tourism and Afro-Bahian culture; and the role of dancers as cultural and political agents. Some essays highlight the important and often overlooked work of Afro-Bahian dancers, choreographers, and educators who have significantly contributed to the promotion, validation, and recognition of Afro-Bahian dance as well as black culture more broadly. Other essays analyze the inclusion of Afro-Bahian dance in the enactment of relatively recent laws that mandate the inclusion of "Afro-Brazilian history and culture" in the school curriculum. Many teachers have approached these laws as opportunities for a deeper engagement of the body in their (non-dance) classes and academic teaching routines, thus challenging the Eurocentric mind-body divide. Aligned with the insight of these educators, the essays in this book take seriously the body as a locus of knowledge production.

The book contributes to democratizing knowledge because its language is accessible to non-dance scholars and to non-academics in general, but more importantly because it contributes to disseminating the knowledge produced by dancers and activists who are non-academics and who have been more often than not overlooked in the studies of dance and black culture. Furthermore, the book also contributes to challenging the geopolitics of knowledge as it makes available in the English language the work of Brazilian dancers, religious leaders, activists, and scholars whose work would otherwise remain available only to Portuguese speakers, if published at all, given the current post-institutional coup conjuncture that is rendering increasingly precarious the support for education and culture in Brazil.

The connection between language and dance is important not only because dance is a language in itself, but also because, in many ways, to learn to dance is similar to learning a language. The younger the one learns a language or dance form, the greater one's mastery of it, and the more authentic and natural it seems. Correspondingly, the later the learning process happens, the more evident become the accents and missteps. Applying this logic to a context in which black bodies have predominantly performed Afro-Bahian dance prevents us from conforming to the detrimental processes of essentialization and stereotyping. One of the greatest contributions of this book is its thoughtful discussion of the construction of authenticity as it pertains to the connections between Afro-Bahian dance, memory, history, and tradition. The concept of "African matrix dances," discussed in several essays, for example, is always dealt with in a way that does not attach, or restrict, to the black body the various dance forms that have become associated with this denomination.

Although words cannot fully convey the magical pleasure that dance brings to the body or its empowering effects on the soul, the chapters assembled in this book get as close as possible to doing just that!

Patricia de Santana Pinho
Santa Cruz, CA, May 2017

Acknowledgments

This book embodies hopeful inspiration, community research, and many levels of translation. For over ten years, we have been honored to participate in conversations, dance classes, performances, professional conferences, outreach, and community programs spanning Brazil, the United States, and Canada through generous support from official, alternative, and personal resources. Lucía M. Suárez and Amélia Conrado began the collection's editorship with Yvonne Daniel as a contributor; eventually, Yvonne joined the collaboration as a committed editor, sharing substantially in the responsibilities toward publication.

The process of translation was an especially critical one for us. Translations of the original texts in Portuguese were made possible by a grant from the Faculty Research Award Fund, H Axel Schupf '57 Fund for Intellectual Life, at Amherst College. Thanks go to Lisa Earl Castillo for early conversations on content and translation and to Sueann Caulfield for reviewing parts of the translations. We are indebted to Mariangela Nogueira's expert guidance with two of the essays, shedding light on how activist language can be translated into academic text. We tip our hats with a solemn bow, to our translator, Elizabeth "Bebete" Martins, who expertly translated the essays from our Brazilian collaborators into English.

Throughout our conversations, we found that across local geographies, many are grappling with similar issues in different ways, which get overlooked in general global discourses; the local work, which impacts global conversations, is central to this collection's ethos. We hope that this first text (in English) addresses these issues for English speakers, and that the eventual Portuguese translation will do the same for Portuguese speakers. We remain grateful to all the participants that have been in conversation and expect this to be an initial or one of many sites of cross-reference and the interlocution of action and theory.

Thanks go to the many colleagues and friends that participated in conferences and panels, providing provocative questions, interesting points of view, and challenging the role of the arts in community work and civil society. The conversation with John Chasteen, Yvonne Daniel, Lucía Suárez, Jeff Packman, and Danielle Robinson at the Latin American Studies Association panel in Toronto incited the direction the project took. Special thanks go to Lester Tomé, the panelists, and the audience, for their critical inquiry and enthusiasm. We particularly thank Sonia Alvarez and Gloria Bernabe-Ramos for the support and assistance at CLACLS (Center for Latin American, Caribbean, and Latino Studies at University of

Massachusetts), and Marguerite Harrison and Malcolm McNee at the "Five College Afro-Luso-Brazilian Faculty Seminar".

In particular, the seminars on "Dance and citizenship," which Lucía and Amélia developed together through intense international brainstorming and that Amélia organized in Bahia, gave foundational space to significant conversations. For such ongoing collaborative work in Brazil and the United States, Lucía solemnly thanks Amélia.

Many were part of the panels that took place during two "Dance and citizenship" conferences in Bahia, Brazil, as well as part of the working group organized by Amélia in August 2012. Lucía and Amélia especially wish to thank the administrative colleagues and scholars who have assisted in their research collaborations in Brazil: Beth Rangel (Federal University of Bahia [UFBA] and former director of Escola de Dança da Fundação Cultural do Estado de Bahia [EDUFUNCEB]), Ricardo Biriba (UFBA), Suzana Martins (UFBA), Nadir Nóbrega (Federal University of Alagoas [UFAL]), Alberto Olivieri (Ruy Barbosa College), Nanci Helena Franco (UFBA), Pilar Zambrano (Cauca University, Colombia), Piedade Videira (Federal University of Campina Grande [Universidade Federal de Campina Grande, UFCG]), Carlos Eugenio Soares (UFBA), Inaicyra Santos (The University of Campinas in São Paulo, Brazil [Universidade Estadual de Campinas, UNICAMP]), Maria Cecília de Paula (UFBA), Margarete de Souza Conrado (University of the State of Bahia [Universidade do Estado da Bahia, UNEB]), and Neuber Leite Costa (UNEB).

Funding for the second "Dance and Citizenship" conference, which paid for scholars to visit from Brazil and the United States, was made possible by UFBA and the Foundation of Research and Support (Fundação de Amparo à Pesquisa do Estado da Bahia, FAPESB, #001/2013). We all, but especially Amélia, give thanks for these resources and for support from the Federal University of Bahia's Department of Education, III (Grupo HCEL-Linha Historia, Memória e Diversidade) in Salvador, Bahia, Brazil.

Lucía thanks the Ford Foundation for generously funding her field research in Bahia, Brazil, and her students in the Mellon Research Seminars at Amherst College, for stimulating discussions about research, human rights, dance, and tourism. Special gratitude goes to Julian Ricardo for his exemplary dedication to research, synthesis, and translation. A nod goes to Rafael Calderón and Carlos Ramírez, exchange students from Spain, whose thoughtful questions made emphatically clear the need for this kind of study across languages and cultures, and the long road that awaits us all as we aim to build a better world that truly values dialogue and human possibility.

Lucía is grateful for the support garnered by the Cultural Agents Initiative at Harvard University, by which continued conversations with Doris Sommer underscore the relevance of this kind of collective. Deep gratitude goes to Leah Hewitt and Karen Sánchez-Eppler, the best colleagues and friends imaginable. Lucía is profoundly grateful to her daughter, Arianna Lucía, who has lived the language, dance, and struggles of this collection as her own, bringing innocent joy to a long and fascinating journey of critical inquiry. Lucía gives thanks, always, to her parents for their exemplary dedication to a life of honesty, goodness, and fairness, filled with laughter and hard won negotiations.

Lucía and Amélia are also grateful to Neal B. Abraham and Five Colleges, Inc. for support, which funded Amélia's visit to New England and fostered the expansion of central questions that have been developed in this book.

Amélia emphasizes her deep appreciation for continuous backing from the Federal University of Bahia (UFBA); she is also grateful to Five College, Inc. for her connection to other dance and Brazilian studies scholars during her New England visit. In addition, and especially, she gives thanks to her nuclear family, Biriba, Raína, Raissa and Tainan, as well as her extended family for their unconditional love and support.

Yvonne thanks Lucía for her persistence in garnering critical international dialogues and for researching the histories of Afro-Brazilian dancers; Amélia for shepherding the fresh voices of scholarship on African Diaspora dance in the Americas; and Intellect Press for solid support and appropriate swiftness in dispersing these important findings across the globe. She thanks her four sons and their families for excusing her for time away in order to complete this meaningful project.

We, the three editors of this collection, thank each other publicly for the immeasurable mutual support demonstrated within this shared research and unique writing experience, and we thank the many interlocutors who continue to share their research, writing, and support. In short, we remain deeply grateful for the experience of producing this collection, which has allowed us to further cultivate community in serious and creative ways. We have been honored to work in continued solidarity with colleagues near and far, and we are forever appreciative of the intellectual curiosity and generosity of spirit (presenting research, sharing activist work, collaborating in critical analyses of socio-political work) our contact has generated. We thank all our professors and masters before us for their pioneering examples – particularly Katherine Dunham and Mercedes Baptista, on whose shoulders our work stands and who still inspire our continued labor, commitment, and enthusiasm.

Our appreciation is extended to the Iowa State University Publication Endowment, ISU Foundation, for their partial support toward the publication of this collection. Finally, we thank the anonymous readers for their incisive and supportive critiques. Special gratitude goes to Jelena Stanovnik, Jessica Lovett, and the staff at Intellect for believing in this project from the very beginning, and Naomi Curston for seeing it through with efficiency and care, and making the process of publication an earnestly edifying experience.

Introduction

The state of Bahia, situated in the northeastern region of Brazil, occupies a significant place in the imaginary of Africa in the new world. For over half a century, the region, and especially its capital, Salvador, has been an important geographic center from which dynamic representations of the African Diaspora have been, and continue to be, cultivated. Star singers such as Caetano Veloso, Gilberto Gil, and Daniela Mercury have globalized Bahia's rhythms. Internationally acclaimed folkloric dance companies, such as the Balé Folclórico da Bahia featuring the *Orixás* (divine spirits of African-based religions) and *capoeira* presentations (a self-defense practice that is also performed as a dance spectacle in theaters), have established the Brazilian northeast as a geography of African-descendent memory. Bahian Carnival associations, called *blocos afros* or "African blocks," support African-descendent communities by highlighting African heritage and black pride through music, dance, theater, and art. *Blocos* such as Ilê Aiyê and Olodum have proven the need for, and capacity of, grass roots organizing. *Terreiros* (houses of worship), such as Casa Branca and Ilê Axé Opô Afonjá, are long-enduring, and still active Afro-Brazilian religious communities. The city and its surrounds serve as an international mecca for African Diaspora roots tourism, enthusiastically welcoming cultural programs and university exchanges that are focused on Afro-Brazilian history, music, and dance.

In addition, international conferences (such as the ones held by ASWAD [Association for the Study of the Worldwide African Diaspora] in 2005 and the Caribbean Studies Association in 2007) and annual summer study programs (such as Viver Brasil's "Dancing at the Source") connect activists, dance practitioners, students, and scholars through a shared interest in Afro-Bahian culture. More specifically, the prominence of the FUNCEB (Fundação Cultural do Estado da Bahia, "Cultural Foundation of the State of Bahia"), state-sponsored dance school, Bahian and Bahia-centered choreographers and dance teachers (such as Mestre King, Luiz Badaró, Rosângela Silvestre, Jelon Vieira, and Clyde Morgan) and international dance ethnographers (such as Molly Ahye, Susan Cashion, Yvonne Daniel, and Linda Yudin)[1] have actively created a global interchange of Afro-Brazilian dance arts. That is, Bahia is a central geographic site from which the local and global work of culture bearers keep Afro-Brazilian traditions alive. Aside from entertainment, dance functions as educational and cultural value systems, both of which provide Afro-Bahians, and those who practice the traditions, with the means to foster self-esteem, self-respect, and self-worth.

Despite the glitter of tourism and the splendors of Afro-Brazilian performance, the lives of African-descendent community members throughout Brazil remain disproportionately poor and marginalized. In addition, the labor of Afro-Brazilian dance has been overlooked, as it has been historically subsumed by "*Axé* music"[2] or as part of "sun, sand, and sex" tourism.

However, Afro-Brazilian dance embodies the cultural and socio-political significance of Bahia; it serves as an important and critical platform from which to examine identity, education, and memory, and expose race in Bahia. This collection pays homage to the hard work of dance.

Dancing Bahia: Essays on Afro-Brazilian Dance, Education, Memory, and Race reframes the labor of dance behind and beyond the tourists' gaze and commercialized representations of blackness in Bahia, thus challenging simplified and oversold notions of black artists' lives. Locally, in segregated neighborhoods, Afro-Bahian individuals and communities negotiate survival innovatively outside the confines of debilitating prejudice. Through case studies, historical analyses, and autobiographical essays, *Dancing Bahia* encourages readers to join the interrogation of local and global dynamics that have revealed continued and new sociocultural and economic circumstances, structuring the ways African Diaspora identities are performed, valued, internalized, and/or negated.

This collection gathers dedicated dance activists, practitioners, and scholars, who have worked extensively in Bahia over the last four decades, to examine the particular ways in which Afro-Brazilian dance has responded to socio-political notions of race, nation, and community, resisting stereotypes and redefining African heritage and Afro-Brazilian traditions. The essays that see light in this collection reflect an expansive, never-static series of investigations and creative partnerships that span lifetimes and multiple projects. They are the result of working groups and collaborations within the United States, Brazil, and Canada that were originally organized by professors Lucía M. Suárez and Amélia Conrado. Collection contributors, and many others from our wide-spanning African Diaspora, Latin American, and Latinx studies colleagues, as well as dance communities, have dialogued and debated during the Latin American Studies Association in Toronto (2010), in conferences at the Federal University of Bahia, Brazil (2009–11), during a Five College Residency in Massachusetts (2014), and in numerous other, less formal venues (2006–17). As a result, *Dancing Bahia* examines artistic departures that represent, recall, and reframe Afro-Brazilian dance arts, and the lives of those impacted by them.

Through long-standing cross-cultural conversations, we have meditated on the lessons that can be learned in Bahia from the work we do collectively and among the city's extensive socio-politically active dance communities. These essays present a glimpse of the complex history of Afro-Brazilian dance as the grounding language for education, memory, and new creative enterprises. The voices herein represented are plural. They foreground different experiences from different points of view, within varying, yet interconnected ways of investigating and activating equality and inclusion through Afro-Brazilian dance. Our collection exposes the flexibility that has been necessary to keep Afro-Brazilian dance practices alive. A number of Bahian dance practitioners and African Diaspora theorists emphasize the fact that the survival of African heritage has depended on its malleability to meet its community needs. Thereby, we have avoided conventional charted histories and dance categories in favor of relaying the unique experiences and particular perspectives of our working group of dance artists and dance researchers. Our shared premises are: African origin dances have morphed alongside important Portuguese and Indigenous dance traditions in Brazil, reflecting the mixed realities of the people throughout northeastern Brazil especially, and the Afro-Brazilian dances that have resulted from this history are not only representative of an art form, but also a formula for cultural and community survival.

Contributors to *Dancing Bahia* have consequently focused on key themes inherent in their everyday experiences working within local communities throughout Bahia and its immediate surroundings. Broad premises such as the individual as cultural agent, dance education as social activism, and culture bearers as keepers of African-descendent memory shape the organization of the collection; specific topics are brought to light with examples in each essay. In Part I, "Bahian Dance in Action," the contributors concentrate on specific dances and analyze their research findings in terms of cultural agency and social activism. In Part II, "Memory, Resistance, and Survival through Dance Education," the findings derive from provocative education studies that challenge the official status quo. Part III, "Reflections: Paths of Courage and Connections," examines dance artists' personal perspectives on social activism and social tensions, and in Part IV, "Defying Erasure through Dance," the author observes religious and social tensions, yet focuses on the recuperative, uplifting work of those who cultivate cultural memory. All essays address Afro-Brazilian identity and cultural practices that complicate personal and cultural memory, often contextualized within the backdrop of race and popular tourism practices of Bahia.

Our collection exposes varied professional voices; they are expressly diverse in tone, but the common methodology has revolved around ethnographic fieldwork, that is, intense and long-term cultural immersion, in addition to educational observation and testing. Since all contributors have participated as dancers as much as we have observed either as education specialists, cultural theorists, or anthropologists, the core methodology of our studies has been participation, dancing, and music-making.[3] Our findings provide readers with a realistic understanding of the different experiences that result from studying dance and community at different historical and political moments.

The majority of our interlocutors speak mostly of cultural resistance and emphasize the importance of heritage, history, and memory as well as a reliance on elders and dance specialists to pass on such knowledge. Our authors underscore these sentiments and attach them to notions of viable citizenship. We, the editors, aim for conversation and understanding among new readers that assist in understanding as we have learned in the process of organizing and publishing this collection. We especially encourage students to incorporate this knowledge into their training and future intellectual pursuits.

Afro-Bahian Knowledge

The work of putting together this collection has involved documenting the memory of African-descendent or Afro-Bahian knowledge, which has been affected by discrimination as "*coisas de negros*" ("black stuff"), the pejorative associations that linger in Bahian society's racist mentality. Seeking to offer a discussion informed by both theory and practical experience for those interested in the subject, the editors and contributors primarily approach Afro-Brazilian dances within the concept of a black activist movement. In Bahia especially, black activism is an important foundation on which dance performers, researchers, and teachers base their actions, practices, choreographic and educational content, inspiration, and creativity. In addition to revealing artistic, cultural, and educational values, Afro-Brazilian dances are responsible for disseminating an aesthetic that is as much something intelligible as it is a feeling that arises from the African presence in Brazil.

The African presence is one of the great blessings that came out of the highly exploitative and violent enslavement of different ethnic groups during the process of European colonization in Brazil. Although the abusive past has left a horrible mark on Bahian history and society, Brazil's national culture has benefited exceedingly from the West and Central African diversity and creativity received. Despite the violence, genocide, prohibitions, and castrations imposed by enslavement, Africans and African-descendent communities have resisted, using strategies such as escape, insurgency, maroonage, secret societies, religious organizations, as well as dance and music-making. Afro-Brazilian ancestors have left a historical and cultural legacy that has been passed down through generations of ritual customs, languages, and diverse forms of knowledge. In Bahia, those involved with the remembrance and representation of African-descendent livelihood form part of an ever-shifting, creative network of dance practices rooted in Bahia through genuine rituals, educational performances, and tourist venues.

We say "Afro-Bahian knowledge" because of the centrality and concentration of African-based culture that is the identity and the terrain of Bahia. Customs and understandings of African heritage circulate not simply among phenotypical Afro-Bahians, but Bahians of all colors and shades, all classes and professions. Degrees of respect for such culture are varied, but Bahians learn from birth and residence about Iemanjà and her water rituals at Praia do Rio Vermelho on February 2; they look forward to popcorn feasts in July within public ceremonies for Omolú and the health he fosters in individuals and communities. They do not worry about people praying as they wade at the bottom of water falls where Oxum reigns in the sparkle and trickling of cascading streams. Despite more recent stigmatized assaults from fundamentalist Christian religious sects, Bahians recollect and hold many African understandings, even alongside Protestant and Catholic traditions. Thereby, there is distinct cultural knowledge in Bahia.

Notes on Translations and African Origin Dances

Dancing Bahia is a project of translations: first, translation for all authors of non-verbal bodily practices and understandings into words; then translations between Portuguese and English. Our project is also one of dialogues between different communities that refer to similar issues with varied language/word choices. We, as editors, have respectfully conserved the national preferences and current vocabularies of both Brazilian and US American contributors. For example, we have left each author's solid understandings and preferred usage of "Afro," "Black," "African," "African descendant," "Afro-Bahian", or "Afro-Brazilian," instead of attempting to construct a unifying translation of such important recurring terms. We have also supported the documented arguments of Brazilian or US colleagues with additional editors' references, primarily noting those that have not reached each nation's literature in translation yet. Lastly, but significantly, both contributors and editors have worked in ongoing, intermittent dialogue with our professional translator, Elizabeth "Bebete" Martins, whose artful expertise has clarified so many nuanced understandings beyond non-native language users on each national side. These exchanges initiated deep and thoughtful conversations and permitted insertion of thorough body, word, and analytical translations.

It is our intention that *Dancing Bahia* provides a foundational conversation that references distinct models for honoring and utilizing African-descendent dance practices, offers several pertinent and innovative pedagogies for improvement in historical and cultural education, and augments the diverse and effective regional studies of the most populous African Diaspora site outside of the African continent. *Dancing Bahia* shares the fruitful yield of ideas and potential solutions that have resulted from respectful debate, cooperative dialogue, and collaborative international study that have focused on one geographical site. It has been a profound and provocative, touching and intriguing experience for each of us, which has only further confirmed the importance of Afro-Brazilian dance arts.

Most public audiences and some scholars outside of the dance discipline think that dance has only a few genres – for example, social/popular/recreational dance, ballet, and perhaps modern concert dance; however, African and African Diaspora dance have several genres. Once in the Americas, black dancing bodies with shared African movement principles had to address both European and Indigenous movement principles. Some African bodies rejected the European and Indigenous dance qualities they encountered, so that their dances continued to promote African heritages alone. Other African bodies projected a mixture of forms, called Creole forms, and still other African dancing bodies bypassed their African heritages and assumed or projected European heritages.

What characterizes those dances that retained most of their African heritages has been outlined by three scholars of African arts: historian of African arts Robert Farris Thompson (1974), African dance artist/scholar Kariamu Welsh (Asante) (1985),[4] and dance critic and artist/scholar Brenda Dixon-Gottschild (1996). In the 1970s, Thompson's pivotal work involved his analyses of African sculptural and textile arts in which he consistently saw motion and movement. He knowingly aligned motion and movement with African dance, since it is seminal to African life in general. In doing so, he gave the dance world uniform ways of saying what thousands of dance teachers had been saying in thousands of ways over time. Similarly, Welsh had to define African dance as she worked in the 1980s to establish both a technique to prepare the African American body for characteristic African dance movement and an international journal for African-based dance scholarship. She used a different vocabulary, but her characteristics of African dance coincided fundamentally with that of Thompson. Another decade later (in the 1990s), Gottschild used Thompson's vocabulary to unearth African-ness within American ballet specifically, but also in concert or theatrical dance forms in the United States.

In combination and summary of these three authors' detailed definitions of African dance characteristics, we, the editors, list for the non-dance specialist reader the most important indicators of African movement: *an earthiness or downward, flat-footed emphasis within a circular space, mode, or design, simultaneous isolation of many body parts creating poly-rhythms in the body, profound attachment to music in its polyrhythmic fullness, linkage to narration, stories, myths, dramas and tales of the ancestors and spiritual essences within African cosmologies; and a calm, smooth, and "slick" or "cool" attitude that supports and builds contrasting, extreme, and virtuoso performance.* These types of movements are combined in most African-based dancing with vivid colors, visual art motifs, dense rhythmic percussion, call and response singing, and most importantly, a welcoming expectation of participatory engagement, i.e., the community of onlookers is supposed to evolve into fellow dancers, instrumentalists, and singers during dance performances. These general characteristics dominate in African dance heritages, but there are distinctions that identify West and Central African roots, and in some cases, specific ethnic lineages (Fon, Ewe, Jeje, Yoruba, Malê, Congo, Angola, etc.) (see Daniel 2011: 1–4; Daniel in press).

There are many African heritage dance forms. For example, sacred dances are mainly dances of continuity, dances that have been passed on, forgotten slightly, reconstituted or recreated, and repeated over time and geography in African and African Diaspora ritual contexts. From the beginnings of the Americas, these forms have often been written about in terms of the names of African groups that performed them. Afro-Brazilian sacred dance forms are called Angola, Jeje, Ketu/Nagô, Caboclo or inclusively, Candomblé or Umbanda.

Sacred dances contrast in purpose with social dances; however, the division between social and sacred is not as strict in African cultures, as it is in other cultures of the Americas. Speaking generally, many African heritage social dances are historical forms that were written about in the colonial era as *bamboulas, calindas djoubas, chicas,* and *contradanças.* Others have been separated out as "national" dances (e.g., *samba* in Brazil, *tango* in Argentina, or *candombe* in Uruguay, etc.), and still others are called contemporary fad or popular dances (e.g., *samba reggae,* hip-hop, *samba-hiphop,* etc.). Social dances have been further sub-divided into special categories, like combat dances (in Brazil *capoeira* and *maculelê*) or parading dances (e.g., in Brazil *Carnavais, afoxés, blocos afro, bumba meu boi, maracatu,* etc.) and the remaining social dance genres are concert/theatrical dances and tourist dances. Both concert and tourist dances use all categories of dance genres; that is, sacred, historical, national, parading, combat, modern concert techniques, etc. all appear on concert stages, as well as in tourist settings as featured or foundational choreographic material (see full discussion of African Diaspora dance genres in Daniel 2011: 41–188).

In Conversation

Brazilian choreographer, dancer, and scholar Amélia Conrado's study begins our collection's conversation with "Afro-Brazilian Dance as Black Activism." Her study explores the diversity of African-derived dance expression that is found throughout Bahia, and underscores the ongoing relationship between Afro-Brazilian dance and the Black (political) Movement in Brazil. This initiating contribution augments our knowledge of identified meanings found in Afro-derived dances, and references leading scholars and militant activists, whose works have not been translated from Portuguese. Through her text, we are privy to a particular way of reviewing and interpreting the work of Afro-Brazilian dance and of Black studies in Brazil. Specific case studies that have not entered mainstream market culture center on dances and their history as powerful, emotional repositories of traumatic memory, resistance, and psychological release.

Conrado posits here, as elsewhere (2010), that dance performance is historical memory. For example, the performance of the *nego fugido*, which she describes, enacts not only memory, but also the current struggle with which African-descendent populations are still engaged. Conrado underscores that, as translated history, these dance practices give blacks and all others who dance them a visibility that has reshaped Afro-Brazilian lives and inserted pride and respect for black racial identity. Additionally, she emphasizes a recurrent theme in all of our conversations, one of resignification (new meanings to multiple histories and their importance in the present). Afro-Bahian knowledge is, out of necessity, a multilayered and pluralistic process. Her essay reveals how black dancing bodies dance proudly in the direction of freedom, releasing all sorts of shackles that would hinder freedom's progress. Thus, she re-casts the history of Afro-Brazilian legacies in today's dance culture.

Looking at two critical decades of systematic change with regard to race and Bahia, choreographer, dancer, and anthropologist Yvonne Daniel shows how and why dance performances have been at the crux of cultural citizenship. Through a case study on an important Bahian dance artist, Isaura Oliveira, Daniel highlights the character and trajectory of race in Bahia during the 1980s and 1990s, a decade of germinating arts activism and dance/music protest. She uses choreographic analysis to explicate the experiences of this dedicated dance artist. What follows serves as a revealing commentary on Bahia and the social conditions of that time. Most importantly, however, Daniel's analysis places Bahia at the top of efficacious socio-political dance performance. Through both the performances of courageous dancers and choreographers and the persistence of dance organizations since the 1980s, Bahia has moved decisively in the attack on race. "Dance Artistry and Bahian Forms of Citizenship: Isaura Oliveira and *Malinké*" demonstrates how the Bahian model of "dance and community performance" generated similar performances in the university and the arts market of Bahia; that model has educated and influenced Bahians, Brazilians, and the world.

In "Pedagogies of the Body within African Matrix Education of Salvador, Brazil: Perspectives and Challenges of an Emancipatory Project," Colombian-born and Brazilian-trained dancer and education specialist Pilar Echeverry Zambrano offers an ethnographically grounded analysis on the pedagogies that emphasize dances of African origin. Her case study is based on three years of Bahian fieldwork and the effects of an elective dance program supported by the State of Bahia (EDUFUNCEB). She scrutinizes the changes promised by the thematic and discursive education model for inclusion of Afro-Brazilian culture to see if concrete effects result, like freeing and understanding an inclusive body. She questions education policies that are supposed to decrease colonial traditions that marginalize and stigmatize young black bodies.

Echeverry Zambrano's essay attaches a defining script to a new (once again diverse) collective of Afro-Brazilian dancers. She suggests that African and Portuguese consolidations of sovereignty, hierarchy, politics, spirituality, etc. form the base of Brazilian culture and this consolidation professes to be celebratory. As she tells the story of African matrix dance history, she reveals that it is an accidental, but formative coalition of dance artists who, in fact, must struggle within the parameters of tourism and income-generating stereotypes. Nonetheless, Echeverry Zambrano confirms, within the context of Brazilian socio-political realities and limitations, that African matrix dance is an important collaborative effort that renews hard-work attempts to teach and keep alive Afro-Bahian knowledge and Afro-Brazilian dance arts. It is through addressing methodologies and contradictions that this study exposes, for example, the connections between colonial pedagogical principles and contemporary emancipation pedagogies as well as the ongoing efforts to build communities and utopian bodies within the framework of Bahia's tourism practices, and the underlying struggle for economic survival of black students and teachers.

In another ethnographically based essay, dancer and education and social movements scholar Piedade Lino Videira describes the perspectives and challenges that Afro-Brazilian educational settings offer with regard to contemporary and innovative teaching practices that are being generated, offered, and tested. "African Matrix Dance: Repertoire Options for Approaching Race and Ethnic Relations in Brazilian Schools" exposes new strategies for education of different actors and corporealities, using Videira's native Afro-Amapá community. This essay introduces the neighborhood of Laguinho, which is part of the history of being black in Macapá, the capital city of Amapá State, and underscores the Afro-Brazilian manifestations of a neighboring northern territory of Brazil. Like other Brazilian states and pocket territories throughout Brazil, Amapá has community sites of black life experiences, culture, and memories that are analogous to, yet different from, Bahian experiences. By examining organized black Brazilian social movements through education and using her own community's *marabaixo* dance and cultural festival, this study makes a case for the conscious formation of an integrated Brazilian society, actively and honorably including African heritage dance and culture through a plural education model.

Canadian based, US American co-authors Danielle Robinson and Jeff Packman relate how an after-school program that is dedicated to preserving local heritage and instilling cultural pride is reversing the emphasis on the past and ensuring cultural memories for the future. In "After-School *Samba*: Cultural Memory and Ownership in the Wake of UNESCO

Recognition as Intangible Heritage of Humanity," music, dance, and anthropology specialists Robinson and Packman analyze the practices and goals of local *samba* performers in the outskirts of Bahia (called the Recôncavo), where elder music and dance specialists lead classes with aims to empower and inspire their students as eventual, responsible stewards of their regional traditions. The authors analyze one school's response to local, national, and international efforts to celebrate, preserve, and (arguably) control Bahian *samba de roda*. Since *samba de roda* was recognized by UNESCO as a masterpiece of oral and intangible heritage in 2005, numerous professional *samba* groups have formed and longstanding ensembles have, in some cases, capitalized on the increased marketability of the practice.

In this essay, the activities and efforts of two *samba* performers are examined as they teach *samba de roda* to local school children in a program intended to counter damaging trends, e.g., the lure of monetary gain, the increased attention from NGOs (non-governmental organization) and various governmental agencies, and debates over notions of authenticity. Drawing on several years of fieldwork and the ideas of education theorist Paulo Freire, the authors argue that this program engages in a localized "pedagogy of the oppressed" within the larger and more powerful educational, economic, and social structures that historically have served to maintain the hegemony of the area's white, educated, economic, and cultural elite.

Dancer and anthropologist Deborah A. Thomas contributes an essay in an experiential and impressionistic voice. In "Dancing into the Politics of Race: From Bahia to Kingston," Thomas addresses relationships within dance and politics and explores performing politics. She is concerned with racial self-making and nation-building as she shares her Bahian experiences and compares these with her Jamaican background and research. She recounts her immersion into Bahia, Bahian dance, and the political connections between the two. She leaves poignant commentary on Brazil's "racial democracy" – the foundational tenet of Brazilian nationalism – and her own understandings of race and national belonging through dance performance.

Activist, dancer, and dance education scholar Nadir Nóbrega Oliveira offers her essay as an examination of the effectiveness of the 2003 law that was instituted in Brazil to make the teaching of black history and culture compulsory in elementary and secondary school curricula as a remedial measure, due to historical and ideological neglect in this field. Nóbrega Oliveira offers an analysis of the problems to which teachers of Afro-Brazilian dance are subjected in order to implement and execute African dance language in Bahian schools. In "Why Not Me? Reflections on Afro-Dance and Law No. 10.639," Nóbrega Oliveira gives personal examples of the plight she and others like her must negotiate regularly. Despite some advances in Brazilian society, Afro-Brazilian culture is still considered vulgar and exotic by many; African-descendent communities continue to be severely exploited; and Afro-Brazilian culture is routinely ostracized in educational and professional environments. Tracing her own development as an Afro-Brazilian dancer, and her decades of work in community projects throughout some of Bahia's poorest communities, Nóbrega offers a first-hand account of the challenges "shadow communities" must overcome, and the ways that dance is central to this process.

The closing section, "Negotiations: Afro-Bahian Memory, Storytelling, and Dance," by dancer and cultural studies theorist Lucía M. Suárez, highlights the workings of human rescue within and against the current violence and anti-Afro-Brazilian media madness that distresses the lives of Bahia's majority African-descendent population. Focused on a complex repertoire of stories that merge traditional, African-origin, and Afro-Bahian storytelling and dance, this study demonstrates how active sites of memory, resistance, and cultural agency present a poignant contrast to media-hyped disempowering narratives of crime and disposability. Through ethnographically based case studies and the powerful interventions of Griot Dona Cici (master storyteller Nancy de Souza e Silva), dancer Negrizú (the name he prefers to use, also known as Carlos Pereira dos Santos), the alliances facilitated by the Pierre Verger Foundation, and Afro-Bahian memories honored by co-artistic directors Linda Yudin and Luiz Badaró (Viver Brasil Dance Company), Suárez makes the case that Afro-Brazilian education and spectacle are political acts of memory and possibility in motion (see also Suárez 2013).

The passing, in 2003, of Law 10.639 highlighted the importance of African-origin knowledge. It established guidelines to include Afro-Brazilian and African history and culture systematically throughout the entire national primary and secondary school curricula. Supposedly, this would have opened doors for those with African-origin knowledge to enter the education system with their experience and practice. As reported by Dona Cici in Suárez's essay at the end of this collection, the desired outcome was not completely achieved. However, this was not unexpected. Consequently, new modalities of education, memory, and resilience continue to surface. The stories that Suárez has gathered (which include oral histories, survival parables, and Afro-Brazilian dance collaborations) expose the complex, interrelated narratives that play a pivotal role in the resilience necessary to confront blatant and ongoing racism and violence in Bahia and beyond.

Closing Considerations

In a 2005 interview, shortly before her death, world-renowned dancer and anthropologist Katherine Dunham pondered, "… expressing the meaning of your life … the meaning of the people that you came from… dance does this you know" (Nine Network 2007). She was talking about the myriad ways in which dance embodies history, tradition, and memory, as well as the ways through which dance changes the present and creates possibilities. She believed in the importance of dance in the lives of young people who otherwise had all doors of opportunity, and therefore citizenship, foreclosed to them. A pioneer for African and African Diaspora dance, Katherine Dunham was an active cultural agent who made connections between continental Africa, the Caribbean, Brazil, and the United States. She worked tirelessly through social activism for her communities. For Dunham, dance, citizenship, community, social activism, and political responsibility were all intertwined.

Following Dunham's lead, *Dancing Bahia* offers a much needed, critical, and scholarly investigation of the ways that dance continues to be central to the imaginings of Bahia, serving as a pivotal, political tool in a continued national and local quest for implementations of civil and human rights. Throughout the dance analyses offered in this collection, the concern has been with the monumental courage it takes to face racism, expose its presence, and create interconnected spaces of education, memory, political possibility, and social mobility. Dancing is viewed as labor and artistic production that permits engagement with and understanding of others, allies who join in the dance, enduring the outside world with consummate resilience. Such dancing creates a dancing community with humanistic values and confers and confirms an implied cultural citizenship, which dancing performers of all colors and creeds feel inevitably, regardless of dance genre.

Especially throughout our conversations here (but also in our lectures and publications elsewhere), we have suggested that dance, itself, is a place of translations that connects, creates, and restructures the way we view ourselves in space, in our communities, and across the restrictions of difference. We have relied on knowing claims that African dances are contagious forms that pull audiences or onlookers up from their seats and transform them into participating performers. We have argued here specifically that Afro-Brazilian dance is an ideal, historical act of resistance and an exemplary, educational act of freedom for the present and the future. While African heritage dances are often performed inside social and cultural spaces that exude latent and overt racism – subtle, ridiculing, blasphemous and insidious – but racism nevertheless, Afro-Brazilian dancing happens regularly and defiantly in Bahia.

We, the editors of this volume, consider ourselves fortunate disciples of Katherine Dunham's teachings and hard-working collaborators in the continuous efforts of both our teachers and our peer colleagues, as we explore and support new ways in which dance continues to evolve and activate social change.

Lucía M. Suárez
Amélia Conrado
Yvonne Daniel

References

Conrado, Amélia (2010), "Danças Afro-Brasileiras: Diálogo, pensamento, e arte-educação na contemporaneidade," in François Soulages, Alberto Olivieri, Ricardo Biriba, and Ariadne Moraes, *O sensível contemporâneo*, Salvador: Federal University of Bahia, pp. 121–34.

Daniel, Yvonne (1995), *Rumba: Dance and Social Change in Contemporary Cuba*, Bloomington: Indiana University Press, pp. 21–22.

——— (2011), *Caribbean and Atlantic Diaspora Dances*, Urbana: University of Illinois Press.

——— (in press), "Mentoring notes on African Diaspora dance styles and continuities," in Kariamu Welsh, Esailama Diouf, and Yvonne Daniel (eds) *African Dance and Diaspora*

Communities: Indelible Stories of Hot Feet, Perpetual Motion and Social Change, Urbana: University of Illinois Press, pp. 278–305.

Gottschild, Brenda Dixon (1996), *Digging the Africanist Presence in American Performance: Dance and Other Contexts*, Westport: Greenwood Press, pp. 11–19.

Nine Network (2007), "KETC | Living St. Louis | Katherine Dunham," YouTube, https://www.youtube.com/watch?v=7vyx6ue7K6o. Accessed December 22, 2017.

Suárez, Lucía M. (2013), "Inclusion in motion: Cultural agency through dance in Bahia, Brazil," *Transforming Anthropology*, 21:2, pp. 152–68.

Thompson, Robert Farris (1974), *African Art in Motion*, Berkeley: University of California Press.

Welsh, Kariamu (1985), "Commonalities in African Dance: An aesthetic foundation," in Molefi Kete Asante and Kariamu Welsh Asante (eds), *African Culture: Rhythms of Unity*, Westport: Greenwood Press, pp. 71–82.

Notes

1   These are exemplary but by no means exhaustive, as the composition of dance practitioners and ethnographers is a powerful and extensive one.

2   "*Axé* music" refers to Afro-Brazilian religious music that is employed within popular, commercial music. *Axé* is central in the Candomble religion, signaling "vital power," "powerful force," or "essential essence within everything."

3   See "observing participant" versus "participant observer" in Daniel (1995: 21–22).

4   The author no longer uses Asante.

Part I

Bahian Dance in Action

Chapter 1

Afro-Brazilian Dance as Black Activism

Amélia Conrado

Político

IBGE

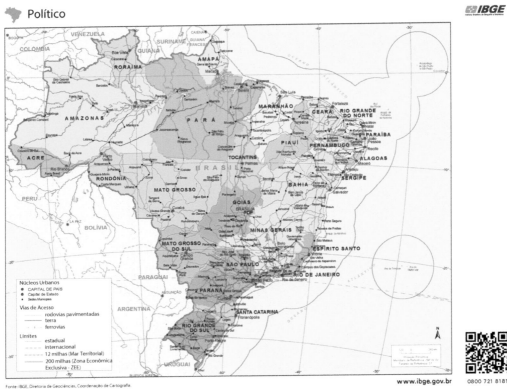

Figure 1: Map of Brazil.

Introduction

This essay outlines a brief historical background of African dance in Brazil and its importance for the struggles of blacks, both in the past and in the present. Racism and racial discrimination still exist in Brazilian society, and must be addressed and overcome as soon as possible. I draw from studies on education and black identity formation to show how dance can lead to significant black consciousness and consequently to a positive transformation of black people and the social attitudes of others. This essay examines the ways that black Bahians across several Brazilian states have engaged in their cultural practices, such as drumming sessions, rituals, and *capoeira*, as manifestations of ethnic identity and cultural resistance. Where the practices persist, they incorporate new aesthetic concepts and forms, which broaden the meaning of these cultural legacies without losing their origin purposes. In identifying many Afro-Brazilian dances, this chapter provides a sturdy dance background for concentration on Bahia and its seminal position as the activism and affirmation center of African legacy art, culture, and heritage in Brazil.

Afro-Brazilian dances are diverse expressions within the corporeal patrimony of Brazil. These varied cultural forms are practiced, conserved, and disseminated by a community made up of groups or individuals who identify with Afro-Brazilian heritage and wish to affirm their identity and be recognized as full Brazilian citizens who transmit knowledge through their cultural expressions. These expressions include religious rituals such as Candomblé, Umbanda, and Xangô; entertaining and ritualistic game/dances such as *capoeira* and *maculelê*; choreographies found in *afoxés*, *maracatus*, *congadas*, and *bumba meu boi* celebrations; and in popular, street or community forms like *frevo* or *jongo*. In addition, there are new, contemporary formats that are Afro-Brazilian recreations and innovations by individuals and dance/music companies and schools, as in the cases of Balé de Cultura Negra do Recife – Bacnaré (Pernambuco), Balé Folclórico da Bahia (Bahia), and Cia Étnica (Rio de Janeiro).

To understand the complexity that Afro-Brazilian dances involve, I raise the following questions:

- What did African legacy dances represent for enslaved Africans?
- How are danced cultural expressions perceived in historical and contemporary discourses?
- What role do Afro-Brazilian dances play in the construction of racial identity today?

To address these questions, I have consulted studies on the relationship between education and black identity (Siquiera 2006; Kabengelê 1986); studies on black activism (Junior and

Melgaço 2007); documentation by historians (Reis 2002; Mattos 2008); and research completed by dance scholars (see Tiérou 2001; Nóbrega Oliveira 2007; Martins 2008; Videira 2009; Suárez 2013 among others). I also draw from my own experiences as an Afro-Brazilian dance teacher, choreographer, and researcher who actively participates in the socio-political Black Movement of Bahia.

The Meaning of Dance for Enslaved Africans

Prior to European occupation, ancient Indigenous peoples dominated the territory now known as Brazil with their ways of life, forms of social organization, and diverse knowledge systems. European colonization greatly reduced Indigenous populations in South America, imposed a new cultural model, and transformed values within the new territories. Despite the genocide, many ethnic groups survived and are still present in the twenty-first century. According to theater and dance researcher Clélia Neri Côrtes (1996), there are 240 Indigenous groups living in Brazil today. Referring to the European "civilizing" model, Côrtes points out that Jesuit pedagogy, which favored writing and reading, lasted until 1758 when the Jesuits were expelled from Brazil by the Marquis of Pombal. Their model emphasized a lack of dialogue among the civilizations that formed early Brazilian society: Amerindian, European, and African. Côrtes adds that the Jesuit model of education was characterized by domination of "the other" and the interdiction of the body (see Freire 2014).[1]

In 1539, in a letter to King John III of Portugal, there is a request for the importation of Africans from the coast of Guinea, for a fee. Although colonizers often confused African ethnic groups, called "nations" in the African Diaspora,[2] with the ports from which Africans had departed the continent (such as Cape Verde, Mina Coast, Ajudá, and others), enslaved Africans or blacks in Brazil came from all over West and Central Africa, which included regions such as Minas, Ardras, Daomés, Sudaneses, Cambindas, Angolanos, Congos, etc. With them came their dances, songs, and customs. The continuity and recreation of their dance practices and the transformations that they underwent during the enslavement, migration, and colonization processes became the foundation of what we now call *danças afro* (African dances); they are historical memories preserved in dance performance.

Researching records in Pernambuco from 1674 of the Irmandade de Nossa Senhora do Rosário dos Homens Pretos da Paróquia de Santo Antônio (the Brotherhood of Our Lady of the Rosary of Black Men of St. Anthony Parish), historian Leonardo Silva (1988: 15) found documents that refer to the coronation of Angolan, as well as Brazilian-born blacks (*crioulos*) as kings and queens. These data suggest that the coronation proceedings subsequently gave rise to *maracatu* and similar parade-type processions with dancing, singing, and playing of musical instruments. L. Silva observes that the first known cortege of dignitaries from the Kingdom of Congo to Brazil was documented by Gaspar Barleaus in 1643, who described a delegation that visited Recife to meet with the Dutch Count João Maurício de Nassau[3] and address issues

Bahia

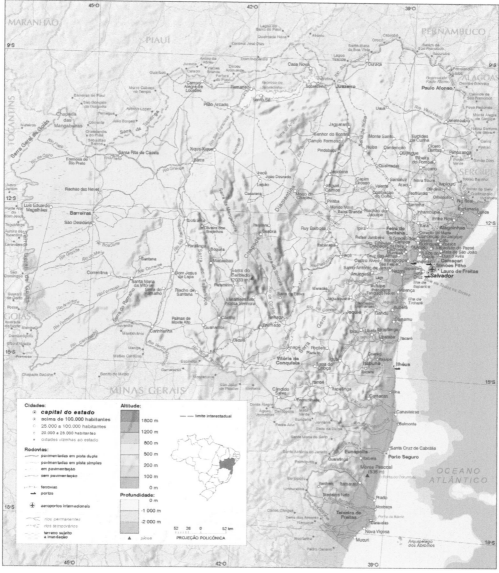

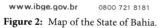

Figure 2: Map of the State of Bahia.

involving the King of Congo and Count of Sonho. Count Maurício de Nassau describes the occasion: "[…] we saw their original dances, flips, fearsome sword flourishes, flickering eyes simulating anger at the enemy. We also saw the scene in which they represented their king sitting on the throne and witnessing the majesty in dogged silence" (1988: 17).

Additionally, I conducted research for IPHAN (the Historic and Artistic Institute), a dossier on *samba de roda*[4] within the interior of Bahia, and found that "there is no scarcity of documentation of black drumming and other musical and choreographic sessions" (Conrado 2008: 32). My discussion refers to studies by historian João José Reis that mention an 1808 document concerning a massive festival that took place in the Santo Amaro region, with African and black or African-descendent music and dancing and a significant number of whites, all with the consent of local slave owners and to the annoyance of provincial police authorities (2002: 105). Within the context and dynamics of a society dominated by enslavement practices, transformations took place as a result of both internal and external pressures, affecting slave trafficking and the institution of slavery itself. The Free Womb Law (Lei do Ventre Livre, 1871[5]) and the Sexagenarian Law (Lei dos Sexagenários, 1881) were only able to legitimate and confront on their own terms what was left of [the] Masters' dominion over their slaves, putting on the horizon the end of slavery itself" (Mattos 2008: 152). Such pressures forced the Portuguese Crown to take an action that could no longer be postponed, and Imperial Law No. 3353, known as the Golden Law (*Lei Áurea*), was signed by regent Dona Isabel on behalf of Emperor D. Pedro II, proclaiming the abolition of slavery on May 13, 1888.

Of course, abolition was cause for great celebration by the formerly enslaved population. Many of these celebrations remain etched in popular memory to this day – in the form of dances, poems, and songs. However, the historical literature on slavery in Brazil reveals that celebration was not the only meaning given to such festivities. For the colonial population, the festivities also signified resistance, just like running away, murder, and suicide constituted extreme individual forms of African and African-descendent struggles against colonial slavery (Mattos 2008: 168).

In my later fieldwork, I have observed other examples of historical memories that are preserved through dance performance. One is the annual performance of a dance called *parafuso* or the "dance of the screws". It is usually presented at the Laranjeiras Cultural Festival (*Festival Cultural de Laranjeiras*) during the period of Three Kings' Day (*Folia de Reis*) in January.[6] The dance of the screws was created just for men, who move to the rhythm of the music, gyrating tirelessly, wearing white dresses, shoes, hats, and white makeup on their faces. Their "dresses" are actually long full petticoats. Members of the group explain that during the time of slavery and in the middle of the night, Africans would steal young ladies' petticoats from the clotheslines of the master's houses. They would cover their whole bodies with the petticoats in attempts to simulate ghosts, awaken and frighten the colonists, and then try to escape through the woods. When the Golden Law was signed, groups of African-descendent men dressed in petticoats came out frolicking and dancing, thereby revealing the "secret" of the hauntings. This is still preserved in the oral memory of dance groups that perform the *parafuso*.

In attempts to confirm the story, I found a citation in a 1985 publication that briefly describes the *parafuso* dance: "Black slaves, their faces covered with *Tabatinga* (paint used to whitewash houses), wearing white petticoats of Irish linen and lace decorated with toothpick folds [...]" and "[...] humming and making a huge fuss, in a twisting back-and-forth dance, they took to the streets to make fun of their masters, who had been defeated on May 13" (Fundação Estadual de Cultura 1985: 13).[7]

There are other examples of African heritage in Brazilian dance culture that refer to the memory of the struggle and the quest for freedom from bondage, which simultaneously reveal the complexities the dances involve. I highlight two significant corporeal expressions: *maracatu* dance practices and the *nego fugido* (black runaway) dance variations. *Maracatu* is an artistic or cultural event from the state of Pernambuco that involves a large number of groups; *nego fugido* is a smaller event that takes place in the interior of the state of Bahia. I consider both as dance expressions that have moved across historical time to the present, retaining tremendous vitality.

Memory and History through the Lens of *Maracatu*

Maracatu is most known as a traditional dance in the form of an African royal procession, practiced in the northeastern state of Pernambuco. "*Maracatu* street presentations display much grandeur with ornately costumed characters, such as kings, queens, vassals, ambassadors, spearmen, *baianas*, cortesans, and ladies of the imperial palace. The protagonists of *maracatus* are representations of enslaved Africans and their Brazilian descendants, who also worshiped the Africanized forms of [the Catholic] religion" (Conrado 2013: 2). *Maracatus naçãoes* or *maracatu* nations, so named by the communities from which they come, are forms of identity affirmation and ethnic belonging, signaling the organization of black resistance. There are many *maracatu* variations; for example, *maracatu nação Estrela Brilhante, nação Porto Rico, nação Cambinda Velha, nação de Luanda*, and *nação Elefante*.

Dance education scholar Margarete Conrado draws attention to the meaning of *maracatu* as a dance that mixes festive and warlike characteristics, calling it a "beautiful war" (2013: 14). The prefix "*marã*," in the language of the Tupi-Guarani, means "war, confusion, disorder, revolution." "*Catu*," also in Tupi-Guarani, means "good, beautiful." Other authors attribute the origin of the dance or event name to the musical instrument called *maracá*, which is an indigenous rattle. Silva, in his study of the institution of the King of the Congo and its presence in *maracatus*, traces the dance to the beginning of Brazilian enslavement practices in 1530, in the captaincy of São Vicente. I consider it a processional dance that represents the coronation celebrations of Kings of Congo, organized by the Irmandade do Rosario (Brotherhood of the Rosary) in the colonial period and linked to Catholic festivals of the Three Kings.

In his doctoral research on *maracatu rural* (rural *maracatu*) or *de baque solto* (loose-beat *maracatu*), José Antonio Leão explains that the culture of *maracatu* unfolds in several ways (2011: 36–37). The name of this form refers to the loose playing of drumsticks on the snare drum and it differs from the *maracatu nação* or *de baque virado* (reverse-beat *maracatu*) because of its particular musical sound, but also because unlike the *maracatus naçaoes* versions, *maracatu rural* includes the fusion of Indigenous and African representation. *Maracatu* performances incorporate an orchestra consisting of bass drum, snare drum, *cuica gonguê*, and *ganzá*,[8] as well as unique stock characters, such as the *caboclos* of the sword,[9] who embody the local customs and everyday life of the region known as Nazaré da Mata. Thus, regional residents participate in the process of preservation, reconstruction, and dissemination of their culture; however, Leão attributes the historical origin of the *maracatu rural* to the mixture of Indigenous, European, and African cultures around the end of the nineteenth century (2011: 37). This fusion is found within many cultural practices, such as *pastoril, bumba meu boi, cavalo-marinho, caboclinho, folia de reis,* etc.

Maracatu would come to be associated with the most widely used term, "*nação*" or "nation," which (again) marks the identity and ongoing presence of African peoples everywhere it was performed. Repression of "all things African" led blacks to seek a time and space where they could come together, recall and affirm their cultures, a space and time for organized cultural resistance. *Carnaval* celebrations became that annual time and space for popular African-based festivities. Current "traditional" groups even undergo a religious ritual before coming to the streets and plazas during Carnival, repeating the connections between African royal processions and spirituality (Conrado 2013: 14). Today, *maracatu* is performed in addition to *Carnaval* time, during cultural encounters, academic events, and festive community occasions, especially in commercial/tourist events.

The fundamental principles of events such as the *maracatu dances* weave together the meanings of existence, spirituality, playfulness, learning, knowledge, continuity, and renewal. Across time, the strength, beauty, and magnificence of *maracatu* dancing bodies reveal the persistent desire for freedom and the preserved memories of traditional and historical African continuity that accompanied each beat of the song. All of this takes place within a political perspective, which marks black organizations that struggle to deconstruct the negative representations that racial prejudice has historically imprinted onto Brazilian society.

Memory and History through the Lens of *Nego Fugido*

Nego fugido is another dance that documents the complexities within dance performance, as it also provides proof of memory across generations. For this analysis, I utilize the limited literature available, consisting of a few recent academic studies and my own research and fieldwork observations.

Zilda Paim, a native researcher from the area where the *nego fugido* is staged in the state of Bahia, explains the manifestation of *nego fugido* as a black narrative of the Palmares (Maroon) War (1999: 69). African-descendent performers re-enact how white colonists pursued escapee or maroon Africans in their hidden villages, called *mucambos*. When the colonists attacked, the maroon groups fought in defense. During the conflict, they imprisoned a colonial oppressor. As the struggle intensified and the persecution of blacks increased, the African escapees would flee through the bushes, camouflaged in skirts made of dried banana leaves, to hide from their oppressors. By Paim's accounts, the provincial government promised blacks the end of persecution, if blacks handed over their colonial prisoners. In turn, the government would release one enslaved captive whom it had imprisoned.

It is the fulfillment of this agreement that blacks celebrate in the festive ritual of *nego fugido*. Everything takes place in a public square. First the prisoner, who has been under their guard, is released; he or she comes out dressed in white, and is accompanied by songs, dances, and war cries. Then, blacks who had remained hidden in the woods, hungry and thirsty, would return to their villages, asking for forgiveness and alms from the community.

In the work of scholar and playwright Nelson de Araújo (1986), the *nego fugido* is linked to other historical events, including the Tailors' Revolt (Conjuração Baiana) and black conspiracies against the colonial regime during the nineteenth century, when enslaved Africans and their descendants were armed and fought in uprisings that shook the province. According to Araújo, *nego fugido* represents the memory of these struggles for freedom. He stresses that "it was in Acupe[10] that one of the richest popular performances in terms of significance and dramatic content was created" (1986: 82). The songs that are part of this performance are possibly based in Jeje-Nagô[11] traditions (according to community understandings) and were influenced by the Portuguese language. In addition, "they merge elements of dance, singing, recitation, and instrumental music that create boundless movement and great complexity" (1986: 83). Another highlight of this drama is that all participants, who are usually black, accentuate their color by covering their bodies in a mixture of cooking oil and coal. They chew red tissue paper to create an image that looks like blood dripping from their mouths.

Two documentaries of *nego fugido* were recorded by filmmaker and researcher Pires Neto in 1997 and 1998. He states that "[n]ego fugido is street theater created by teenagers, fishermen's children, currently led by Dona Santa. They act out the freedom struggle of slaves" (2005: 183).

In the state of Sergipe, we find important expressions of Afro-Brazilian culture such as the *cacumbis/cucumbis*, *samba-nego*, the dance of São Gonçalo do Amarantes, the *samba pareia*, and *maracatu*.[12] In the state of Pernambuco, there is the dance of *frevo*, during *maracatu* celebrations and the religious dance of the Pernambucan Xangôs.[13] All of these interpretations and/or variations of the *nego fugido* enact the memory of the struggle for freedom during the enslavement period. When performed today, they underline current struggles for equality. These danced memory performances are powerful and emotionally relived through performers' bodies. Staged theatrical plots and dance dramas are drawn from the struggle for freedom and serve to teach performers and audiences. *Nego fugido* variations additionally reinvigorate the collective energy needed to combat and overcome historical injustice. It is no secret that such performances have been appropriated and exploited by members of Bahia's elite cultural industry.

Afro-Brazilian Dance Expressions in Historical and Present-Day Discourse

Melo Morais Filho's depiction of a popular event on the eve of the *Folia de Reis* in Bahia contains an example of the racism that was hegemonic in the Brazilian social sciences and influenced studies of African-descendent cultures during the late twentieth century: "Clashing with the magnificent concert (of white musical groups), there are growing groups of *cucumbis*, black men and women dressed in feathers, growling African tunes and making barbaric sounds with their crude instruments" (1988: 175). *Cucumbis* or *cacumbis* are words of Bantu[14] origin used in Bahia to describe "traditional festivities of blacks, who, dressed in furs and feathers, participated in a procession in which they celebrated the puberty rite, as well as representations of the death and resurrection of the chief's son" (de Castro 2005: 214). In the short passage cited above by Morais Filho, the tone of scientific discourse is clear; such language was propagated for many years in the literature about African descendants in Brazil. It was a discourse that placed black and white populations at two ends of a hierarchy; thus, the black "clashed" with the "magnificent concert." Morais Filho even uses the word "growl" to refer to Afro-Brazilian singing, which is a literal association of human beings with animals.

Despite mistaken views of nineteenth- and twentieth-century social scientists, researchers such as Melo Morais Filho left clues for contemporary studies, which, of course, have moved beyond these views. For example, contemporary scholars extract deeper, hidden meanings from his studies, which disparaged blacks. His references have been reclaimed to underscore how racism was impregnated in academic discourse and to exhibit other interpretations inadvertently readable "between the lines." Beginning with the efforts of those who never identified with or felt included in scientific discourse, Afro-Brazilian communities created strategies for organized struggles in the form of a black socio-political movement. One of these strategies was to encourage African-descendent community members to become scholars in different discipline areas. That training has enabled them to break through institutional and paradigmatic barriers in academic fields, giving rise to research and studies that rewrite and retell the history of Afro-Brazilian legacies. From such perspectives, formed inside African-descendent communities, the Afro-Brazilian legacy has been one of a truly civilizing nature, in comparison to the discriminatory and unjust practices of the Portuguese legacy in Brazil. As these studies advance, scholars are unveiling the "formula" that has sustained racism in the modern world. Among these studies, and struggling against the neglect of this topic, lies the work of Cuban ethnologist and political scientist Carlos Moore. It is from his work, "Racism & society: New epistemological bases for understanding racism," that I draw a definition of racism: a "phenomenon that emerges freely from man's consciousness, and therefore is derived from what we call culture [which has] played a *causal* role in the unfolding of the plot that [has] culminated in the brutal clash between the West and the rest of planet" (Moore 2007: 216). Analyses by the Senegalese historian/anthropologist/physicist and activist scholar Cheikh Diop moved in the same direction much earlier, according to

Moore, drawing attention to a global barbarism caused by a domination model that was marked by genocide, the gigantic Atlantic slave trade, and an imperialist expansion of Europe over the rest of the world (Moore 2007: 216).

It was in the second half of the twentieth century that scientists emerged from black activism beginnings to tell their perspectives on Brazilian history, which contrasted with official history, i.e., history recounted from the European perspective. For the specific field of dance, I highlight the scholarly works of other dance scholars and activists, including Nadir Nóbrega Oliveira (1992),[15] Maria Zita Ferreira (1998),[16] Edilson Fernandes de Souza (1995),[17] and myself (1996). These cited works serve to illustrate the importance of the decade of the 1990s for solid research on Afro-Brazilian dances and the arrival of legitimate academic specialists who were also products of the Brazilian Black Movement. These studies shaped and continue to shape the historically informed activism that presently finds voice in the Dançando Nossas Matrizes Movement (Dancing Our Roots Movement or DNM), which I will address more fully in the next section of this essay.

Resignification of Afro-descendent Dance and the Construction of Racial Identity

In the first half of the twentieth century, the Vargas dictatorship imposed the discourse of modernization based on European ideals; however, black activism did not lower its weapons. It created newspapers and organized black fronts. A major example was Teatro Experimental do Negro or TEN in Rio de Janeiro, which was created in 1944 and led by activist and playwright Abdias do Nascimento in 1944. TEN was a milestone for the affirmation of blackness through the arts: it was theater performed by black men and women, directed by a black director, and featured themes related to racial issues. Afro-Brazilian dances, songs, and poetry were interwoven into its scenic design. After the success and recognition achieved by TEN, other black arts groups and companies emerged and new Afro-choreographies appeared.

Dancer/choreographer/teacher Mercedes Baptista was deeply influential in the development of Afro-Brazilian dance movement. Born in 1920 (exact date unknown), she was a poor black girl inspired by films with international icons Shirley Temple and Judy Garland (1922–69). She dreamt of fame and sought a career in classical ballet in order to achieve this (Silva Junior 2007). She was the first black dancer to join the Municipal Theater's ballet company in Rio de Janeiro. She faced exclusion in her career because despite being talented and dedicated, she was always dancing in the background chorus, and was rarely given prominent positions. She knew it was because of the existing racism in Brazilian society. Fortunately, at the same time, the contemporary Black Movement began to emerge in Rio de Janeiro, seeking to enhance the cultural and social identity of the black population. Baptista approached the movement and became part of TEN in 1948, as a ballerina, choreographer, and collaborator. Thus, she engaged in the theory and practice of Brazilian black culture, becoming an activist artist.

The first Congresso do Negro Brasileiro (Congress of Black Brazilian Culture) in 1950, with its extensive programming, had as its guest in the field of dance the US-born, international choreographer Katherine Dunham. She was invited to give lectures, teach classes, and watch artistic performances of Afro-Brazilian cultural groups. More important was her performance with her professional company of black dancers, which contributed significantly to a change in how black artists saw themselves and their opportunities in Brazil.

Baptista met Katherine Dunham in Rio de Janeiro and received a scholarship to study at the Dunham School of Dance in New York, which was a prominent center of dance training and research between 1944 and 1957 (see Dunham, also Peron, in Clark and Johnson 2005: 479, 625). After working with Dunham for a year and a half, Baptista returned to Brazil and began to do more research on Afro-Brazilian culture. She frequented houses of Candomblé to learn about Afro-Brazilian religiosity, which, along with what she learned from Dunham, assisted her in the merging of dances that came from people in the streets and what she had learned about ballet and modern concert dance. As a result, a new phase in her dance was born.

In 1953, Mercedes Baptista founded her dance group, Balé Folclórico Mercedes Baptista (Mercedes Baptista Folkloric Ballet), which trained generations of dancers and was recognized nationally for its artistic innovation. Among numerous choreographies based on African heritage and cultures in Brazil, some of the most successful works from the 1980s are: *Orungá e Iemanjá*, *Visita de Oxalá ao Rei Xangô*, and *Mondongô*, among others. Mercedes Baptista died in Rio de Janeiro on August 18, 2014, at the age of 93, in Rio de Janeiro (see Silva Junior 2007; museuafrobrasil.org n.d.).

Turning to Brazilian and, more specifically, Bahian contexts, these dance artists moved and created within the the particulars of mid-twentieth-century political circumstances. This was marked by a military coup, which resulted in the establishment of another dictatorship that lasted from 1964 to 1985 by means of a succession of generals who each served as president. The dictatorships persecuted activists, intellectuals, artists, students, and leaders who were suspected of opposing the established order. Any cultural or political event that was different or went against the established standards of the existing order was placed under surveillance and participants were severely repressed.

The Unified Black Movement (MNU), originating in Rio de Janeiro and expanding to other areas, such as Bahia, Sergipe, Maranhão, and São Paulo, emerged at the height of the dictatorships, representing various fronts in the struggle and the reaffirmation of Afro-Brazilian values and culture. As a result of connections among a group of young black men who were inspired by ideas emerging from the US American Black Movement, a Carnival group, or "*bloco afro*," called Ilê Aiyê was formed in Bahia in 1974.[18] Ilê Aiyê paraded on the streets of Curuzu district, clashing with police and the press and becoming the target of criticism. They persevered and became the pioneering epicenter of a political project in which art and culture were perceived as appropriate and effective weapons with which to combat racism and racial discrimination. The word "*ilê*" in Yoruba means "home"; and "*aiyê*" means "world"; thus, in the conception of this cultural group, "Ilê Aiyê" is "The Black Home."

The trajectory of this group followed a number of different strategies: educational, economic, and political. One of the most important was the creation of the Mãe Hilda (Mother Hilda) School, named after one of the founders of the *bloco* and a priestess in the Candomblé religion. The school's courses included content that is neglected by official public schools in Brazil, where African descendants are the majority. African dance classes, in which the dancers do research and restage dances, occupy a central place in the school pedagogy. In addition to the Afro-centric curriculum of *blocos afro* schools, special attention is given to teaching about historic struggles for equity, ethnic-racial identity, human rights, and citizenship.

Also, Ilê Aiyê supports vocational projects for children and adults, including crafting percussion instruments, computer training, sewing workshops, and making fashion handbags and shoes. The production of these items opens economic opportunities, as it also follows an African aesthetic. For example, there is a focus on hairstyles and makeup that are popular among African-descendent women and men and classes in cosmetology and styling yield jobs and careers for at-risk youth and marginalized or unemployed adults.

Additionally, each year, Ilê Aiyê's Carnival show is preceded by research and study of resistance movements to Portuguese colonialism: in Angola, Guinea-Bissau, Mozambique, and countries connected to the African Diaspora. Research results are disseminated through bulletins, Carnival song texts, and education journals; they additionally serve as a base for the creation of music, costumes, and float theme designs. Through Ilê Aiyê, Afro-Brazilians were, and continue to be, encouraged to release the upset and potential despair of their historical marginalization, and to learn about and be proud of their African history and heritage. Ilê Aiyê is responsible for a resignification process through music and dance at Carnival time, which has affected local and global African-descendent communities.

There are many other examples of resignification of Afro-Brazilian artistic creations that play a role in transformation to the contemporary stage. For example, in Pernambuco in the 1970s, the famous Brazilian playwright Ariano Suassuna founded the Armorial Movement, a militant artistic and political force that valued and defended the culture and art of Brazil's northeast, bringing popular arts onto the stage and having them recognized as erudite. The Balé Popular do Recife (Popular Ballet of Recife), inspired by the Armorial Movement, was created in 1977, and later, its Escola Brasílica de Expressão Artística began in 1983. Additionally, the Primitive Ballet of Black Art in Pernambuco was fundamental for the training of Afro-Brazilian youths in the metropolitan area of the capital, Recife. As they became qualified in pre-professional classes, emerging artists would join the Ballet company, created in 1982 by masters Zumbi Bahia and Ubiracy Ferreira. Through the teaching of Afro-Brazilian and popular street and community dances, this group worked to valorize a black aesthetic, suggesting that an Afro-Brazilian or black aesthetic was equal to any other aesthetic. Also noteworthy is Bacnaré or the Black Culture Ballet of Recife, which was founded in 1985 by Ubiracy Ferreira and recreated a dance movement language by referring to the Afro-Brazilian cultural universe.

Marlene Silva's work as a pioneer in the teaching of African dance in the state of Minas Gerais is yet another example of resignification and the construction of a proud and formidable Afro-Brazilian identity. She is responsible for training many professionals who work in the field of Afro-Brazilian dance in the capital city, Belo Horizonte. As a student of Mercedes Baptista, Silva has dedicated 45 of her 70 years to displaying, conserving, and innovating within Afro-Brazilian dance culture.[19] Baptista in Rio and Silva in Belo Horizonte taught Afro-Brazilian dance, both nationally and internationally, as translated history, giving blacks *and all others who dance these dances* a visibility that has reshaped Afro-Brazilian lives and inserted pride and respect for black racial identity.

Bahian Influences on the Construction of Afro-Brazilian Identity

The state of Bahia houses a significant number of Afro-Brazilian dance schools, performing groups, and techniques. Viva Bahia is one performance example. Created in the 1960s, the group is a pioneer in the training of its cast and in the public production of performances featuring Brazilian community and street dances and Afro-Brazilian dances; Emília Biancardi, an ethnomusicologist, is the founder and continues as director. The Balé Folclórico da Bahia, created in 1988, is directed by Walson Botelho and José Carlos Arandiba and has received much international recognition, but it is the late Raimundo Bispo dos Santos or *Mestre King* who is considered "the father of African dance in Bahia." He is known first because he was the first male to graduate in dance from the Federal University of Bahia (UFBA); his work marks the beginning of an Afro-Brazilian repertoire that combines Afro-Brazilian/Bahian dance materials with modern dance in presentation for the concert stage. (He died in Bahia on January 13, 2018.)

An important mobilizing force that began in Salvador in 2011 was the Collective of African Dance Teachers. With the goal of connecting Afro-Brazilian dance professionals, the group promoted an event entitled "Dancing our roots: A dialogue among Afro-Brazilian dances" ("Dançando Nossas Matrizes" or DNM). DNM's agenda is the dissemination of dance and public policies designed for the black population in Bahia and Brazil. In the same vein, Afro-Brazilian dance professionals came together in two iterations of the "Dance and citizenship seminar: Memory and tradition in Brazil and Latin America", in 2010 and 2013. DNM continues to offer a forum for ongoing examination of the myriad ways through which dancers, teachers, and activists retain, validate, and augment Afro-Bahian dance forms. This process is at the root of racial identification and resignification and cannot be defined with one simple narrative.

In the field of public policy, some of the major demands of the Black Movement have been met by important federal laws. Beginning with racial quotas in public universities, both to equalize educational opportunities for all students and to combat the inequalities of the past, laws and education policies have been instituted. In addition, during the government of President Luis Inácio Lula da Silva, from 2003 to 2011, the Secretariat of Identity and Cultural Diversity (SID) was created under the Ministry of Culture. SID's objectives are to coordinate, produce, disseminate, and promote Brazilian cultural diversity. Also within the government, the Institute for National Artistic and Historical Heritage (IPHAN) began the process of mapping intangible cultural heritage in order to safeguard Afro-Brazilian and Indigenous heritages and establish policies for their promotion and dissemination. Among the cultural events entered in IPHAN's registry are manifestations of culture such as *jongo*, *frevo*, the *samba* groups in Rio de Janeiro (*partido alto*, *samba de terreiro*, and *samba-enredo*), the *tambor de crioula* of Maranhão, *capoeira* masters, and the *roda de capoeira*.[20] Accompanying these policies and substantive, but beginning actions, there has been an increase in the theoretical literature on Afro-Brazilian artistic expressions.

Meanwhile, at the level of daily realities, Bahian dance professionals live with the uncertainty of whether there will be public or private calls for proposals that include the category "African dance" or "Afro-Brazilian dance." Their everyday routines involve many hours of rehearsals, experimentation, and creation. They are endlessly uncertain of whether it will be possible to bring their corporeal-artistic discourse to the public. They often have inadequate rehearsal space; they rarely know whether they will obtain minimal financial resources; and they face challenges that can include a lack of adequate food for those who work with their bodies, which, depending on the type of choreography, is extremely exhausting. They are affected by the racist attitudes and discriminatory practices against black people and black culture that still linger in the twenty-first century. To combat this persistent reality, it remains critical that there is an active and ongoing relationship between Afro-Brazilian dance and the Black Movement in Brazil.

The activists of the black cause in Brazil, regardless of skin color, are those individuals or organized groups that work toward the ideal of eradicating racism, discrimination, and prejudice in society; they are committed to change positions and discourses, whether in the family environment or in the various institutions where Afro-Brazilians interact, such as the university. These professionals, who are conscious of the value and social place of the language of dance, exercise the power of political and cultural representation.

To re-emphasize the relationship between Afro-Bahian dances and black activism, I draw from the conceptualization of the Black Movement, according to professor Ana Célia da Silva, one of its founders in Brazil: "We can consider the black movement as all entities or individuals who fought and fight for black freedom, developing strategies of occupation of spaces and territories, denouncing, defending and developing concrete actions for the achievement of fundamental rights in society" (Silva 2011: 116). Also, I find an explanation for working in Afro-Brazilian dance in Maria Zita Ferreira's studies ([1998] 2008), which promote the socio-political recuperation of the oppressed through dance. Ferreira presents teaching methodologies that feature Afro-Brazilian dance in schools in order to reveal the rich repertoire that encourages exercise in creativity, sensitivity, and cultural memory through corporeal expression. Ferreira insists that "when we defend dance – a part of the common sense of black and popular-class people who rely on previously established methods and techniques – it is because we believe it is a practice that incorporates all forms of organizing knowledge, in a broader sense of education" (2008: 32). In short, studying Afro-Brazilian dances from the past has led me to understand their expansion, complexity, and value in the present.

Emphasizing what I have stated earlier, dancing Afro-Brazilian forms is to remember, and also to celebrate, African ancestry and struggles for freedom. It is to move our bodies to the sound of this memory, with emotion and strength. It is to stage the fight that was once for freedom and now is for a dignified place in society with rights and social justice today. Dance can be used to learn and now reinvigorate a collective strength, to maintain the ability to fight, and to combat still prevalent historical injustices. However, for dance to exist, it is essential to preserve and take care of the agent of its creation and diffusion: the human being in motion, alive, creative, and critical.

Conclusion

In looking back on Brazil's historical past, marked by European colonization and the enslavement of Africans and their children, I observe that if "luck" allowed Africans to survive, it was precisely their bodies, the only "commodity" of value for the colonizing oppressors, which also safeguarded their dances, customs, rituals, struggles, and knowledge. What made their cultures unique in relation to other contexts and cultural realities was a sense of collective strength that incorporated communication between the natural and supernatural worlds and among the living, the dead and nature. African and African-descendent communities depended on bodies dancing for their dynamic and collective strength! African-informed dances expressed and continue to express a sense of celebration for the successes of community life, while also transmitting mythical, real, or imaginary stories that serve as lessons and foundations for transferring ethical values, whether in the realm of spiritual beliefs or in the transcendence of these beliefs to shape psychological and social imaginations. So, celebration through dance, in addition to its festive meaning, contains resistance.

Looking at present circumstances, I am convinced that it is essential and urgent to recognize the importance of various forms of Afro-Brazilian cultural expression that have survived attempts at homogenization, repression, and prejudice. Afro-Brazilians are taking advantage of what African ancestry promotes, which is the possibility of transmitting knowledge to the generations that follow as a way of affirming and reconnecting to an ethnic and cultural identity. The understanding of this dynamic by new generations is what underpins both contemporary discourse and the black population's historical pursuit of spaces where its culture is preserved. This is where the dance has a prominent place.

For the legacy of African dance traditions to persist in Brazilian society, it was necessary throughout history for African descendants (who were immersed in knowledge through their dances) to develop concealment strategies. They disguised religions, customs, and traditions that had been persecuted for a very long time. This led them to find ways of reinterpreting their cultural legacies and of creating spaces for cultural organization and resistance. They developed ways to come together, to remember, and to affirm their cultures that consistently included a political sense of black militancy. This discourse forged collective struggles for the transformation of the social, economic, and educational lacunae that originally created inequality and distanced people from one another in society.

I marvel at the many ways that the contemporary Black Movement has engaged with the field of dance. Communities, social workers, scientists, and all those involved in this movement collaborate in building a black epistemology, based on deep understanding of the existential dimensions that underpin this danced form of cultural expression. Today, many Afro-Brazilians participate and identify ethnically; many even transcend the issue of skin color, but above all most take a political stance and contribute to the struggle against racial prejudice. This struggle demands the deconstruction of the negative social effects of Brazil's history. This struggle is not only about blacks, but also about all who live in a society. It is concerned with where all of our minds have been, and where they continue to be, as we all are affected by racism.

I think that black militancy never dropped its weapons, but continued to fight an unequal war from the past to the present. Yet, there are positive changes that, although small in relation to the whole, are in themselves immeasurable. A few examples will illustrate and provide a conclusion to the ideas I have developed here.

I refer first to the victory within the struggle for racial quotas in Brazilian universities, where many young black men and women have won the right to study – to become doctors, lawyers, teachers, dancers, anthropologists, economists, etc. Black participation in academic life is transforming mental frames and values and is promoting change, although we know that it might take centuries to eliminate color and/or racial prejudice. Another example is the victory of the black community in its struggle for the inclusion of Indigenous, Afro-Brazilian, and especially street and community dances, within the official curriculum of the School of Dance at the Federal University of Bahia (UFBA). Under the direction of professor Dulce Tamara da Rocha Lamego da Silva, an opening was approved for a full-time faculty position at the rank of assistant professor in June 2016. The application process publicized the need for, but also identified several qualified scholars in the study of the body with emphasis in popular, Indigenous, and Afro-Brazilian dance.[21] Marilza Oliveira da Silva and Vania Silva Oliveira emerged at the top of this very competitive selection process and were hired.

These and other examples are concrete victories of a collective Afro-Brazilian struggle. In different social sectors throughout Brazil, but especially in Bahia, varied kinds of work, volunteering, and study are, in fact, strategies of resistance that define – and strategies of achievement that solidify – the important role of a militant. Again, Afro-Brazilian dance is aesthetic and cultural, but indelibly associated with political activism.

References

Anon. (n.d.), "Dançando Nossas Matrizes um diálogo entre as danças afro brasileiras," http:// cufanabahia.blogspot.com.br/2011/06/dancando-nossas-matrizes-um-dialogo_01.html. Accessed January 17, 2014.

Araújo, Nelson de (1986), *Pequenos Mundos: Um Panorama da Cultura Popular da Bahia*, Recôncavo, Salvador: Universidade Federal da Bahia (EMAC) and Fundação Casa de Jorge Amado.

Bertolino, Júnia (n.d.), "Circulação de Ideias, Gestos e Saberes," *Revista Terreiro Contemporâneo*, revistaterreirocontemporaneo.blogspot.com.br. Accessed January 23, 2018.

Bhabha, Homi K. (1998), *O Local da Cultura* (trans. Myrian Ávila, Eliana Lourenço de Lima Reis and Glaucia Renata Gonçalves), Belo Horizonte: UFMG.

Biriba, Raissa (2010), "Dança e Cidadania," YouTube, http://www.youtube.com/watch?v=wFA_eL994MY. Accessed January 17, 2014.

Castro, Yeda Pessoa de (2005), *Falares Africanos na Bahia: Um Vocabulário Afro-Brasileiro*, 2nd ed., Rio de Janeiro: Topbooks Editora e Distribuidora de Livros Ltda.

Clark, Veve and Johnson, Sara (eds) (2005), *Kaiso!: Writings by and about Katherine Dunham*, Madison: University of Wisconsin Press.

Conrado, Amelia (1996), "Dança Étnica Afro-baiana: Uma educação movimento" ("Afro-Bahian ethnic dance: An education movement"), MA thesis, UFBA.

——— (2004), "Danças populares Brasileiras: Valor educacional, cultural e recurso para pesquisa e recriação cênica," *Revista da Bahia*, 32:38, pp. 36–46.

——— (2006), "Dança étnica Afro-baiana: Educação, arte e movimento," in Maria de Lourdes Siqueira (ed.), *Imagens Negras: Ancestralidade, Diversidade e Educação*, Belo Horizonte: Mazza edições.

Conrado, Margarete de Souza (2013), "Percursos de resistência e aprendizagem nos cortejos de Maracatu," Ph.D dissertation, Salvador: Federal University of Bahia.

Côrtes, Clélia Neri (1996), "A Educação é como o vento: Os Kiriris por uma educação pluricultural," Master's thesis, Salvador: Education Department, Federal University of Bahia.

Cunha Junior, Henrique (1992), *Textos Para o Movimento Negro*, 1st ed, São Paulo: EDICON.

Dossiê Iphan: 4 (2006), *Samba de Roda do Recôncavo Baiano*, Brasília, DF: IPHAN, http://portal.iphan.gov.br/uploads/publicacao/PatImDos_SambaRodaReconcavoBaiano_m.pdf. Accessed October 31, 2017.

Dunham, Katherine (2005), "The Dunham schools," in Veve Clark and Sara Johnson (eds), *Kaiso!: Writings by and about Katherine Dunham*, Madison: University of Wisconsin Press, pp. 479–80.

ELMO MELO DE MENEZES (2011), "PARAFUSOS," YouTube, https://www.youtube.com/watch?v=4Tzeauo94bw. Accessed April 13, 2015.

Ferreira, Maria Zita (1998), *Dança Negro, Ginga a História*, 2nd ed., Belo Horizonte: Mazza Edições.

Francisco Eugênio Carvalho Dias (2011), "Apresentação do Grupo Folclórico Parafusos de Lagarto/ SE em São Cristóvão no dia 08072011", YouTube, https://www.youtube.com/watch?v=ic2fOLKd9ko. Accessed April 13, 2015.

Freire, Paulo (2014), *Pedagogy of Hope*, London and New York: Bloomsbury.

Fundação Estadual de Cultura (1985), *A Indumentária Folclórica*, Sergipe: Núcleo de Pesquisa Folclórica.

Gomes, Nilma Lino (2015), "Diversidade étnico-racial, inclusão e equidade na educação brasileira: Desafios, políticas e práticas," http://www.anpae.org.br/iberolusobrasileiro2010/cdrom/94.pdf. Accessed July 4, 2015.

Jecupe, Kaka Werá (1998), *A Terra dos Mil Povos: História Indígena Brasileira Contada por um Índio*, São Paulo: Peirópolis.

Leão, José Antonio Carneiro (2011), "Saber Brincante: Cosmovisão e ancestralidade como processo educativo," Ph.D. dissertation, Federal University of Bahia.

Martins, Suzana Maria Coelho (2008), *A Dança de Yemanjá Ogunté sob a Perspectiva Estética do Corpo*, Salvador: EGBA.

Mattos, Wilson Roberto de (2008), *Negros Contra a Ordem: Astúcias, Resistências e Liberdades Possíveis (Salvador, 1850–1888)*, Salvador: EDUNEB and EDUFBA.

Moore, Carlos (2007), *Racismo & Sociedade: Novas Bases Epistemológicas para Entender o Racismo*, Belo Horizonte: Mazza Edições.

Munanga, Kabengelê (1986), *Negritude Usos e Sentidos*, São Paulo: Editora Ática.

Oliveira, Nadir Nóbrega (1992), *Dança Afro: Sincretismo de Movimentos*, Salvador: EDUFBA.

—— (2007), *Agô Alafiju,Odara! A presença de Clyde Wesley Morgan na Escola de Dança da UFBA, 1971 a 1978*, Salvador: Fundação Pedro Calmon.

Paim, Zilda, (1999), *Relicário Popular*, Salvador: Secretaria da Cultura e Turismo, EGBA.

Peron, Wendy (2005), "Katherine Dunham: One woman revolution" in Veve Clark and Sara Johnson (eds), *Kaiso!: Writings by and about Katherine Dunham*, Madison: University of Wisconsin Press, pp. 624–28.

Pires Neto, Josias (2005), *Bahia Singular e Plural: Registro Audiovisual de Folguedos, Festas e Rituais Populares*, Salvador: Secretaria de Cultura e Turismo, Fundação Cultural.

Portal do Governo (n.d.), "Mercedes Baptista", http://www.museuafrobrasil.org.br/pesquisa/hist%C3%B3ria-e-mem%C3%B3ria/hist%C3%B3ria-e-mem%C3%B3ria/2014/07/17/mercedes-baptista. Accessed July 29, 2016.

Reis, João José, (2002), "*Tambores e tremores: A Festa Negra na Bahia na primeira metade do século XIX*," in Maria Clementina Pereira Cunha (ed.), *Carnavais e Outras F(r)estas. Ensaios de História Social da Cultura*, vol. 1, Sao Paulo: UNICAMP/CECULT, pp. 101–55.

Rodrigues, Nina (1988), *Os Africanos no Brasil*, 7th ed., São Paulo and Brasília: Nacional and University of Brasília.

Silva, Ana Célia da (2011), *A Representação Social do Negro no Livro Didático: O que Mudou? Por que Mudou?*, Salvador: EDUFBA.

Silva, Leonardo Dantas (1998), *Estudos sobre Escravidão Negra*, Recife: FUNDAJ, Editora Massangana.

Silva Junior, Paulo Melgaço (2007), *Mercedes Baptista: A Criação da Identidade Negra na Dança*, Brasília, DF: Fundação Cultural Palmares.

Siqueira, Maria de Lourdes (ed.) (2006), *Imagens Negras: ancestralidade, diversidade e educação*, Belo Horizonte: Mazza Edições.

de Souza, Edison Fernandes (1995), "Representações sociais da cultura negra através da dança e de seus atores" ("Social representations of black culture through dance and its actors"), MA thesis, Rio de Janeiro: Universidade Gama Filho.

Suárez, Lucía M. (2013), "Inclusion in motion: Cultural agency through dance in Bahia, Brazil," *Transforming Anthropology*, 21:2, pp. 153–68.

Tiérou, Alphonse (2001), *Si sa Danse Bouge, l'Afrique bougera*, Paris: Maisonneuve et Larose.

Videira, Piedade Lino (2009), *Marabaixo, Dança Afrodescendente: Significando a Identidade Étnica do Negro Amapaense*, Fortaleza: edições UFC.

Notes

1 Translator's note: "interdiction of the body" (*interdição do corpo*) is a concept coined by Brazilian pedagogue Paulo Freire and refers to educational practices that prohibit corporeal expression.

2 In Brazil, "nations" refers to the gathering of ethnically or culturally related blacks. Africans and their descendants eventually organized and called themselves "nations" to differentiate the distinct, but often related ethnic groups that sometimes combined and at other times, remained separate in the African Diaspora; these nations were ethnic amalgams, not political nation-states.

3 Translator's note: The Dutch occupied a large part of Northeastern Brazil from 1630 to 1654.

4 *Samba de roda* is a type of *samba* in which participants form a circle and pairs of dancers move to the center and, after dancing together for a while, bump navels and choose new partners alternately in succession.

5 Translator's note: The Free Womb Law freed all children born after its promulgation; the Sexagenarian Law freed slaves over the age of 60.

6 Laranjeiras is a historical city in the north-bordering state of Bahia, called Sergipe. It is also a sugar area with a strong African presence and history of enslavement. Its large number of dances and festivals reveal elements of Indigenous, European, and African heritages and reflect the African corporeal memory of the city and its extended vicinity. One aspect worth mentioning is that all of the participants in these dances today are African descendants.

7 See also ELMO MELO DE MENEZES 2011; Francisco Eugênio Carvalho Dias 2011.

8 Translator's note: The *cuíca* is a percussion instrument frequently used in *samba*, consisting of a drumhead with a string attached inside. The *gonguê* is also a hand-held percussion instrument that looks like a bell-shaped stick that produces sound when hit with a piece of iron. It is frequently used in *maracatu* orchestras. The *ganzá* is a cone or cylindrical-shaped rattle instrument made of tin-plate and is very common in popular Brazilian orchestras.

9 Translator's note: *Caboclo* generally refers to rural northeastern small land holders or wage laborers of mixed Indigenous and European heritages. Editors' addition: Also among Afro-Brazilians, it refers to mixtures of African and Indigenous peoples and religions.

10 Translator's note: Acupe is a community in the municipality of Santo Amaro da Purificação, state of Bahia, whose population is of mixed Indigenous and African heritage.

11 Jege and Nagô were and are distinct, but related African nations.

12 *Cucumbis*, also called *cacumbis*, are processional dances of Afro-descendants in furs and feathers celebrating both puberty and funereal rites. *Samba-nego* is a popular black music,

dance, and theater genre, traditionally performed in the town of Laranjeiras, Sergipe. It represents the memory of battles among blacks, Indigenous people, and colonial oppressors. *São Gonçalo do Amarantes* is a popular dance that pays homage to the Portuguese saint; it has many variations and is popular in the interior of Brazil. *Samba de pareia* is a unique way of dancing *samba*. The word "*pareia*" means "as a pair" and points to the pairs of women who face each other, forming squares and performing specific footwork while dancing *samba* and exchanging places. This style originated in Mussuca, a black town in Laranjeiras, Sergipe.

13   *Frevo* is a dance and music that originated in the state of Pernambuco in northeastern Brazil, which has spread to other regions. "*Frevo*" is derived from "*ferver*" (to boil), and describes an accelerated rhythm and incredibly fast dance with many steps. Dancers hold a small umbrella that helps with balance. "Xangôs Pernambucanos" is how Afro-Brazilian religion is identified in the state of Pernambuco. It is believed that Xangô, the *Orixá* (deity) of fire and justice in Afro-Brazilian mythology, became so popular that people began to designate the locale as a religious site.

14   According to Yeda Pessoa de Castro, an ethno-linguist and specialist in African languages in *The Bantu in Brazil*, these people became known as Congos and Angolans, who currently account for numerous ethnic groups and languages distributed between those territories (2005: 34). This is one of several factors that identify *cucumbis* and other African-origin dance groups, for example, *congadas* and the dances of Angola rites within Candomblé. In many places, these groups are named incorrectly after their language heritage, Bantu, which is *not* an ethnic group.

15   Nadir was born in Salvador, Bahia, and graduated from the School of Dance at the Federal University of Bahia (UFBA). She is an activist, choreographer, and dancer who has performed frequently in Brazil, and on the European and African continents.

16   Ferreira is a teacher and dancer from the city of Floriano in the state of Piauí. She graduated from the School of Physical Education of the State of Goiás (ESEFEGO).

17   de Souza studied at the Federal University of Uberlândia in the state of Minas Gerais. He holds a doctorate in the field of physical education and before his academic career (in the 1980s), he was a dancer within Balé Primitivo de Arte Negra de Pernambuco (The Primitive Ballet of Black Art of Pernambuco).

18   Translator's and editors' notes: Ilê Aiyê was the first *bloco afro* of the 1970s; it was inspired by themes reminiscent of earlier revolutionary Carnival groups, e.g., Filhos de Gandhy in 1949. Huge floats carried the main performers and incorporated large numbers of followers. Many other *blocos afro* were created over the following decades.

19   See Bertolino, Júnia, 2014. Bertolino is an African dancer, journalist, and anthropologist, who holds a post-graduate degree in African Studies and Afro-Brazilians from the PUC-MINAS (2010). She is director and choreographer of the dance company, Baobab, and has written consistently about Marlene Silva. See the online magazine: http://revistaterreirocontemporaneo.blogspot.com.br/2011/08/danca-afro-brasileira-1.html.

20   *Jongo* is a circle dance originating in Congo/Angola culture, disseminated and resignified by Africans in the colonial period and currently danced in the southeast of Brazil, particularly in the state of Rio de Janeiro. It is accompanied by drumming and call and response singing that pays homage to the ancestors and to everyday life.

Samba de partido alto, samba de terreiro, and *samba-enredo* are all traditional *sambas* from the state of Rio de Janeiro. *Samba de partido* is characterized by the ability of master singers to improvise verses in the form of challenges and jokes; *samba de terreiro* is a *samba* that takes place in the sociocultural space of a backyard or a Candomblé compound; and *samba-enredo* is characterized by free-form songs, verses, and improvisation and the music of the *escolas de samba* (*samba* schools) and Carnival groups that come from peripheral communities outside of Rio. The musical intent is plot-driven, that is, the songs narrate a particular historical or cultural theme or they pay homage to important people in Brazilian culture. *Tambor de crioula* is another type of Afro-Brazilian circle dance/music from the state of Maranhão in northeastern Brazil. One person dances a solo in the center and calls another to dance next, through a movement called "*umbigada*" (from the word for navel) or "*punga*." The dance is typically accompanied by wooden drums that are held between the legs of the drummers.

21 The head of the selection committee was professor Amélia Vitória de Souza Conrado of the UFBA School of Education (FACED), and committee members included professors Evani Tavares Lima of the Federal University of Southwest Bahia (UFSB) and Ausonia Bernardes of the Faculdade Angel Viana. Of the 21 candidates who applied for the position, fifteen participated in the first stage of the competition and eight continued on to the additional examinations and evaluations. The two new hires are black dancers and choreographers with extensive artistic experience, socially relevant dance projects, and have offered courses in numerous Afro-Brazilian communities and professional schools.

Chapter 2

Dance Artistry and Bahian Forms of Citizenship: Isaura Oliveira and *Malinké*

Yvonne Daniel

Introduction

In honest homage to the entire Bahian community, this essay describes both pleasant and unpleasant vignettes to explicate a history of dance and "race"[1] in Bahia. Through the dance experiences and life history of one of Bahia's treasured black dance/theater artists, Isaura Oliveira, I examine dance practices and race within a complex dance environment that luxuriates in vibrant colors, delicious smells, exquisite sounds, and exciting activities, but also that same environment harbors deep prejudices. This essay reveals how individual dancers and corporate dance communities in Bahia have used dance practices to influence the requisite arrangements for diversity and respect within a political order. Race was core – both to Isaura Oliveira's first one-woman show, *Malinké*, and to what I experienced and observed in Bahia during the time just before and just after Brazilian military dictatorships ended in 1985.

Isaura Oliveira's choreography and memories display the distinct character of Bahian dance practices; they also represent the work and attitudes that I observed within Bahia's artistic community prior to advancements from the revolutionary education laws of 2003 and 2008 that boosted efforts to acknowledge African historical and cultural heritages in the whole of Brazil. At that previous time, many of Bahia's dance companies were engaged equally between dance performance and community service, and many Bahian dancers exercised as much socio-political commitment as they dedicated to dancing. Thus, there was a consistent relationship between dance performance and "community performance,"[2] which, in turn, exposed the socio-political dimensions of dance. In reviewing Isaura's experiences in relation to Bahian dance practices, varied models of citizenship have surfaced and prompted me to refine my earlier conclusions on dance communities and citizenship (see Daniel 2005: 267–68, 271–74, 2011: 189–93). Bahia's form of citizenship epitomizes its particular spirit and permeates both joyous and difficult events with calm and resolve. Before opening the curtain on Bahia through Isaura's experiences, I briefly review my conclusions regarding dance and citizenship.[3]

Forms of Dance Citizenship

Regardless of genre, dance generates a unique set of feelings that performers experience in the process of dancing and that they act upon thereafter. The feelings are first felt as individual, but contagious exhilaration inside the body; those feelings produce a kindred collective, which ultimately results in a sense of connectedness and shared solidarity, a kind of shared citizenship. Such feelings are most closely contained in anthropologist Victor Turner's term *communitas*, which refers to the sense of collective well-being and bonded belonging that surrounds group membership and mass group activities within kinship and religious communities, public festivals, as well as other secular events among non-kin.[4] Attachment, belonging, and commitment exude from within the dancing body and engulf dancers, musicians, other community members, and occasional visitors. *Communitas* fosters relationships and consequently (more often than not) integrates performers into the social or religious group. *Communitas* is generated while dancing and music-making, but its effects within dancing communities *last beyond the dance event.*[5] As the group continues to perform (weekly, monthly, or even annually), relationships are cemented and both kin and non-kin are bound, such that each performing participant takes on agreements and responsibilities as if she, he, or they were a member of a family, tribe, or clan.

Dance groups that remain together over time become dance communities – special, heart-felt groups that perform dance, make music, and maintain a sense of attachment and resultant citizenship. Granted, the citizenship these dance communities offer is not the official or political citizenship vested in rights and responsibilities within nation-state organization, but it is an alternative or "cultural" citizenship that becomes a shared responsibility or even exceeds the attachments, loyalty, and connectedness that are most often grounded in political citizenship.[6]

Notions of citizenship have apparently had a very long history in parts of Brazil and such notions have taken a variety of forms. Historian Yuko Miki suggests that notions of citizenship should be added to notions of resistance that have served as meaningful behaviors for African Diaspora communities and have permeated so much of the literature. In her study of nineteenth-century maroons, Miki documents African descendants running not toward the wilderness of actual or somewhat guaranteed freedom, but disappearing into or re-entering territories of enslavement, in order to express their rights to freedom and a citizenship that was presumed, although not assured (Miki 2012). Miki states:

> The São Mateus *quilombolas* [maroons] confronted the exclusion from citizenship experienced by enslaved people throughout postcolonial Brazil [...]. As such, for the *quilombolas*, marronage signified not only an act of slave resistance, but also a political expression [...]. [T]he *quilombolas* decision to live and act as free agents with the rights of citizens cannot be appreciated under the rubric of slave resistance alone.
>
> (2012: 497–98)

Comments of other scholars add to my further contemplation of citizenship among African-descendent dance communities in Bahia. For example, political scientist Michael Hanchard states, "...contrary to the [...] notion that citizens are abstract bearers of rights, [we] ... need to conceive of citizenship as that which would inhere in concrete persons" (Hanchard 1999a: 75).

Also, anthropologist Renato Rosaldo's words remind me to adhere to "vernacular notions of citizenship" rather than replicate the approach and evaluations of those who exert power. Rosaldo states:

> In Latino contexts the term *"cultural"* calls attention to the range of claims that citizens (especially groups subordinated by race, gender, and class) make against the state [...]. The term *"citizenship"* ranges from the formal rights of citizens with respect to the state, such as voting, to more colloquial or vernacular matters that revolve, for example, around the distinction between first- and second-class citizens or the desire for recognition as a full member of a group.
>
> (Rosaldo 2003b: 3, original emphases)

Therefore, I hesitate to continue using the term "alternative citizenship," with its possible inference to hierarchy and power and in light of the varied situations and forms that citizenship has taken among northeastern/Bahian Brazilians in particular. While occasionally different from cultural understandings held by Bahians and visitors to Bahia in the 1980s and 1990s (as readers will see), Rosaldo's, Hanchard's, Miki's, and others' thinking on citizenship have assisted my conclusions on late twentieth-century behaviors in Bahia. I use "cultural citizenship," Rosaldo's term, to describe what I observed and experienced, but also to focus on the strategic role of Bahian dance artists and dance arts organizations before and after 1985.

Cultural citizenship accrues in all sorts of dance communities and is not restricted to the Latin American or African Diaspora communities discussed here. Cultural citizenship prioritizes members' actions toward both social and artistic responsibilities, thereby providing connectedness and a tremendously satisfying sense of well-being and wholeness. The dance arts, i.e., dancing, dance drama, and music-making, balance concerns of the self and the group, and produce a spirit of togetherness that ultimately generates feelings and convictions surrounding citizenship. Dance arts produce feelings and notions of belonging that are similar to those attached to legal citizenship; however, political organization requires additional actions to attain legal citizenship. Like nerves that fire throughout the body so that muscles produce both autonomic and intentional movement, dance communities produce sufficient "firing" motivations and consequent behaviors to generate cultural citizenship. With the addition of overt political or socio-political activity, dance communities become fully engaged *within* a political order – whether or not they satisfy legal requirements for citizenship.[7]

Performing Race and "Nation"[8] for the Nation-state

Malinké: Representaçao de Uma Negra en Traje de Ensaio ("*Malinké*: A representation of a black woman in rehearsal clothes") was Isaura Oliveira's startling evening-length choreography, which she performed between August 17 and 25, 1988, in a major venue for showings of professional contemporary arts, *Quarta da dança* (Wednesday Dance), sponsored by

Figure 3: *Malinke Woman Isaura*. Courtesy of
Aristides Alves, *A Tarde* newspaper, August 24,
1988.

Fundaçao Cultural do Estado da Bahia ("The Cultural Foundation of the State of Bahia").
Here, Isaura expressed through dance what she and many Bahian artists were feeling in the
1980s, especially those who were simultaneously pursuing success in the commercial arts
market and a University degree in dance or theater. In her solo choreography, Isaura
confronted common everyday behaviors that ridiculed or negated the crucial cultural and
material input made by the African Bahian population. She confronted both spoken and
unspoken rules about when, where, and how black artistry could be staged. And, she
confronted official positions that excluded the study and validation of a black aesthetic within
University curricula. Her choreography focused on the African Brazilian, Afro-Brazilian, or
black[9] dancing body in challenging circumstances, expressing pivotal societal views.

Malinké, the main title, was critically important because it was the first indication of
the choreographer's intent for public understanding. It referenced a mostly Muslim nation
of Mande speakers, an African people from the ancient Mali Empire, who spread across
West Africa from the thirteenth to the seventeenth century and were later trafficked in great
numbers to the Americas. In Bahian slavery, Malinkes were also called Mandingos and Malês,
and were preferred for their literacy and full range of capabilities; they were simultaneously
feared for their vindictiveness in captivity.[10] Malês led the largest slave rebellion in Salvador,
Bahia, in 1835 and *Malinké* thus referenced this courageous history and emphasized Isaura's
major interest in African peoples within the choreography.[11] Additionally, "representation"
in the choreography's subtitle clearly referred to more than a solo black woman dancer;

it suggested African Brazilian women, as well as Malinkes, and a representation of many African descendants. With "rehearsal" in the subtitle, and especially in a creative space and time for dance and dance audiences, the idea of something unfinished seemed potentially critical to the choreographic content as well.

In Isaura's words, *Malinké* was ultimately an artistic critique of "[…] the narrow spaces available for the black body at that time" (Oliveira 2012).[12] Ballet, modern concert dance, and, to a lesser extent, European-derived or Portuguese folk dance were well-represented in Brazilian curricula and in the arts market, while Afro-Brazilian dance was primarily relegated to the streets. Isaura's dream for her graduation concert was a narrative choreography that displayed the daily struggles of a black woman dancer and through her, the struggles of diasporic Africans, especially women. It proposed to sum up her/their frustrations and joys and to reference smart, determined Malinke/African descendants. Isaura's provocative solo was also an attempt to widen a lens on the plight of black dance students at the Universidade Federal da Bahia (UFBA or Federal University of Bahia), as she joined the social protest forces that were brewing at that time in Bahian society.

"Isaura Oliveira faz '*Malinké*' no teatro do ICBA" (*A Tarde*, August 10, 1988).
"A dança a negra Isaura em Malinké" (*Correio da Bahia*, August 17, 1988).
"Malinké, Um espetáculo ultrapassando fronteiras" (*A Tarde*, August 24, 1988).[13]

Translation:

"Isaura performs '*Malinké*' at Theatre of ICBA"
"The dance of the black woman Isaura about *Malinké*"
"*Malinké*, a performance crossing boundaries"

According to most press reviews and estimations of dance contemporaries, *Malinké* was masterful in concept and execution, but its preparation spawned an unfortunate series of events. Through several succeeding scenes, a black ballet dancer changed costumes and sets, music and movement qualities, historical eras and contemporary spaces, to convey the layers of hurts and indignities she and other black Bahian women experienced in daily life, in staged performance and concert activities, and in the university setting. With each change of costume, another dimension of the black dance artist or the African Bahian woman emerged: first ballet dancer, then the mother of poet Luis Gama, a fictitious female Malê warrior, and finally US African American singer Billie Holiday. While sifting and analyzing what Isaura told me, I found that attractive and unattractive dimensions of Bahia were also revealed in each character's section within the choreography.

Isaura created the original story and choreography, collaborated with a professional team of Bahian artists, and performed the full-evening solo. Aninha Franco, a well-respected script writer, was inspired to help build a theatrical team because of the provocative and relevant topic and the talent she observed in Isaura's initial approach and plans. Antonio Godim, who was researching "blackness" for his MA thesis in theater (recommended by

Franco), joined as theatrical director. Set designer Márcio Meirelles's collaboration resulted in a series of stunning sets with distinct levels and specific colors for each black woman character. Armando Pekeno and Paulo Fonseca, both from Balé Teatro Castro Alves, co-choreographed with Isaura, separately, for specific music within the piece.

The music changed according to each personage the black dancer portrayed. Chico Buarque de Hollanda's popular song about "A ballerina doesn't, and everybody else does"[14] was particularly apt accompaniment for the first scene, as it matched the feelings of African Bahians in that era, especially those espoused by the popular *blocos afros – Carnaval* dance arts organizations of Bahia. For example, lyrics spoke of "bad teeth" and "lice in the hair" that prevailed among thousands of poor people, except for the ballerina who had beautiful teeth and clean, styled hair. The ballerina in the first scene represented dancers with crisp ballet technique, and also elites, "whites," the wealthy, the powerful. "Everybody else" in the choreography stood for capable African Brazilian dancers with little or no opportunity for technical training, and also the black population, the white, "brown," and black low-income class, or what is popularly called "the 99 percent" today. Isaura also used Billie Holiday's recording "Strange Fruit," Miriam Makeba's "The Reason is Your Skin," and instrumental music by Bira Reis. Aninha Franco and Isaura selected prose excerpts and poems that served as a richly textured narrative for the ensuing drama.

In honor of a strategic and memorable mentorship with Cida Linhares, a ballet teacher apart from the University, Isaura choreographed and performed a technically solid and ultimately surprising ballet section.[15] The choreography began with the black ballet dancer in a long, layered black, gray, and white gown. Her ballet aesthetic was pronounced through *arabesques, developés*, classical positions of the feet, etc. that projected softness and yet, strength, symmetry, and balance, and coincided with musical theater movement that followed the tradition of ballet; in other words, she used a bit of off-centered and grounded movement, but technically, the movements honored a ballet base.

As with all dance students of the era, Isaura had to perform in both balletic and modern concert dance works to demonstrate proficiency for graduation. Previously, she had had to endure literally thousands of comments about her big *bunda* (backside, bottom, butt), her inappropriate profile or silhouette, and her "lack of technique" (read: ballet technique).[16] She was uncomfortable in ballet technique, mainly as a result of the ongoing, debilitating critiques of her body and many other black bodies. In other words, many African Brazilian dancers had been harassed at the hands of university officials who represented Bahian society at large. Thus, in the choreography, ballet itself (in addition to the character of the ballerina) became an important protagonist. The black ballet dancer represented Isaura's university student position at the time, but her balletic dance also relayed, as subtext, the supposed superiority and actual prestige that ballet enjoyed. Ballet has been the protagonist of many a black dancer's attempt to join the professional dance world throughout the major part of the twentieth century.[17]

A definitive choreographic change occurred when the black ballerina began to pirouette; suddenly, as if a hurricane or tornado had grabbed her, the dancer's elegant, layered white, black and gray gown was torn and ripped away and the ballet dancer was turning furiously in browns, reds, and black. The ballet dancer was transformed, as if manifesting an *Orixá* or *Caboclo* spirit.[18] She was Luiza Mahim, a nineteenth-century African Brazilian woman primarily speaking the words of her son, revolutionary poet Luis Gama, with her back to the audience when the turns stopped. (Long sections of the narratives were published in the press; all lauding the choreographed messages of historic black struggle and black pride.)

The black dancer in rehearsal clothes was looking into a mirror for inspiration from history – black women's histories. Her words and phrases relayed a legacy of marginalization, insecurity, dismissal, and subservience – to ballet technique, to men, to a domineering society. That legacy was answered in bodily frustration, hurt, and anger. She began to tease her hair with an African hair pick, and to stare at and pointedly stroke her dark skin. These movements were gradual at first, but became relentless, ultimately climaxing with a full "Afro" hairstyle, unseen bruises, and extreme agitation – apparently because of the color of her skin. Isaura's long, crimped hair became a gigantic bush and her *canela* (cinnamon) skin color made a racial image undeniably clear. Two conceptions of race were portrayed: a contemporary black dancer's conception of her place in the world as a strong, strikingly beautiful, creative and efficient mover, an empowered woman, and Bahia's conception of her as a beautiful "thing" or part of a dismissed group of African Brazilians.

Malinké stretched in content from race to validation of women: the black woman dancer and her physical force, the African-descended woman and her critical, but unheralded role in Bahian society, most Brazilian women in the fight against machismo for gender equality, body control, and equal regard, and African Bahian women who remained at the bottom of the social totem pole. A fictional woman leader in the Malê rebellion appeared. She had fought against the Portuguese and referenced not only African Brazilian women from a past and contemporary Bahia, but also the fight of black dance students in UFBA's Dance Department. Gama's words, "I Am You," framed the scene, referenced "representation" in the title, as well as shed light on neglected historical documentation. The Malê woman warrior reported that black and mulatto merchant women, who sold food in the streets, were able to send messages to guerilla fighters in undetected ways. She highlighted the role of black women who worked in colonial households and relayed what was strategic for underground, rebellious black movements.[19]

Race and gender inequality were at the core of Isaura's choreography and simultaneously simmering at the core of Bahia in the 1980s. Tensions grew, overtly expressed in the mesmerizing focus on the skin of the black dancer. Miriam Makeba's repetitive refrain, "The reason is your skin," haunted the choreographic sections, indicating how tightly gender was woven into issues of race. Between the compilation of narratives and the dance movement sequences, the audience understood the black woman dancer as representative of the black population of Bahia, which totaled 85 per cent and was identifiable and physically present, but routinely marginalized – not recognized for its distinct culture and not given acknowledgment for its national contributions.

To further address the conflicts surrounding ballet technique and racism, the choreographic team developed a mirror section at the end of the ballet section, including a dance section behind a costume rack. Theatrically and stylistically, Isaura and Armando Pekeno developed a metamorphosis of the ballet dancer to Luiza Mahim and then, to the revolutionary Malê woman warrior. Pekeno's thrust was "[...] a choreography about skin [and] became the ritual of celebration [...]" for who the black dancer really was and for what those two militant characters stood (Oliveira 2014). Isaura and Pekeno emphasized Pekeno's mixture of modern concert dance and Afro-Brazilian *Orixá* and *Caboclo* traditions (or *dança afro*[20]) through three Makeba songs; then, as the black dancer arose from in front of the mirror and receded behind a costume rack, which was filled with rehearsal costumes, they incorporated the improvisational techniques of Leda Muhana and Betti Grebler.

At the time, Muhana and Grebler were creating a new technique, "Tran-Chan," that emphasized a combined scientific, body-centered, and personal-centered approach to choreography.[21] Behind the costume rack, Isaura revealed only her knees, lower legs, and feet. Through the juxtaposition of ballet footwork and Muhana and Grebler's studied weight changes, Isaura performed an impressive new dance to symbolize the obscuring racist critiques and hegemonic evaluations of her body by Bahian society and UFBA's Dance Department. Her lower body (the seen body) was controlled with feet positions, locomotor sequences, freezes or long balances; her upper body (the hidden body) made radical costume changes behind the scene. This was technically challenging, but choreographically intriguing and Reis's experimental music with percussion, saxophone and flute befitted the unique scene of the "body-less black dancer." And I would add that this image and sequence corresponded to the troubling situation of a negated or "black-less" Bahia.

By this time in the choreography, the black dancer was consumed with upset and grief, but also, eventually, with resolve. As she emerged from behind the costume rack, yet another costume and character were revealed as the result of choreographic collaboration with Paulo Fonseca (who was known for his strong modern aesthetic within classical ballet). The first part of this section could not have been executed without the use of a wall as a prop. Fonseca used the wall for body designs that were contorted, off-balanced, totally irregular, alluding to the hanging bodies in trees that were the subject of the song Billie Holiday was singing – about lynching in the US south, called "Strange Fruit." Fonseca and Isaura augmented their design to include the agony and disappointment of Billie Holiday's life as well. The potential victory of self-pity – or a weakened spirit from utter devastation – could have been imminent; however, the team did not end with tragedy.

In the very last section, Márcio Meirelles's important set design visually established the bustling playfulness of black nightlife, which was intermittently thrown into shock with the insurmountable pains of life in the African Diaspora – not just African Brazilian lives. The black woman dancer was transformed again, this time looking full of vivacious energy in a long, sparkling, green gown – bubbling, proud, and excited – as if situated in a nightclub or lounge of Salvador, Rio de Janeiro, New York City, or Chicago. The choreographic team's projection of Billie Holiday continued, this time in her joy and achievements. The fashionable barroom lady on the stage was left enjoying life (as most African Brazilians do).

Her beauteous spirit was last witnessed smiling and gently laughing while sipping from a glass of wine and savoring the vital black life surrounding her.

The black dancer danced for and as Billie Holiday, who achieved success despite her addictions and afflictions; she danced for and as Miriam Makeba, whose songs successfully focused international eyes on an imprisoned Nelson Mandela and South African apartheid in the 1980s; she danced for and as Luiza Mahim and other real and fictitious black Brazilian women throughout history and literature. She danced for and as each symbolic woman character and the thousands of African Brazilians who "make it" daily, despite prejudicial estimations of their worth, staggering psychological debilitation, and fundamental limitations on their existence.

The audience was given only one "rehearsal" version where the strong, free spirit in vibrant green ultimately continued dancing as an unperturbed African Bahian woman. This transformed black woman dancer certainly became the model for active resilience within harsh, "unlovely" circumstances, but she also represented possibilities. As Isaura wrote: "... not finished yet was the idea. The light going down showed... [us still] in pain, but we were thinking!!!!! We just did; we continue doing; we did not finish yet!" (Oliveira 2014). Accordingly, the choreography remained a "rehearsal" in which Isaura could play the part differently at another time and reach the same or not-so-similar conclusions. This version's ending indicated joyous fearlessness – the political hope of the era – and triumph over imminent obstacles.

The black dancer portrayed alienation as a ballet dancer; power and transformation as an *Orixá* or *Caboclo* spirit; fear, frustration, and anger as the African Brazilian in the mirror; courage, endurance, and nightmarish suffering behind and transiting away from the costume rack and against the wall; and utter and sustaining joy within the lady in green. The dancing character experienced serial transformation and projected growing strength; her message was resilience and persistence in hopes of full liberation for Malinke/African descendants.

For pursuing this graduation project with the probability of publicly critiquing UFBA's Dance Department and dramatically unearthing Bahia's hegemonic denial of deep-seated racism and misogyny, Isaura was formally dismissed from the Dance Department's special work program for graduating senior student teachers and was denied permission to perform her scheduled choreography. Under the guise of both a failing grade in ballet technique and new administrative rules, there was "no longer room or placement possibilities" that were available to her. In response to this devastating blow, Isaura calmly, yet firmly took another (higher) path. She was non-confrontational, but fighting nonetheless as she successfully mounted her militant University project a year later – in collaboration with Bahia's top theater artists, which garnered rave reviews (Oliveira 2012).[22] For example:

There is a tenuous and subtle border between artistic languages. There are doubles and multiplicities that operate between their universes. There is an artist with her own reflexive solitude establishing [the fact that she would be] exceeding the limits of this border, synthesizing these forms of transcending expression, augmenting the global repertoire of humanity. There is an hypnosis, a sexual energy seducing the public, changing or catalyzing the energy. All this can be fully observed in *Malinké*... with Isaura Oliveira....[23]

Malinké is still a work in progress; however, it already has excess of possibilities to appear and make the public uncomfortable, provoked.[24]

When the Dance Department closed its doors to her and her university situation became public on campus as well as within the larger Bahian community, director Yeda Pessoa de Castro welcomed Isaura into the Center for African and Asian Studies (CEAO) within UFBA. Isaura's new graduation project at CEAO covered the history of and artistic productions by African Bahian dancers in the 1970s and 1980s. Through what she called "N'Bunda," an historical investigation of those professional dancers with black *bundas* was completed. Its name helped to extend Isaura's public fight with Dance Department officials who were originally and consistently upset about her *bunda*. From her safety net in CEAO, they could not ignore news about her research project and also, about her documentary video. While Isaura interviewed African Bahian dance specialists to write "N'Bunda," she created "Kubungula," a documentary video of their personal histories and perspectives.[25] Isaura also received unsolicited and overwhelming public support, most prominently in 1988 at a City Hall celebration in Bahia. A unique festival award within a dance competition in Rio followed this accolade, and Isaura was acclaimed "Newest Honored Choreographer." Isaura received public and professional, national and international attention. Through *Malinké*, Isaura had danced race, African nation, and gender![26]

Developing Black Artistry in Bahia

Isaura's experiences during childhood and adolescence were midway within a continuum of Bahian possibilities. Her life contained more commonalities than rarities among African Brazilian children, i.e., growing up black in Bahia did not necessarily mean growing up uneducated and poor in a *favela*.[27] Still, Isaura's upbringing as a middle/upper-class, black Bahian was privileged when compared to that of many other African Bahians. She was brown-skinned with long crimpled hair, a fairly broad nose, and full lips; she enjoyed a private school education; she had more than her daily living requirements; and her family included two loving parents, seven siblings (two brothers, one sister, and four cousins), and many close kin. Despite this stability and respectability, Isaura stated "[a]s a young girl, I always knew that I could never be Queen of Corn in São João festivals or a Miss Universe" (Oliveira 2012).[28]

From the beginning, Isaura displayed an undeniable streak of independence and creative artistry. She grew up dancing with her father, moving spontaneously to recorded music that he would bring home. He noticed her creativity early and encouraged her improvisations. He participated in all-family and neighborhood dance competitions with his daughter as his partner, and usually won. They were "notorious" as a dancing duo – inventive and rhythmically astute. Through her father and his insatiable love of dance music, Isaura was saturated with the music of Martinho da Vila, Jackson do Pandeiro, Elza Soares, Luis Gonzaga, and *samba* and Brazilian country music galore. Additionally, she was "at home" with the Jackson Five, James Brown, Miriam Makeba, Hugh Masakela, and other African American and African popular music stars of the day. She was addicted to musicals on film: Brazilian musicals with Grande Otelo and Oscarito and US American musicals with Fred Astaire, Gene Kelley, and all the "tribal dancing" within Tarzan movies. She was not enamored with the screen characters of Tarzan or Jane, but she waited breathlessly for the staged virtuosity of Tarzan's "natives." She devoured dance of all sorts and beginning at around 11 or 12 years old, she began orchestrating family and neighborhood productions. Her sense of social justice surfaced early also; at age 14, she created her first theatrical solo about the freeing of enslaved Brazilians.

Her mother modeled Bahian womanhood of the era, which taught Isaura to be strong, but not to directly confront, to be quiet and not to show tears. She taught Isaura to sew, brought her attention to fabric textures and colors, and inspired Isaura to design costumes for all of her performances. Her mother also impressed her with a special sense of spirituality. The family majority were Catholics who later converted to Protestant fundamentalism, but her mother deepened Isaura's independent spiritual quest with private journeys to the ocean, where they always left a white rose.[29] At other times, her mother left her with one of the midwives who had assisted at Isaura's birth, like Dina Roxa, Tia Isabel, or Tia Duzinha. Through Dina Roxa, her mother, and especially her grandmother, Isaura learned the properties of herbs and plants, which revealed a *Caboclo* heritage within her African and Portuguese roots.[30]

One could imagine that Isaura's youth would fit an idyllic picture, but it didn't. Isaura's father fought her decision to become a professional dancer and refused to pay for dance lessons. He preferred that she study engineering to help the family construction business, since Isaura had proven to be an excellent student. Over time, Isaura defied the rules and struggled against limitations, machismo, and later, the Protestant evangelism she witnessed in Bahian society and in her household. She treasured her freedom to do what she wanted in theatrical dance. Secretly, the supportive parents of a best friend, who was taking lessons in ballet, jazz, and tap, paid for Isaura's first dance lessons. Thus, formal dance training for Isaura began relatively late – at around 14 years old – with the study of jazz and tap; and early dance classes remained a life-long secret to avoid her father's anger. Classes also caused irritation because they were regimented and fully structured. Isaura preferred improvisational, creative dancing. She excelled despite her preference because she worked hard – always; however, she fought the mainstream culture around her. Regardless of whether Bahian childhood and youth were equated as quite comfortable or exceedingly difficult, neither type was free of prejudice against dark-skinned people or "things African," and this was jarring for Isaura, now a university student and a child of the new 1980s Bahian generation – a race-sensitive generation.

I should emphasize here that while Isaura's experience in university dance was difficult and offensive, it was not unique. Many dance students have entered the university system and discovered their love of dance bombarded with rules and regulations, biases and preferred tastes, and certainly at a feeling level, their commitment to the art was challenged. Isaura and her contemporaries had had a history of white dominance and notions of black inferiority that had repeatedly squashed challenges for change, but they were experiencing new attitudes, laws, and protections. For example, racial prejudice was deemed a crime in Brazil for the first time, beginning in 1988 (Hanchard 2006: 14, 1999a: 59–61; Butler 1999: 41–46). For Isaura's generation, this and similar changes represented mounting ammunition and they were ready to shoot for other possibilities.[31]

In Isaura's words, her university case was "a fight against bad education"; however, it was also part of an ongoing political strategy (Oliveira 2012).[32] Isaura's dilemma on the university campus was the same dilemma of black Bahian artists in the streets within *blocos afros*, as well as African Brazilian people across the nation-state. It was representational of many who founded dance arts organizations in the 1970s and 1980s, where they could communicate

Figure 4: *Black Woman, Looking for Her Space.* Courtesy of Vera Godin.

bodily what they called "blackness" or what they could NOT say directly in the midst of a highly censored dictatorship. Isaura's dilemma was in the dance tradition of Raimundo Bispo dos Santos or *Mestre King*, who, in the 1970s, had designed and organized Afro-Brazilian dance classes, called *dança afro*, in the curriculum of Serviço Social do Comércio (SESC), an off-campus education site in the black community (Yudin 2005: 6).[33] Through *dança afro* – a combination of US modern concert dance and Afro-Brazilian Candomblé dance vocabularies (often called "folkloric" outside its religious contexts), Mestre King communicated non-verbally and definitively to a prejudicial system that Bahian dance courses – at UFBA or elsewhere – should include the fullest representation of Bahian dance expressions – namely, *capoeira*, related *maculelê, samba, Orixá* dances, and the new and innovative mixture, *dança afro*. Respect for African Brazilian culture was needed in addition to the North American modern dance techniques and European-based dance history that were already offered.[34]

Within the mushrooming Afro-Bahian dance context of the 1980s, Isaura's choreography was distinct. It was dance/theater and a challenge for the university and Bahians at large to accept. Her first one-woman show demanded respect for the black body – diasporic or continental, female, male, or transgender, dancing or not dancing. Isaura aimed for acceptance of Malinke/African descendants.

Race in Bahia

Multiple scenes in Isaura's *Malinké* pointed repeatedly to race, which was the pivotal concern that Bahian activists were consciously inserting into political organizing of the late 1980s (da Silva 1999; Hanchard 2006: 1–29). *Malinké* was a powerful example of highlighting and identifying with African Brazilian culture in order to halt deplorable commentary about the black body and black aesthetics. It encouraged profound shifts in cultural values that might break through prevalent ideas and abusive behaviors. However, dance in the University and the arts market reflected social relations in the wider Bahian society of the 1980s; the mainstream systematically rejected blacks, dismissed black contributions, and marginalized black art, aesthetics, and artists, except perhaps in sports and tourist enterprises (Santos 1999; da Silva 1999; Scott 2001: 5–6; Daniel 1996).

African Brazilian history recounts centuries of black agency that is often minimized or erased, e.g., many *quilombos* or maroon encampments throughout Brazil (not just the famous *Palmares*), revolts and rebellions, black newspapers, congresses and conventions, as well as artist organizations – all of which assisted African descendants and gave voice to ongoing attacks, first on slavery and later, on neo-colonialism and racism (Leal 2001: 294–99; Butler 1998: 88–133; see also Miki 2012: 495–528). Despite the fact that most institutional efforts by African Brazilians to address racial inequality and improve conditions ended in defeat, their continuous historical presence speaks through the incessant waves of black action against racism. The first Brazilian centers to combat racism on a national scale were São Paulo (e.g., through Frente Negra Brasileira or FNB, the Black Brazilian Front of 1931) and Rio de Janeiro (e.g., through Teatro Experimental do Negro or TEN, the Black Experimental Theater organized by Abdias do Nascimento in 1944) (do Nascimento [1979] 1989: 161–68; Leal 2001: 294; Butler 1998: 115–33, 168–71; Hanchard 2006: 6–9). Also, since the turn of the twentieth century, the Brazilian cultural intelligentsia – a group of white sociologists, artists, and writers (e.g., Gilberto Freyre from Recife, Argentinean artist Carybé living in Rio and Bahia, Jorge Amado from Bahia, Pierre Verger from Paris and later Bahia, etc.) had, in effect, appropriated African Brazilian culture as their private research reserves, thus inhibiting or delaying the empowerment of African descendants to collate and disseminate their own histories and contributions (see also Scott 2001: 88–89). This critique does not dismiss the extraordinary efforts or demean the important contributions that each of these scholars and artists have made to Bahia, Brazil, or to the African Diaspora literature; however, I am not aware of attempts on their parts to share authorship, specialization, or position and most importantly, to assist or promote African Brazilian community representatives as knowledgeable specialists (see also Butler 1998: 42–44, 206–07).

The formal challenge to unjust racial conditions in Bahia started mushrooming in the 1970s with Núcleos Culturais Afro-Brasileiros (Afro-Brazilian Cultural Centers), *bloco afro* Ilê Aiyê in 1974, and Dia Nacional da Consciência Negra in 1978 (Leal 2001: 297).[35] At that time, African Brazilians endured racial indignities routinely. Dictatorships and military rule had barred any discussion that portrayed Brazil negatively and the myth of a non-racist, "democratic" Brazil was strongly defended. Many middle-class Bahian families did not recognize their own African history and heritage, nor did they come in direct contact with African Brazilian associations, such as the major *terreiro* communities. It was equally true that many Brazilians simultaneously embraced "things African," like *samba*, dark-skinned soccer great – Pele, Bahianas in Candomblé attire, etc. As in the dance of the Yorubá divinity Iemanjá, when she holds one palm up and the other palm down and continuously alternates positions, Bahians maintained a similar wave-like attraction to and rejection of African elements. Interest in Africanity came to Bahian shores, but with equal energy, rushed back to Atlantic Africa.

Some Brazilian artists were exiled for their outspoken critiques of racial inequities and others emigrated to liberal international sites (e.g., Abdias do Nascimento to Yale and State University of New York [SUNY] Buffalo Universities; singers Caetano Veloso and Gilberto Gil to London; Chico Buarque de Hollanda to Italy; theater artist Thereza Santos to Bissau [Guinea Bissau] and Luanda [Angola]; dancers/*capoeiristas* Jelon Vieira and Loremil Machado to New York City; etc.). On the other hand, during the decades of interest here, many lower-class, dark-skinned Bahians identified with blackness and celebrated it defiantly in the streets at Carnival time. "African consciousness" or lots of history, education, and cultural sensitivity were missing within the understandings of mainstream Bahians in the 1980s.

Colonial framing of many issues and neo-colonialism did not advance the treatment of race either. Certainly after 1832, Brazilian history displayed efforts to establish the nation-state, but also it displayed deep-seated fascist thinking from Italy and Germany. Such biased attitudes permeated official positions during the 1920s to 1940s and affected democratic efforts that surfaced between 1930 and the end of dictatorships in 1985 (see da Silva 1999; dos Santos 1999; Graham 1999; Hanchard 1999a; Santos 1999; Winant 1999). The radical moves of the 1980s and early 1990s were about racial equality in all social spheres through *Movimento negro* or MN organizations or through what became the Workers Party (PT), the Democratic and other political parties, trade unions, and interest groups (Winant 1999: 103–05).

By the 1990s, significant change was "on stage," but much of the official view was still "an act." Repressive leadership was officially over; democracy was in process; and more attention was being given to black cultural events in Bahia and throughout Brazil. The significant impetus for change came mainly from public dance activities and the negative responses surrounding the centennial celebration of the abolition of Brazilian slavery in 1988. Many African Brazilians said, "*Cem anos sem aboliçao*" (one hundred years without abolition). They looked forward more so to the celebratory recognition of the 300th anniversary of the death of Zumbi in 1995 (Leal 2001: 294, 297–98).[36] Still, black monologues shifted gradually into Brazilian dialogues about racial inequality with the development of political party strategizing, labor organizing, and Black History tourism. Bahian officials saw the focus on race come from the background to the foreground of Brazilian politics. They also recognized the material wisdom of exploiting their advantages within the support of celebratory traditions that were native or historical to their region, i.e., black traditions.

Bahian dance organizations in the university, the arts market, and the streets were revolutionary interest groups that acted with developing political groups in consciousness-raising agendas that celebrated blackness, featured African Brazilian identity and history, and espoused political goals to fight racial inequalities. Inside the University, the attempt to promote African Brazilian culture with Candomblé dance movements, other Afro-Brazilian dance vocabularies (e.g., *capoeira*, *maculelê*, or *samba*), and continental African and US Diaspora dance forms – all stimulated official opposition and unofficial political activism. Black dance teachers (developed and trained outside the University by Mestre King and his followers in community education centers) and black popular dancers and musicians led students and the Bahian public from *blocos afros* in conscious shifts of perspective through sensitive displays and portrayals of African heritage and African Diaspora history. Performance scholar Anna Scott cites a *bloco afro* leader as saying: "[...] a *bloco afro* can draw thousands and get them to listen to and understand the history of Africans worldwide within the span of a few refrains" (Scott 2001: 5). Parading during *Carnaval* publicized international perspectives on race and racism; parading highlighted comparable situations of injustice and struggle, educated the Bahian public on inequality and freedom, and conversely, advertised and spread African Brazilian situations to an international audience. In other words, global inequities were danced and sung in stark comparison with local Bahian examples, and both situations were condemned appropriately.

By the late 1990s, early perspectives had faded with new interdisciplinary analyses of race in Brazil. At first, Frank Tannenbaum's legal and cultural treatment of Latin American slavery ([1946] 1963) had augmented Gilberto Freyre's classic *Casa Grande e Senzala* ([1946] 1956), which was a meticulous history of the Brazilian colonial period that exposed "black grandmothers in the closet," but also lodged the myth of Brazil's "racial democracy." As a privileged white compatriot of blacks, Freyre saw his native Brazil with little overt racism, which he felt he had come to know well from living in the United States as a teen and young adult. Tannenbaum narrowed the argument to the differences in Portuguese and Spanish laws that he felt explained enslavement practices and accounted for Brazil's "docile" form. Carl Degler, writing almost 30 years later (1971), stirred the controversy again by attributing the inequality that obviously existed to socio-economic reasons; but broader examinations replaced all these views (Degler 1972; do Nascimento [1979] 1989; Hanchard 2006; Butler 1998; Caldwell 2007). For example, Hanchard's (1999a) academic and political activist collection provided an historical review and comprehensive interpretations of how power and power politics had guided motivations and events to reach an explicit understanding of official nation-state and everyday racism in Brazil.[37]

In addition to academics, public dialogue among community scholars and political activists by the end of the 1990s had made many Brazilians aware that racial inequality greatly influenced national policies. In Bahian society particularly – where most dark-skinned, impoverished, and (previously) politically impotent black Brazilians lived, it took cultural and political workers from MN organizations and street demonstrations, usually in the form of dance arts, to progress effectively toward the eradication of racial prejudice, discrimination, and segregation. Many personal prejudices, social norms, and governmental misdoings had yet to be conquered before "a lived democracy" was in place.

Also, as a result of technological advances by the 1990s that spread popular culture worldwide (e.g., long-playing records, early beta videos, and 8mm film with sound for personal use in the 1980s, and high8, VCR video recordings, personal computers, and email in the 1990s), African Brazilian culture grew in popularity.[38] Likewise, Brazilians were influenced by African Diaspora musical currents of the 1960s and 1970s, e.g., US rhythm and blues, US rock and roll, Jamaican *reggae*, Cuban/Puerto Rican *salsa*, Trinidadian *calypso*, Dominican/Haitian *merengue* and popular music on the African continent, e.g., from Mozambique, Zaire, Ghana, Nigeria, etc. Bahians combined these foreign elements with their own music and dance and created new Afro-Brazilian dances. African-based music launched black culture as "world music," such that Afro-Brazilian dance music held a prominent position, not only for Brazilians, but also for global others. At home in Bahia, racist attitudes were sometimes camouflaged by the contagious popularity of Afro-Brazilian dance music; however, the political struggle against racial inequality remained a paramount theme within Bahian dance organizations – in the university, the arts market, and the streets. Bahian musical styles of politicization matched Brazil's stereotyped style: soft and sweet, persistent and resilient, and deeply affective and effective.[39]

Artistic Renderings of Bahian Cultural Citizenship

At the end of the twentieth century, Bahian dance arts organizations, called alternately *blocos afros* and *afoxés*, advanced the political development that was crisscrossing the nation.[40] Most organizations began in the 1970s and 1980s after *bloco de índios Apache* spawned *blocos afro* Ilê Aiyê, which then spawned Olodum and others: Agbara Dudu, Araketu, Badauê, Didá Banda Feminina, Malê Debalê, Muzenza, etc. (not in this alphabetical order). As cultural expressions, they formed around African Brazilian identity, the attempt to embrace "African-ness" or blackness, and the struggle for racial equality in Bahia. They used the signature gestures of Candomblé nation dances, sequences from *capoeira* and *maculelê*, and *samba* magnetism to stimulate resistance to oppression and to secure committed resilience, especially while under a dictatorship or military rule. *Blocos afros* had exemplified African Brazilian cultural concerns in the 1970s and had promoted the power and beauty of African Brazilian nations during well-publicized *Carnaval* parading.[41]

A precedence – and historical model – was Filhos de Gandhy, an all-male *afoxé* organization that has had literally thousands of members parading together annually in *Carnaval* since the 1940s. Among a few earlier *afoxés*,[42] Filhos de Gandhy aligned itself first and importantly with Candomblé. Those who performed were from the three related Candomblé *terreiros*, that is, most belonged to the Ketu/Nagô nation in which Oxalá was the leading *Orixá* and became the patron saint for their performing group. Through the judicious peace, rhythms, gestures, and color (white) of Oxalá in that *Carnaval* celebration of 1949, they combined Candomblé symbols with Mahatma Gandhi's principles of non-violent protest (symbolized in white and blue) and proudly and peacefully danced an almost silent and measured parade, as opposed to the usual highly animated and boisterous parade dancing. They disrupted conventional *Carnaval* parading with a powerful, disquieting performance. Determined dancing bodies communicated non-verbally the generalized discontent of the poor, mainly African-derived masses to the political elite of Bahia and the nation-state.[43] Filhos de Gandhy was promoting local political action through global themes within artistic Carnival presentations that encouraged liberation from discrimination and segregation, equality for non-white Brazilians, and persistent political action. Because of Filhos de Gandhy's powerful, resistant parading, politics and dance arts organizations became linked, either heralding or accompanying the social and political action of black performers and importantly, the thousands they influenced.

Within the *en masse*, peaceful, yet resistant form used by Filhos de Gandhy, the new revolutionary Bahian dancers and musicians of the mid-1970s and 1980s injected then-current socio-political content. Under the influence of MN organizations and the National Day of Black Consciousness and under the weight of persistent local problems, Bahian artistic directors of *afoxés* and *blocos afros* directed huge ensemble performances, aggressively emphasizing race and as always, overtly connecting performances to Candomblé and nation dances.[44] Outdoor rehearsals that could involve literally hundreds of performers in black neighborhoods made themes surrounding inequality – discrimination, segregation, and racism – routine experiences for thousands of community members who listened and observed (Yudin c. 2005: 17–19; Scott 1998: 12–14, 2001: 56–57). By dancing and singing about international issues (such as wars in Zimbabwe and Angola, Rasta glory and repression in Jamaica, droughts and conservation efforts in Ethiopia) and comparing these to lingering prejudice about African Brazilian nations, obscured freedom throughout the nation state, and ecological problems in Bahia, *blocos afros* challenged local political and social abuses and communicated publically on sensitive issues within regime borders (either dictatorship or beginning, conservative democratic boundaries).

What was new to the form was an augmented definition of "community," beyond established dance arts organization membership, the required and consistent commitment to social services for needy community members, here called "community performance." *Bloco afro* and *afoxé* performances entertained the public, educated peoples of African descent toward political action, and also encouraged genuine social service. In the 1970s and 1980s, Filhos de Gandhy's model of community articulation and the bid for wholesome social wellness re-appeared within several local groups, albeit in a more openly aggressive or militant form.

Ilê Aiyê was the first of several "new" dance arts organizations that produced performances, promoted African Brazilian culture, and included the less fortunate of Bahia as part of its dance community (Scott 1998: 10; Perrone and Dunn 2001: 84). It countered the all-white majority of Bahian *Carnaval* groups with its all-black membership restriction, beginning in 1974. Antonio Carlos "Vovô" and Apolônio de Jesus started performances in Liberdade, the largest black neighborhood of Salvador, Bahia. They were influenced by ongoing political activities that had been challenging the national political agenda from São Paulo and Rio de Janeiro since the 1930s, but more recently by active political development in Bahia. Ilê Aiyê became (and continues as) a major Bahian dance arts resistance organization that is against the racial inequality that has continued, especially since the dedication of the National Day of Black Consciousness. Ilê Aiyê has contributed hundreds of thousands of hours of community assistance to improve health and social services for the needy and has invested performance profits in non-governmental education and other commercial programs that directly benefit Liberdade residents.

Bloco afro Olodum was founded in 1979 by percussionist Neguinho do Samba, but received its greatest attention after 1986 when Neguinho combined *samba* rhythms with *merengue* and *reggae*, introducing *samba reggae* as a music and dance sensation (Perrone and Dunn 2001: 28, 180–84).[45] Olodum has enjoyed international success through recordings and international celebrity collaborations ever since. Its beginnings were centered in African Brazilian identity and combating racism, especially assisting abandoned children. It bourgeoned into an immense commercial enterprise, with boutiques selling t-shirts and recordings, ostensibly dedicated to assist community health and political development, but also within revised definitions of African Brazilian identity. Over time, Olodum has promoted "Brazilian-ness," abandoning political goals surrounding blackness and/or "African-ness," and has sought liberation for all Brazilians instead.[46]

In the 1980s, these and other *blocos afros* and *afoxés* encouraged Bahians and Brazilians at large (through dancing, song lyrics, costumes, flags and banners, and African nation religious chants and dance gestures) to take serious note of African identity and history, community needs, social discontent, and political views that were being articulated within huge ensemble performances. The powerful significance of thousands of Bahians dancing fiercely in unison (and also improvisationally), routinely singing and underscoring themes of equality and freedom, was not lost on the powers that be in government, the University, or the arts market.

Social service to needy communities was the prominent element of *bloco afro* and *afoxé* performances in the 1980s. Social service emanated from administration offices where directors and a staff attended to dance and music rehearsals, alternative school programs for neighborhood children, health assistance, job opportunities in commercial stores and tourist boutiques, and of course, *Carnaval* preparations (costumes, float designs, fliers, rehearsal schedules, etc.). All of these interests generated new definitions of social responsibility and of citizenship. Direct service to community members became a special type of performance when enacted by dance and music artists – a "community performance" that involved dancing, music-making, social services, and public marking of community issues. That combination resulted in danced political statements and became the signature activity of Bahian dance arts organizations and their members.

Contrasting group with individual artist renderings of "dance and community performance," I return to Isaura Oliveira's recollections, as representative actions of other African Bahian artists working courageously before the supportive laws of 2003 and 2008. According to Isaura, black dance students who matriculated within the federal and state University systems of Bahia organized a black dance company in the mid-1980s, which still exists today (Oliveira 2012).[47] Odundê featured Afro-Bahian dance vocabularies and garnered performance space for African Bahian dancers and African Brazilian issues. Odundê's first illustrious group of dancers included Tânia Bispo, Reginaldo "Conga" Flores, Isaura Oliveira, Neuza Saad, Raimunda Senna, and Rosângela Silvestre. Conceição Castro was the administrative director and both Neuza Saad and Conga (one of Mestre King's assistants and protégés) acted as choreographers, and all danced together. Odundê members grounded themselves in Afro-Brazilian ritual dance under Conga's tutelage, in addition to the founding teaching patterns that combined modern concert dance with Afro-Brazilian nation dances, *capoeira*, *maculelê*, and *samba* moves.[48] In other words, they utilized *dança afro*, which had been organized earlier by Mestre King and supported in the courses and performances of US African American dance professor in residence, Clyde Morgan.

The importance of this cadre of Odundê dancers is found in the invaluable training each dancer received and is seen in the danced personal expressions that have been part of their individual professional signatures forever after. The original cadre shared experiences that influenced their maturation as individual dance artists. Most have worked tirelessly in the movement languages of black Brazilian culture and, as teachers, instilling appreciation and stamina in the fight for African Brazilian culture and performance. For university dance students, Odundê affirmed the fight with UFBA for African Brazilian dance culture to be represented officially in the dance degree curriculum. This has finally come to pass with the hiring of three specialists in Afro-Brazilian dance as part of the full-time dance faculty at UFBA (in 2016).

Despite devastating critiques of their bodies, skin color, abilities, and potential and despite the fact that success did not come quickly, Isaura and hundreds of black independent artists throughout Bahia challenged an unequal system. *Malinké* underscored creative resistance to not only the intolerance and insensitivities of the Federal University and its Dance Department, but also the unjust cruelty of all those in positions of power throughout the Brazilian nation-state – black, brown, and white – who were NOT actively involved in the destruction of racial prejudice and its consequences in the lives of African Brazilians. Additionally, Isaura's courageous stand revealed the heartache of Bahian women – not only the harassed black ballerina or African Bahian women in general, but half of Bahia's potential human resources.[49]

Isaura's *Malinké* was a prime example of how individual artists contributed to Bahia's stake in equality and how artists paid political dues. Isaura refused the status quo and took a brazen public stand. Her *Malinké* in *dança afro* style within the arts community, like *blocos afros* and *afoxés* in the streets, modeled militant, but necessary and effective socio-political action. She was not only interested in her own university plight, but also the plight of African descendants everywhere, and her choreography showed the Bahian public how dance artists worked in the university community for the wider community, and how individual artists and community groups fit into national concerns. The combining of artistic lives with social action toward community well-being did not necessitate an either/or dichotomy, but rather a both/and possibility.

Malinké artistically shouted out how to confront and overcome such ingrained culture. The method involved honesty, determination, and organization. When barriers appeared, Isaura staunchly upheld values pertaining to African identity, Bahian history, and women's rights, and creatively proceeded with an organized choreography, a specific plan. In concentrating on the positive, she did not dwell on the door that closed at UFBA; rather, she proceeded on the open path, which manifested dramatic spirituality within the choreography and overflowing good fortune outside the university. Ultimately, her challenging choreography did not stop her graduation or career development; it aided her growth and advertised her strategic enterprise. Isaura modeled attachment to the principle of equality and the value of fairness. In her soft and gentle, yet fierce and courageous Bahian manner, she demonstrated expertise and creatively highlighted UFBA's limited curriculum in hopes for better education for those coming after her. Through a race-focused and gender-focused choreography (and her two accounts of black dancer histories – "N'Bunda" and "Kubungula"), she served the community by addressing inequality in the curriculum and everyday racism in her Bahian world.

Conclusion

Thus, the artistic production and community service of both individual artists and corporate dance groups in Bahia contributed to new notions of citizenship for the 1980s and beyond. Bahian dancers and dance arts organizations became communities based on both the feelings members experienced while dancing and music-making together and the socio-political commitment members accepted. Each community used the dance arts to consummate not only performance, but also "community performance." Combined artistic and socially motivated activity stated bodily that Bahian dance communities would shoulder responsibilities that were normally reserved for other segments of society. Their artistic-socio-political endeavors were responses to the inequalities that prevailed in Bahia, and their unconventional concerns or non-artistic activities publicized the commitment to social responsibility of dance arts communities. Beyond the *communitas* – the bonds of affection and attachment – dancers, musicians, and participating others experienced within ongoing performances, Bahian dance arts communities augmented their boundaries to include others in need of bonding and care. Additional firing motivations that thrust Bahian dance communities into simultaneous artistic and socio-political action resulted in deepened understandings and enlarged views of citizenship. Members of dance arts organizations certainly believed they were acting more like citizens than many other Bahians.

What I came to understand by reviewing Isaura's life, examining Isaura's emblematic choreography, and analyzing her work in relation to the development of Bahian dance arts organizations from the 1970s to the 1990s, was that a unique set of dance practices had evolved: dance practices that required "community performance" or social service. Regardless of the type of involvement or degree of activism among solo artists or among *bloco afro* or *afoxé* members, help and assistance arrived at community destinations where they contributed to understandings of African legacies and contemporary social situations in the African Diaspora. Isaura's audiences came away provoked, sensitized. Members of Bahian dance arts organizations fully understood the power of dance and dance music and used those for huge communities of need nearby. That type of commitment replicated the basic *communitas* that has existed within most dance communities over time *in memoriam*; it also demonstrated Bahia's distinct *communitas* version and its ongoing character. In Bahia, that level of involvement grew into something larger, which I identify as an addition to customary feelings of cultural citizenship. Performing participants first bonded as a dancing and music-making community and cared for one another in familial ways, regardless of actual kinship. Then, the concerns and feelings of the wider community took hold and socio-political action became part of the responsibilities of dance arts organization membership.

In effect, Bahian dance arts organizations generated a second version of cultural citizenship that involves firing motivations and actual social service but, of course, does not confer legal citizenship. Where racism, gender discrimination, and poverty overwhelmed local Bahian community members and their ability to act socially or politically, dance arts organizations added direct community service to their corporate goals and required a membership that was committed to actively addressing and resolving such problems.

Bahia's solo artists and dance arts organizations have influenced succeeding generations of dancers and musicians since the last decades of the twentieth century; they continue to challenge the status quo and improve the wellness of African Bahians. Because of this, I view Bahia's danced cultural citizenship as one of the most formidable models of citizenship. Through dancing, music-making, the public marking of needs, and direct community service, Bahian dance arts organizations echo cooperative ways of living and being fair. Through both dance performance and "community performance," Bahian dance artists and company directors speak non-verbally for the neediest members of their local communities by incorporating an abundantly generous and powerful form of citizenship and by publicizing that form across Brazil and the world.

Bahia's current status is different from the 1980s and early 1990s; however, my hope is that it has taken responsibility for its bigoted history, as many previous colonial sites have done at least officially, and is working rigorously against the maintenance of a culture of prejudice, discrimination, segregation, racism, misogyny, or inequality. Additionally, I hope this volume's spotlight on Bahia demonstrates how striking the Bahian model of cultural citizenship is and how integral dance practices are to that model. While the model is not totally successful (as in Isaura's university performance that was cancelled originally or in the excesses and other problems found over the years in *blocos afros*), it still provides citizens everywhere with a framework that functions as a firm and sensitive commitment to equality. In the most humane and humble ways, Bahian dance communities of the 1970s, 1980s, and 1990s taught social responsibility in opposition to racial prejudice and marginalization, and inspired many "to do good." The results were, and still are, shared community responsibility for social wellness and a sense of genuine citizenship, played out powerfully in artistic and socio-political ways.

References

de Almeida, Lino (2005), *A Bahia do Afoxé Filhos de Gandhy*, Bahia, Brazil: Pólo Industrial de Manaus por Sonopress-Rimo Indústria e Comércio Fonográfico: CDBA multimedia.

de Andrade, Marilia and Canton, Katia (1996), "Overview of dance research and publications in Brazil," *Dance Research Journal*, 28:2, pp. 114–22.

Averill, Gage (1997), *A Day for the Hunter, A Day for the Prey: Popular Music and Power in Haiti*, Chicago: University of Chicago Press.

Bastide, Roger (1978), *The African Religions of Brazil*, Baltimore: Johns Hopkins University Press.

Browning, Barbara (1995), *Samba: Resistance in Motion*, Bloomington: Indiana University Press.

Buarque, Chico (1988), "Edu Lobo," CD, Biscoito Fino, https://www.discogs.com/Edu-Lobo-Chico-Buarque-Dan%C3%A7a-Da-Meia-Lua/release/7881642. Accessed November 1, 2017.

Butler, Kim (1998), *Freedoms Given, Freedoms Won: Afro-Brazilians in Post Abolition São Paulo and Salvador*, New Brunswick: Rutgers University Press.

Caldwell, Kia (2007), *Negras in Brazil: Re-envisioning Black Women, Citizenship, and the Politics of Identity*, New Brunswick: Rutgers University Press.

Daniel, Yvonne (1996), "Dance performance in tourist settings: Authenticity and creativity," *Annals of Tourism Research* 23:4, pp. 780–97.

—— (2005), *Dancing Wisdom: Embodied Knowledge in Haitian Vodou, Cuban Yoruba, and Bahian Candomblé*, Urbana–Champaign: University of Illinois Press.

—— (2011), *Caribbean and Atlantic Diaspora Dance: Igniting Citizenship*, Urbana: University of Illinois Press.

Deflem, Mathieu (1991), "Ritual, anti-structure and religion: A discussion of Victor Turner's processual symbolic analysis," *Journal for the Scientific Study of Religion*, 30:1, pp. 1–25.

Degler, Carl (1972), *Neither Black nor White: Slavery and Race Relations in Brazil and the United States*, New York: Macmillan.

Diouf, Esailama (2011), "Staging the African: Transcultural flows of dance and identity," Ph.D. dissertation, Northwestern University.

Emery, Lynne ([1972] 1988), *Black Dance from 1619 to Today*, 2nd rev. ed., Highstown: Dance Horizons and Princeton Book Company.

Freyre, Gilberto ([1946] 1956), *Masters and Slaves: A Study in the Development of Brazilian Civilization* (trans. Samuel Putnam), 2nd ed., New York: Knopf.

Gaspar, David and Clark Hine, Darlene (eds) (1996), *More than Chattel: Black Women and Slavery in the Americas*, Bloomington: Indiana University Press.

Gomez, Michael (2005), *Black Crescent: Experience and Legacy of African Muslims in the Americas*, Cambridge: Cambridge University Press.

Gottschild, Brenda (1996), *Digging the Africanist Presence in American Performance: Dance and Other Contexts*, Westport: Greenwood Press.

Graham, Richard (1999), "Free African Brazilians and the state in slavery times," in M. Hanchard (ed.), *Racial Politics in Contemporary Brazil*, Baltimore: Duke University Press, pp. 30–58.

Guillermoprieto, Alma (1990), *Samba*, New York: Knopf.

Hanchard, Michael (1999a), "Black Cinderella: Race and the public sphere in Brazil," in *Racial Politics in Contemporary Brazil*, Baltimore: Duke University Press, pp. 59–81.

—— (ed.) (1999b), *Racial Politics in Contemporary Brazil*, Baltimore: Duke University Press.

—— (2006), *Party/Politics: Horizons in Black Political Thought*, London and New York: Oxford University Press.

Karasch, Mary (1996), "Slave women on the Brazilian frontier in the nineteenth century," in David Gaspar and Darlene Clark Hine (eds), *More than Chattel: Black Women and Slavery in the Americas*, Bloomington: Indiana University Press, pp. 79–96.

Landes, Ruth ([1947] 1994), *City of Women*, Albuquerque: University of New Mexico Press.

Leal, Gilberto (2001), *"Fáírgá/Ífaradá*: Black resistance and achievement in Brazil," in S. Walker (ed.), *African Roots, American Cultures: Africa in the Creation of the Americas*, Lanham: Rowman & Littlefield Publishers, Inc., pp. 297–99.

Lister, Ruth (1998), *Citizenship: Feminist Perspectives*, New York: New York University Press.

Maddox, Camee (2015), "Drum, dance, and the defense of cultural citizenship: *Bèlè's* rebirth in contemporary Martinique," Ph.D. dissertation, Gainesville: University of Florida.

McAlister, Elizabeth (2002), *Rara!: Vodou, Power, and Performance in Haiti and Its Diaspora*, Berkeley, Los Angeles and London: University of California Press.

Miki, Yuko (2012), "Fleeing into slavery: The insurgent geographies of Brazilian *Quilombolas*, 1880–1881," *Americas*, 68:4, April, pp. 495–528.

do Nascimento, Abdias ([1979] 1989), *Brazil, Mixture or Massacre? Essays in the Genocide of a Black People* (trans. Elisa Larkin Nascimento), Dover: Majority Press.

Oliveira, Isaura (2012), personal communication, May and September.

——— (2013), personal communication, February.

——— (2014), personal communication, April.

Perrone, Charles A. and Dunn, Christopher (eds) (2001), *Brazilian Popular Music and Globalization*, 2nd ed., New York and London: Routledge.

Reis, João José ([1986] 1993), *Slave Rebellions in Brazil: The Muslim Uprising of 1835 in Bahia*, Baltimore: Johns Hopkins University Press.

——— (2001), *"Quilombos* and rebellions in Brazil," in S. Walker (ed.), *African Roots, American Cultures: Africa in the Creation of the Americas*, Lanham: Rowman & Littlefield Publishers, Inc., pp. 301–13.

Rosaldo, Renato (2003a), "Cultural citizenship, inequality, and multiculturalism," in Linda Alcoff and Eduardo Mendieta (eds), *Identities: Race, Class, Gender, and Nationality*, Malden and Oxford: Blackwell Publishing, pp. 336–41.

——— (2003b), *Cultural Citizenship in Island Southeast Asia: National and Belonging in the Hinterlands*, Berkeley: University of California Press.

dos Santos, Ivanir (1999), "Blacks and political power," in M. Hanchard (ed.), *Racial Politics in Contemporary Brazil*, Baltimore: Duke University Press, pp. 200–14.

Santos, Thereza (1999), "My conscience, my struggle," in M. Hanchard (ed.), *Racial Politics in Contemporary Brazil*, Baltimore: Duke University Press, pp. 188–99.

Scott, Anna Beatrice (1998), "It's all in the timing: The latest moves, James Brown's grooves, and the seventies race-consciousness movement in Salvador, Bahia, Brazil," in Monique Guillory and Richard C. Green (eds), *Soul: Black Power, Politics, and Pleasure*, New York: New York University Press, pp. 9–22.

——— (2001), "'*A Fala que Faz*/Words that work': Performance of black power ideologies in Bloco Afro Carnaval in Salvador, Bahia, Brazil, 1968–present," Ph.D. dissertation, Northwestern University.

da Silva, Benedita (1999), "The black movement and political parties: A challenging alliance," in M. Hanchard (ed.), *Racial Politics in Contemporary Brazil*, Baltimore: Duke University Press, pp. 179–87.

Suarez, Lucía (2010), "Citizenship and dance in urban Brazil: *Grupo Corpo*, a case study," in M. Diouf and I. Kiddoe Nwankwo (eds), *Rhythms of the Afro-Atlantic World*, Ann Arbor: University of Michigan Press, pp. 95–120.

Tannenbaum, Frank ([1946] 1963), *Slave and Citizen*, New York: Vintage Books.

Thomas, Deborah (2011), *Exceptional Violence: Embodied Citizenship in Transnational Jamaica*, Durham: Duke University Press.

Turner, Victor (1969), *Ritual Process: Structure and Anti-Structure*, Piscataway, New Jersey: Aldine Transaction Publishers.

—— (1982), *Celebration, Studies in Festivity and Ritual*, Washington, DC: Smithsonian Institution Press.

Vaughan, Umi (2012), *Rebel Dance, Renegade Stance: Timba Music and Black Identity in Cuba*, Ann Arbor: University of Michigan Press.

Walker, Sheila (ed.) (2001), *African Roots, American Cultures: Africa in the Creation of the Americas*, Lanham: Rowman & Littlefield Publishers, Inc.

—— (2012), Personal communications on telephone and over email, September and November.

—— (2013), *Conocimiento desde adentro: Los afrosudamericanos hablan de sus pueblos y su história*, Cauca, Colombia: Universidad de Cauca.

Winant, Howard (1999), "Racial democracy and racial inquiry," in M. Hanchard (ed.), *Racial Politics in Contemporary Brazil*, Baltimore: Duke University Press, pp. 98–115.

Yudin, Linda (2005), "Divine innovation: The emergence of contemporary Afro-Brazilian dance from Salvador, Bahia," unpublished paper.

—— (2012), Personal communication by email, September.

Notes

1   In this essay, words that denote *socially constructed ideas* – "race," "black," "white," "brown," "nation" – are enclosed within single quotes only once for this acknowledgement; in this case, race synchronizes with Brazilian racial categorization in the 1980s and 1990s, when "blackness," "African-ness," or Africanity was not recognized squarely.

2   A term I explain fully later.

3   This essay is dedicated to Mercedes Baptista, Marlene Silva, and Isaura Oliveira, three Afro-Brazilian dance treasures. I thank Isaura for the precious time we have spent on this project. *Axé!* Her generosity, and that of Aninha Franco, Gracinha Santana Rodrigue, Lais Morgan, and all my Brazilian consultants over the years, has been extraordinary and Bahia is in my heart because of them. I also thank Kelly Sabini, who first called my attention to dance and citizenship in 1991 and to Anna Scott for her still unpublished, but insightful Ph.D. dissertation on dance in Bahia (2001).

4   Turner's work popularized the Latin *communitas*; see Turner (1969, 1982).

5   Turner most often referred to *communitas* within the liminal or liminoid state of "betwixt and between" during ritual and other performances. See Deflem (1991), where the type of *communitas* I refer to is described as "normative communitas, or existential communitas, which is organized into a social system" (1991: 15).

6   See other notions of citizenship in Rosaldo (2003a: 336–41, 2003b: 1–15), Lister (1998), Suarez (2010: 95–120), Thomas (2011), Maddox (2012), and Walker (2013).

7   I have identified three models of cultural citizenship in dance communities thus far: (1) the strong engagement and sense of belonging within dance communities almost everywhere, (2) Bahia's direct model of artistic plus socio-political engagement, and (3) the US indirect model of artistic plus dance-school engagement. Here I limit my discussion to the first two models.

8   "Nation" in Bahia and other parts of the Americas refers to African Diaspora people whose names are not always consistent with ethnic groups on the African continent, but who see themselves as distinct African descendants. They are recognized as African heritages or African ethnic amalgams in the Americas, some of which are religious communities, but none is an official nation-state.

9   African Brazilian, Afro-Brazilian, and black Brazilian are synonymous in English for "Brazilians of African descent" with preferences of one or the other appearing in different eras, decades, and locales or with the development of language over time. In this essay, I prefer "African Brazilian" and "black" for people; I leave the shorthand and often hyphenated "Afro" to reference dance, music, or hairstyles. See also Scott (2001: 131–32).

10 "Malês" was the preferred term in Brazil's academia of the 1980s, over "Mandingos," Malinkes, or enslaved Muslims. Among Bahians, "Mandingo" had a widespread connotation of "wearer of talismans" (which some Muslims carried) and from that, of "witchcraft" or "sorcery." This unsettling or pejorative understanding may have accounted for Isaura's use of "Malinké" instead of "Mandingo" or "Malê." Isaura does not remember why she chose "Malinké" except that "[i]t came strong on my ears and on my reading [...]. I wanted to honor African people, our African ancestors..." (Oliveira 2013).

11 See Reis (2001: 306–08), who is considered the expert on Brazilian Malês (see also Reis [1986] 1993) and note that Isaura's title appeared in 1988 just as Reis's academic conclusions were first being circulated. See also Gomez (2005: 93–97, 101–17) and Butler (1998: 190–91).

12 I have known Isaura Oliveira for more than twenty years; however, I conducted specific weekly interviews with her in Castro Valley, California, in May 2012 and November 2012 for this publication. Thereafter, we exchanged emails, conversed by telephone, and engaged in additional interviews in February 2013 and again in April 2014 to confirm information. This quote is from the interview on May 21, 2012.

13 I am enormously indebted to Aninha Franco who provided these headlines, press clippings, and photographs from her personal archives. These provided critical reviews of Isaura's work during that period.

14 From the 1988 album, *Dança da meia-lua*.

15 "Cida was a phenomenal teacher, who guided not only myself, but many others from the student dance community and somehow, made everything [ballet movements and ballet technique] flow positively. Imagine! I received the highest grade on my ballet finals. My arms, my posture, my confidence was there [after Cida's critical training]," said Isaura, when reviewing an edited version of this essay (Oliveira 2014).

16 Brazilian dance researchers Marilia de Andrade and Katia Canton state: "There is a very strong belief among most Brazilian dance teachers, dance students and even the general public that only classical [ballet] training provides the dancer with good technical skills. Although unfounded, this is definitely a predominant opinion" (1996: 116–17; see also 114–22 and Scott 2001: 173–78).

17 This was the case until the successes of: (1) Janet Collins, the first black prima ballerina of New York's Metropolitan Opera in the late 1940s, hired full-time in 1951; (2) Mercedes Baptista, the first black prima ballerina in Rio de Janeiro's Municipal Ballet Theater in 1947; (3) Carmen de Lavallade dancing in the mid-1950s to late 1970s; and (4) Arthur Mitchell, the first and only African American male ballet principal in New York City Ballet from the 1950s until 1970 (Emery [1972] 1988: 313–16, 320–22, 332–33; Gottschild 1996: 64–65, 76–77; https://www.sfgate.com/bayarea/article/Janet-Collins-prima-ballerina-at-Metropolitan-2613780.php; http://www.wikidanca.net/wiki/index.php/Mercedes_Baptista; https://medium.com/@kennedycenter/2017-honoree-spotlight-carmen-de-lavallade-aeb0a25bd863; https://en.wikipedia.org/wiki/Arthur_Mitchell_(dancer). All accessed March 21, 2018).

18 *Orixá* are Yoruba (African) divinities worshipped in varied rites of the Afro-Brazilian religion, called Candomblé; *Caboclos* are the Indigenous divinities of Brazil. Sometimes *Caboclos* are integrated within African religious groups (see Bastide 1978: 219, 257).

19 For studies on African Brazilian women, see Landes ([1947] 1994), Caldwell (2007), Karasch (1996: 79–96).

20 I discuss *dança afro* later in this essay. For critical interpretations of mainstream Brazilian views of *dança afro* (and *bloco afro* movement), see Scott (2001: 112–13, 178–81).

21 Muhana and Grebler emphasized a particular choreographic process that utilized dance movement through weight changes and the embodiment of the personal within performance, a process-oriented and person-centered approach to choreography.

22 N.b. Isaura was graduated in proper standing after mastering ballet exams in 1987; she was able to present her graduation choreography to the public in 1988.

23 Albenísio Fonseca, *A Tarde*, August 24, 1988.

24 Vera Gondin, *Correio da Bahia*, August 17, 1988.

25 Unfortunately, I did not have access to either "N'bunda" or "Kubungula." They were stored in Bahia and Isaura was too immersed with her mother's illness and eventual transition to look for them when she returned to Bahia in June 2012. Isaura made "Kubungula" with financial support from Television Educativa in 1987. ("Kubungula" is the name of a traditional Congo/Angola dance where sorcerers or witches go from door to door in their communities.)

26 After the production of *Malinké*, Isaura received invitations for theater, opera, television, solo commissions, and concerts. She mounted choreographies and performed across Brazil and traveled to France, Belgium, Germany, Italy, and the United States. What she explored in Bahia 1988, her African Bahian identity and her activist sense of justice, she brought to her new home in the Oakland Bay Area of California, where she continues to teach Afro-Brazilian dance and culture and to share Brazilian wellness traditions (isaurabrasil@hotmail.com).

27 Most of this section's information came from an interview with Isaura on May 21, 2012.

28 See also Belo Horizonte examples of black women's lives and expectations in Caldwell (2007: 133–49).

29 Reminiscent of Candomblé practitioners who throw white flowers into the salt waters with hopes that *Orixá Iemanjá* will grant them their requests for the coming year.

30 Some African Brazilians claim Indigenous ancestry with the use of "*Caboclo*."

31 See also life of actress/playwright/activist: Santos (1999: 188–99).

32 Also see da Silva (1999: 179–87) and Hanchard (2006: 3–16).

33 The actual year of the formalization of *dança afro* is not available, marking the need for a documented Bahian dance history – hopefully, one that includes an analysis and critique of both Isaura's "N'Bunda" research project and the detailed research on Brazilian dances found in Scott (2001).

34 For historical development of Brazilian dance (including Bahian *Carnaval* dancing, *samba*, and *capoeira*), see Browning (1995), Scott (2001), Guillermoprieto (1990), and Butler (1998: 171–89). For Candomblé dances, see Scott (2001: 100-105, 133–53), Daniel (2005), and Browning (1995). (Scott's work also includes Isaura Oliveira as a political activist, dance mentor, and field consultant.)

35 See especially do Nacimento in his own words about this development ([1979] 1989).

36 Also in-depth personal communications with anthropologist and Brazilian specialist Sheila Walker over time, but for this specific saying and public understanding, November 23, 2012.

37 See all authors in Hanchard, *Racial Politics*.

38 Remember, CDs, DVDs, cell phones, blogging, texting, "twittering," and other technology were yet to be developed.

39 For dance, dance music, and political development in Brazil, see Scott (1998: 9–22, 2001), Perrone and Dunn (2001: 7–8, 20–21, 25–30). For Cuba, see Vaughan (2012); for Haiti, see McAlister (2002) and Averill (1997); and for the Caribbean and Atlantic Latin America, see Daniel (2011: 93–107, 170–88).

40 The government or *Carnaval* committee assessment of dance arts organizations most often determined if a group was considered an *afoxé* or a *bloco afro* under the guiding rule: the use of Candomblé instruments for *afoxés* and *samba* instruments for *blocos*; however, for views derived from participants see Scott (2001: 262–63); also Crook in Perrone and Dunn (2001: 238), Hanchard (1999a: 76–77), and Telles in Hanchard, *Racial Politics* (1999b: 94).

41 I consulted with dance researcher Linda Yudin, as I did with anthropologist Sheila Walker, in September 2012 by phone and by e-mail, for their recollections and thorough first-hand knowledge of Bahia. These views augmented personal fieldwork and library research for this section.

42 There were several non-white Carnival groups before Filhos de Gandhy, e.g., African Embassy in 1897 and *blocos de indios* (*Caciques do Garcia, Apaches de Tororó*) in the 1960s; see Moura in Perronne and Dunn (2001: 164–70). Walker reports that *blocos afros* in the 1970s and 1980s used Merchants of Bagdad, a non-black *bloco* of the 1950s as a model of what they were *fighting against*. See also Scott's important data from field interviews about *blocos de indios*, *blocos de caboclos*, and *bloco afro* as "performed otherness" within the context of a national dictatorship (2001: 73–89).

43 See the late Lino de Almeida's poignant documentary, *A Bahia do afoxé filhos de Gandhy*.

44 See Scott (2001: 77) for de Almeida's first-hand activist account of the beginnings of *blocos afros* in Bahia.

45 See also Scott's comparison of *blocos* (2001: 204–08).

46 Scott (2001: 171, 264–70). See also dos Santos for an inspiring case of an abandoned child's experiences and successes (1999: 200–14).

47 See also Scott (2001: 161–62).

48 Conga is an outstanding dancer, teacher, and remarkable drummer who had an unusually strong background within Candomblé *terreiros* before turning to university training. At the time discussed here, he was a teaching fellow working on a graduate degree in dance at UFBA, making him the first known black, male Candomblé graduate from UFBA.

49 Caldwell's report contains recent analysis, collects the views of African Brazilian women, and underscores these issues; see also Gaspar and Clark Hine (1996: 79–96).

Part II

Memory, Resistance, and Survival through Dance Education

Chapter 3

Pedagogies of the Body within African Matrix Education of Salvador, Brazil: Perspectives and Challenges of an Emancipatory Project

Pilar Echeverry Zambrano

Introduction

In 2011, the United Nations Educational, Scientific and Cultural Organization (UNESCO) declared the International Decade for People of African Descent (2015–24).[1] Among researchers, this honorific declaration has generated reflections and new analytical perspectives on historical problems, as well as, the contemporary social situation of African-descendent communities. A particular openness to analyses that integrate reviews and evaluations of the past three decades (in which multiculturalism has struggled against racism and a new social awareness) were incorporated into the historical and scientific landscapes of Brazil and Latin America. This study, conducted after the creation of anti-racist policies and campaigns for racial and ethnic rights in education, contributes to the scholarship on perspectives, challenges, and trajectories of African matrix educational projects in Salvador, Brazil, and their impact on the transformation of conventional, Eurocentric, "white"/modern educational systems. Two broad questions about Brazilian education and dance are the initiating emphases of this essay:

- Are African matrix dance and education projects exerting a significant influence on the traditional colonial educational system?
- Does this contribute to the process of overcoming conventional and exclusionary representations of the body in school settings?

I begin with definitions of terms used and an overview or commentary on research to date.[2] "African Matrix" is a recent concept, adopted by the community of African-descendent dance artists in Brazil within or by the end of the first decade of the twenty-first century. It is more specific than the concepts of "African dance" or "black dance," which over time have become broadened and diffused as dance practices were blended, mixed, and reinvented. Current Brazilian understanding considers the African matrix as a set of practices and discourses that belong to a segment of the Brazilian community, who identify as Afro-Brazilians or African descendants, especially in Salvador. These practices and discourses revolve around a political and cultural struggle to dignify, reframe, and make visible their knowledge and their people. This population self-identifies within a culture that develops much of its existential and identity frameworks through body practices or corporeality, associated with aesthetic, political, religious, and historical processes that originated on the continent of Africa. That Afro-Brazilian culture is based on the concepts of ancestry, identity, and struggle against racial exclusion (Oliveira 2007; Conrado 2006). A literature of documented research has accumulated with discussions on the African matrix, dance, education, and the body in Salvador, Brazil. It reveals interesting and, at the same time, troubling trends, both because of the absence of certain topics and the excessive repetition of others.

The first finding is that there are not many texts (a total of 35), but there are several visual examples on YouTube, which I will refer to more specifically later. The written works began to appear in the 1980s and 1990s, with a significant increase in publications after 2000. This coincides with the stages of legal consolidation of multiculturalism in Brazil (in the Federal Constitution of 1988) and the work of cultural projects that demanded attention to "race" in Salvador after the passage of Law No. 10.639 of 2003, which requires all schools to teach about African and Afro-Brazilian culture.[3] For the most part, these texts are the results of research carried out by women intellectuals, who are also African-descendent social movement activists and political movement supporters, or by foreign researchers.

These authors give this scholarship its second general characteristic: its repeated focus on culture, which highlights the particularity of ethnic groups and defines "African" culture and bodies as "universal" categories, collectivizing the notion of community and using these concepts as tools in the political struggle against the myth of Brazilian racial democracy and racism. Because of this tendency, these studies portray knowledge regarding the black body and corporeal arts as an emancipatory vehicle that can transform urban education, i.e., corporeal knowledge is not supposed to be "contaminated" by the classical principles of conventional, colonial education (Echeverry Zambrano 2011).

In sum, these studies offer an "essentialized" version of education about "Africa." Solely in opposition to "white education," they do not take into consideration that a large part of the urban African-descendent community does not identify ethnically, nor the phenomena of inter-relationships and re-readings, which yield new uses of the African matrix in the contemporary school environment (Sansone 2007). The omissions of these studies are understandable, since the reconstruction of representations for African-descendent culture in education needed to establish a basic description and valorization of corporeal knowledge; and, moreover, the political movement of the 1970s in Brazil could not foresee that new challenges and social actors would appear on the scene, bringing different questions. In this sense, my review of the pertinent bibliography demonstrates that the first stage of intellectual work and policy proposals on the subject has passed, and the current need is for detailed historical studies of African Diaspora education and in the process, analyses of how colonial and "white"/modern education have been reinvented and, in some cases, adopted by the African matrix as its own, or, in other cases, criticized and deconstructed.

Considering these tendencies in the literature, I have sought approaches that do not romanticize African matrix education or discuss it beyond the body, the dance, and the community dimensions. I present an overview of the details, historical background, and scenarios of daily praxis and educational innovation in all the contradictory and paradoxical vitality of the classroom. This is an important concern in light of the well-known statistics about Salvador, Brazil's third-largest city, which has the largest African-descendent population (83%), but where 85.8% of the African-descendant population lives below the poverty line (IBGE 2008). Consequently, the city holds the second-to-last place among Brazilian cities with the lowest per capita income: 0.66%, which compared to global data is second only to Namibia, where the rate is 0.74%. The inequality is evident: residents of neighborhoods traditionally considered upscale or wealthy earn 25 times more than residents in the suburbs, where the population is mostly of African descent. The illiteracy rate in the upscale white neighborhood Itaigara is 0.93%, while in the peripheral areas such as Fazenda Coutos and Felicidade, the rate is 12.95%. 97.6% of children aged 7–14 who live in Itaigara attend school, while 82.70% of children from Coutos slums do not (Moreira 2011).

Observing this scenario, my research has sought to shed light on the complex array of perspectives and challenges that have accompanied the introduction of African matrix education in the context of conventional education institutions and conventional efforts toward multiculturalism. New definitions, actors, questions, and ways of being black have emerged in the city and the old and already classic dilemmas of racial exclusion and prejudice are still unresolved within school settings. My ethnographic study concentrated on African dance experiences in city schools, particularly the Dance School of the State of Bahia Cultural Foundation (Escola de Dança da Fundação Cultural do Estado da Bahia, FUNCEB), in Salvador. Data collection focused on the "free courses" program, which was an experience in public education that specifically addressed African matrix dance and brought together a significant population of teachers, students, and education administrators. In addition, the study included the creation of corporeal arts programs in several schools of dance, that is, the incorporation of *capoeira* and Afro-Brazilian ritual dances, called Candomblé or *terreiro* movement vocabularies.[4]

My essay proceeds with a description of the ethnographic site and some references to the particularities of the identified scenario. The next section describes the concepts and components of African matrix dance, corporeal education, and the African-descendent body in Brazil. The final segment presents some of the research findings, starting with pedagogical perspectives, the rich and comprehensive nature of current projects, and a list of the problems that should be addressed and reformulated in order to qualify African matrix knowledge as a source of corporeal production within Brazilian public education.

The Place of Study and a New Methodological Tool

The research was conducted between April 2009 and May 2012, employing ethnographic methodology that included open interviews, field diaries, and participant observation. I had been introduced to and studied African-descendent dances in Columbia; I came to Brazil to deepen that connection and to complete a doctoral degree. I took classes and eventually began teaching dance in the community.

The central research focus was the FUNCEB School of Dance (Escola de Dança da Fundação Cultural do Estado da Bahia) "free courses" program. Founded in 1984 to encourage the development of public dance in the city, FUNCEB offers a significant number of African matrix corporeal practices and welcomes students from various sectors of the city. This site was chosen for several reasons. First, it is the paradigmatic scenario of the work achieved by teachers, dancers, choreographers, and activist community members who have been involved in African matrix dance, are prominent in the field, and well-known both in Salvador and in Brazil. Secondly, FUNCEB's public character, as an educational institution encompasses the African matrix universe within the logic of conventional education.

This school was also chosen because of its location in Pelourinho, the city's historical center, which allows the participation of local social actors, foreigners, and tourists, who comprise a vast and complex landscape of mobility, differentiation, multiculturalism, and subjectivity. The city's cultural and sub-cultural interactions are evident within this school. Its major importance was that it is not an educational setting that is exclusively for people of African descent, which is the case with other famous dance/music schools, such as Ilê Aiyê, Olodum, Didá, etc. The cultural and existential differences intervene among the populations involved, restricting or expanding the ways African matrix corporeal knowledge is taught. This scenario becomes a representative and legitimate space for observing the infinite number of variables that exist in contemporary school settings of Salvador.

In addition to the FUNCEB School of Dance, research also focused on the *capoeira Angola* School, "ACANNE," in Salvador and Porto Alegre. An event called "Dancing our Matrixes," took place in 2011 and 2012 in Salvador and brought together researchers, artists, and supporters of corporeal arts. Also, an event offered by the House of Benin Cultural Center for Black Dance (Centro de Articulação em Danças Negras da Casa do Benin), called the 2012 Cardan project, brought together Brazil's most prominent figures in African-descendent dance to participate in roundtable discussions. Ethnographic records for Salvador, like these, in addition to those associated with the "Day of Black Consciousness" events (2010, 2011), the Carnival of 2010, and the *Santa Bárbara, Senhor do Bonfim* and *Yemanja* celebrations (2010, 2012) were pivotal data resources and, it was especially fruitful to connect with Shirley Santana, a leader of Yemanja Candomblé group in Salvador. These events and their participants were very meaningful in terms of data collection.

The project revealed a heterogeneous methodological approach that I call *Corpografía*.[5] Few Brazilian ethnographic or qualitative research methodologies are effective in studying the body in contexts such as dance schools or within experiences in which the body is a direct and literal tool in the social actor's work and life. Methodologically, in African matrix dance schools, the body is rarely understood through "observation" because many of the relationships and experiences belong to the universe of the performative, incarnate, and kinetic, and many performers/participants also belong to the spiritual world. In such dance performances, the body of the subjects produces knowledge in a non-visible interiority that is not perceptible to the eyes and ears of the ethnographer. This knowledge is created through anatomy, in the biological realm, in the sub-conscience and neuro-physic universes, as well as in the intermediate spaces within the constant flow of complex movement and human relationships. In short, it is not possible to fully understand or record the elements and issues of the African-descendent dancing body without dancing and without entering the Candomblé religious universe, which is the foundation of all the city's dancing. I am describing a tremendously corporeal scenario, where understanding is not derived from simply studying, but from experiencing dimensions of sociability, such as pleasure, religiosity, the party, food, music, and relationships with elemental forces. Understanding is derived from things that are neither measurable nor explainable, but from that which dance practices bring to those who are in search of the meanings of dance behaviors.

In this particularized context, *Corpografía* attempts to implement: (1) tools for addressing both the visible aspects of the body and the non-visible aspects of mediation, as well as the subjective inner life that subjects experience; (2) techniques that insert the researcher's body experiences inside the methodological framework, and use them as important data for analysis, as well as meaningful experiences in the development of the researcher when teaching others; and (3) a means of ensuring that the research findings resonate with participants, in terms of reconciling any divergences between their understandings and lived purposes for the dance and those of the author/researcher. *Corpografía* allows for kinetic learning, that is, the understanding of an external or internal phenomenon through the body. *Corpografía* explains that phenomenon using the body or from the body perspective and develops reasoning and interpretation that incorporates abstractions and sensations equally with tangible research data (Greiner 2005; Wacquant 2002).

Corpografía has some costs. It is physically and emotionally exhausting to dance or conduct corporeal research while at the same time writing about that research. It is also difficult economically, due to the costs associated with bodywork classes, which are generally expensive and have to be paid by the researcher for the entire period of participant observation, since these are not perceived as conventional support items for fieldwork. It is even more difficult to try to bring together two languages that were not made to coincide within the conventions of formal research: the performative, hyper-mutable, and chaotic language of the body and the organized and coherent language of writing. Yet this study's objective was to mix two codes of understanding and expression, and two disciplinary traditions, observing the dialogues and confrontations between them, listening to corporeal voices that cannot be heard by ethnography, performing the exercise of understanding a social reality by sharing corporal knowledge and registering it in the researcher's own "skin" as well as in her/his writing.

Principles within African Matrix Dance, Education, and the Body

The body and the arts related to it involve both political and pedagogical strategies used in the African-descendent community's process of emancipation; both strategies are directed toward the elimination of prejudices about the black body in Brazilian society. Dance and *capoeira Angola* are two strongly identified Brazilian corporeal arts that are connected to West and Central African heritages, which are found as segments of Brazilian Candomblé ritual communities. Both Afro-Brazilian dance and *capoeira Angola* are aligned with African deities, and feature or involve the principles of ancestry, spirituality, identity, rituality, and resistance or political struggle. African matrix dances, including Candomblé religious ritual dances and *capoeira Angola*, inspire many of the pedagogical principles of Afro-educational projects. However, what participants call "African matrix dance" in this study does not refer to aesthetic production alone, but additionally to a political process that is deeply anchored in African-descendent social movements and Afro-educational projects, as well as a living testament to the memory and history of Salvador's African-descendent communities (Oliveira 2007; Conrado 2006).

Thus, African matrix education focuses on the reformulation of Brazilian history so as to include African-descendent communities and their pivotal role in the historical process through which Brazil was constituted. Such education presents African-descendent communities as subjects of political and social resistance in the struggle to combat the idea of racial democracy, which, ingrained in Brazilian mentality and culture, obfuscates the processes of exclusion that are still in place. African matrix education thereby emphasizes the implementation and support for Law No. 10.639/2003, which mandates the teaching of Afro-Brazilian history and culture in schools. In effect, African matrix education works to build respect for the corporeality, spirituality, and epistemology of Afro-Diasporic knowledge found mainly in urban centers of Brazil, like Salvador (Conrado 2006). An important objective of this education, beyond the obvious fight against racism and the restoring of individual and group dignity, is to reinvent representations of the black body and critique images that have historically marked the "black body" as a household instrument, a dirty, hyper-eroticized, sexually available and precarious entity, or as something that needs to be changed and whitened (Lino Gomez 2002).

The pedagogy that evolves from new historical understandings, definitions, and objectives comprises several concepts. Initially, the African matrix concept of "the body" is a set of factors that, together, create an "anatomy" that is highly communicative, expansive, porous, liminal, and borderline. The body comes and goes in accordance with cosmic forces, spiritual planes, historical and political memories that have merged within subjective processes, life experiences, and social struggles. This "anatomy" does not belong solely to the individual; it shares its history with the happenings of the universe including the guidance and instruction from *Orixás* (deities), the indefatigable steps of collective history from the ancestors, and the historical and contemporary marks of political struggle for full emancipation.

The pedagogy of African matrix education allows students, teachers in training, performers, and community participants to observe, sense, and become aware of a version of corporeality that breaks with the modern idea of the body, which is connected to the individual and the physiological (or the structuralist idea linked to the social and the cultural). The African matrix concept of the body is involved in a web of relationships linked by environmental and cosmic threads. As philosopher Mikhail Bakhtin argues, "the material bodily principle is something universal, representing all the people. As such it is opposed to severance from the material and bodily roots of the world; it makes no pretense to renunciation of the earthy, or independence of the earth and the body" ([1975] 1999: 24).

This understanding of bodily experience promotes an educational idea that has rarely been taught or learned in school classrooms or at home. It assumes the corporeality/physicality of the universe in all its magnitude and breadth, as – that which carries forth the earth, reproduces a greater and more complex spiritual order – and a pedagogy of existence in which learning and teaching are to be engaged with the other and with everything. The African matrix uncovers the value of "world body" and "body history" (that is not an individuated/singularized body) and redefines education as a movement that breaks through the impoverished limits of the school setting. African matrix bodily education fills schools with substance, converting knowledge into a live, expansive, breathing organism.

From this view, the body is that which speaks to the whole, and to dance African matrix dance is an act of "knowing with the body," of "living with the body," or of "learning from the body." Learning from the whole is the same as learning from the body. Above all, to dance African matrix dances is to "remember with the body" and to "fight with the body." For African descendants in Salvador, dancing is a process of surviving by means of the body, giving life meaning through bodily actions and establishing dignity through bodily behaviors. Therefore, individuality is the still incomplete and agonizing process of dissolution. The open and incomplete body is not strictly separated from the world; it is entangled in it, mixed with animals, plant life, and other things. It is a cosmic body (Bakhtin 1999: 30); but also, a body that is collective (made up of a living patchwork of community membership) and hyper-temporal (which brings the past into the present and projects toward the future).

In twentieth-century studies of the body, and in the social struggles that yielded those ideas, researchers were concerned with the process of bodily liberation and considered subjectivity as the beginning and end point of this liberation. They centered their attention first on the individual, as the receptacle of bodily power, and second, on the social/cultural group. Along the way, the body returned to the anatomical-social world, where it was again isolated from the natural/material world and the cosmic universe of existence. However, when the African matrix pedagogy references the body, it invokes concepts of the individual, the collective, nature, memory, and the cosmos, all intertwined within daily life. For this reason, body education within the African matrix considers the sum of these categories as they have overlapped in a developmental process, generating the possibility of emancipation as a vital connection to the world, to history, to others, and oneself. Hence, "freedom" within this pedagogy is a network of relationships of well-being that includes the human and extends beyond the human; it is a cosmic and comprehensive anatomy, an anatomy of the whole that re-inscribes the body.

In this universe, dance also has an expanded content, bringing together instrumental and vocal music, literature, drama, poetry, mythology, and body movement. For example, in the African matrix, dancing does not accompany drumming or singing, it is music and singing. Dance does not narrate the myth; it is the dramatic re-enacting of myth and, dance does not represent the story; it is the story. For these reasons, dance became a deeply pertinent focus of political and educational projects, and would become the foundation of the educational and cultural movement that would take African matrix and body concepts into the schools and ultimately, into society.

On the other hand, African matrix dance is a cross between worlds, mentalities pedagogies, subjects, historical moments, human dimensions, corporealities, resistances, and submissions; it is a complex intercultural product. African matrix dance encompasses *a universe of physical and pedagogical encounters*; it is a land of multiple voices that have come from afar to become close, interrelated. In the beginnings of colonial enslavement practices, African descendants, speaking diverse languages, depended most on the common language they shared – dance, the body communication of African ancestors. Diaspora dance, which retained, but also modified original continental traditions, passed through numerous historical processes – experienced daily, diverse meanings and reinventions. For this reason, and as Helena Kats observes:

> [The body in motion] is not about building a single, comprehensive theory, exclusive of any other. The complexity of the dance phenomenon – like so many others that refer to the living – prevents such nonsense […]. A complex system has many interconnections and will probably never be in equilibrium.
>
> (2005: 49–50)

African matrix dance, which undoubtedly comes from a uterus of African descent, has been mixing its cultural essence along the long trail of social interactions with various cultures and ways of thinking. This dance comes from the libertarian corner of Candomblé houses of worship, from the shackles of slave ships, from the decimated bodies of plantation sites, and from adorned bodies drinking the nectar of wisdom in popular festivals. This dance comes from the desire for freedom that was denied by the "white"/colonial system and from the submission to and acceptance of this limited system. In African matrix dance, the everyday events of Salvador's evanescent and forgotten life can be read, and so can the vital memory of African, European, and Indigenous descendants. African matrix dance is the epic consolidation of an African and Lusophone Brazil, as greatness and misery, politics and spirituality, future projects and the flux of cultural and individual continuity and change.[6]

The diagram below shows the multiple intersections among different social actors and traditions of thought mixed in complex ways within the interior of African matrix dance.

African matrix dance, as an intercultural construction, can bring together diverse wisdoms that are sheltered within the process of Afro-Brazilian knowledge and history; however, distinct cultural and pedagogical models contribute to its development. As dance and theater scholar Mariana Monteiro explains in *Espetáculo e devoção, burlesco e teologia política nas danças populares brasileiras* ("Performance and devotion, burlesque and political theology in Brazilian popular dances") (2002), what is understood as "African dance" in Brazil is an enormously diverse range of dance elements and practices, all related to the African Diaspora phenomenon over the last five centuries. According to Monteiro, the development of African dance has been a multicultural history since its inception.

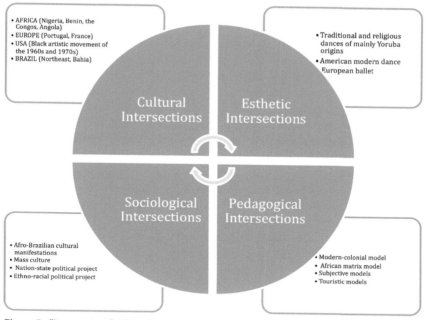

Figure 5: "Intersections," Pilar Echeverry Zambrano.

For example, in colonial times, the Catholic brotherhoods of both African- and European-descendent religious fraternities connected elements from varied African cultures to Catholic rituals and incorporated dance in their ceremonial practice. During the nineteenth and twentieth centuries, modernity, although a progressive impulse, incorporated ethnic and racial cultures in the formation of a homogenizing national culture, converting Native or Indigenous American, European, and African "popular knowledge" into folklore. As part of an assimilation and legitimation process, dances received new names, shapes, pedagogies, and aesthetic meanings. In the mid-twentieth century, the re-Africanization process organized new paradigms within resurgent black political movements. First, Franz Fanon and Aimé Césaire promoted a reinvention of the perception of "blackness" and colonialism. Then, US black aesthetics, seen and heard in literature, visual art, music, and poetry flooded the Americas. Black political perspectives led by Martin Luther King Jr. and Malcolm X, who advanced Fanon and Césaire's earlier reinvention of Africa as a paradigm matrix, helped to unearth and give voice to new perspectives on European, "white" cultural models that were considered "the standards." They inserted the critical presence of African descendants across the Americas.

This socio-political and historical trajectory consolidated thinking about the body with a re-evaluation of dancer/choreographer Katherine Dunham's dance activism. Since the 1930s, Dunham had been fusing African bodily wisdom from her Caribbean research to modern concert dance, and delivering a reinvented black dance to the international arts market throughout the world. Dunham's "new" dance came to Brazil in the 1950s as a concert and cinematic art form (based mainly on Haitian dance and modern concert dance). Brazilian dance artist Mercedes Baptista studied with Dunham and toured with her company before returning to Rio de Janeiro and developing Brazil's black artistic dance forms. Later, in the 1970s and 1980s, Afro-Brazilian Raimundo Bispo dos Santos, called Mestre King, developed a similar, but Brazilian-based style, called *dança afro*.[7]

Later, US African American Clyde Wesley Morgan brought to Salvador both the influences of his performance and technique history with the modern dance company of José Limón, as well as his research experiences in West African dance. All three dance masters (Baptista, King, and Morgan) influenced Brazilian dance training in public cultural centers and in schools and universities. Yet, by the end of the twentieth century, mass commercial culture predominated in Brazil, commodifying African-descendent cultural products and establishing various normative features. These developments eventually created a dance phenomenon within the realm of globalization and tourism. Once again, the African dance matrix was subject to change in its concepts and forms of elaboration (Echeverry Zambrano 2011; Nóbrega Oliveira 2007).

Throughout this brief historical review, the African dance matrix has displayed three characteristic elements of corporeal education: *complexity, as a bodily knowledge system*; *resistance, as a form of political power*; and *reinvention, as an intercultural foundation*. These educational criteria guide body and dance studies and are grounded in a variety of principles, indicators, and related methodologies.

The foot is especially important in African matrix dance, since it marks the intrinsic relationship between the body and the earth, and for dance educators, the foot indicates a pedagogical entry point for instruction. The barefoot on the ground is a fundamental element within African spirituality. The earth, and by extension, the touch of the flat or planted foot, recalls and represents the home of the ancestors.

The connection between the head and the ground also reiterates the important relationship of the body to the earth; the touching of the head to the ground marks that relationship in ritual practice. That physical connection represents the spiritual relationship between the world of the ancestors who live on the earth/ground, called, *Aiye*, and the divine world of deities who come to live in the initiated African descendant's head from their spiritual residence, called *Orum*. The old, the elders, and the dead are a central spiritual community, both in the religious realm and in the universe of bodily practices. Thus, both connections – the foot and the head to the earth – established through bodily gestures and movement sequences – act and function as antenna for transmission of knowledge. I encapsulate the bodily relationship to the ancestors primarily as "Pedagogy of the Foot."[8]

Simultaneously, the drum and other percussion instruments, which are the nexus of communication with the natural, the divine, and ancestral universes, make these three spheres unite. The drum is not only a musical instrument, but also a living entity that emits mantras and sound vibrations at very high frequencies; its complex musical codes act similarly to language codes. This usage of percussion confirms the involvement of bodily arts with spiritual and cosmic communication; percussion and musicality activate ritual life, and also everyday life. The union and deconstruction or blurring of the sacred and the profane I call "Pedagogy of Vibration."[9]

Another approach to the African dance matrix pedagogy involves consciousness of dance movement within the logic of the collectivity, the family, or the dance group and highlights values within African matrix education. The physical example of this is found in Brazilian *blocos*, Salvador's famous Carnival dance/music groups, which emphasize being together as communities and the values learned as a result of togetherness. The belief that human beings learn from one another or together is at the base of social being, and develops to what one person learns, everyone can learn, and what everyone knows is owned by each person, implying a circular route of knowledge eventually, formed by familial transmissions or caring interactions. This suggests circular knowledge transmission within the dance circle or *roda* in particular, and the consciousness within the spinning, turning, and circling of the body or bodies. Circular knowledge strips time, space, and educational hierarchy of their essences.

Additionally, African matrix pedagogy includes telling the history and myths of the deities (*Orixás*), which comprise the entire Candomblé liturgy. Candomblé dances and movements form the base of corporeal arts. I encapsulate this way of investigating past and more current histories as "Pedagogy of Memory."

Finally, the lessons derived from parties, celebrations, and playful interactions, which constitute festive and leisure environments where bodily knowledge also surfaces. These moments have links to the rituality of Candomblé; they are the spaces and times of celebrations, gastronomic abundance, and honorific commemoration. These are not frivolous occasions, but a fundamental part of Salvador's urban life and its multiple forms of playful spiritual expression. In the dance classroom, I refer to these within a "Pedagogy of Pleasure."

To summarize, I draw attention to six specific indicators of *Corpografia*, the approach to African matrix dances, Brazilian education, and the body that this study has tested. Pedagogy of the Foot refers to body education that projects the importance of ancestry and the past. Pedagogy of Vibration refers to education as a daily act of musical connection to the elements of nature through singing, movement, and drumming. Pedagogy of Circularity refers to the wealth of knowledge and sensitivity discovered within collective interactions and encourages the breakdown of bodily hierarchies in order to free expression and creativity. The Pedagogy of Memory reinforces body education as an act of remembrance and contemporary resistance, referencing political and historical victories over slavery, oppression, and exploitation. Lastly, the Pedagogy of Pleasure points to body education that reveals the knowledge within playfulness and celebratory fun. Body and collective learning use the foundation of self-knowledge and add openness to and for the other, as well as sensitivity to the cosmos.

Prospects and Challenges in African Matrix Dance Pedagogy

Here, I present reflections generated by the research and begin to answer the initial questions of this essay; additionally, I present an overview of the various challenges that should be addressed by future research and other teacher training projects. First, the pedagogical system dictated by the African matrix dances that are practiced in Salvador reveals a creative universe of teaching that includes foundational forms belonging to Afro-Brazilian communities and their historical path of emancipation and socio-political resistance. Clearly, principles of life, spirituality, and aesthetics underlie and intertwine with other knowledge taught in classrooms. Structurally sound and innovative methodological tools for teaching, such as *Corpografía,* are recommended to expand understanding of body learning. This creative, innovative, comprehensive, and contemporary view of the importance of the body has been converted into a pedagogy for the teaching of diverse knowledge and different cultures and languages. Such a pedagogy can contribute to the process of overcoming colonial/modern education models. The research described here has provided a curriculum guide for the teaching of African matrix dance. Training of both dance and non-dance teachers involves sensitizing minds and bodies to the bodily arts and their internal knowledge. Playful knowledge, the relationship with the foot, the principles of circularity, collective learning, and the theme of emancipation are used in educational agendas as valid tools for understanding, if not, resolving contemporary challenges and conflicts surrounding Afro-Brazilian students, their history and cultures.

As a life practice (which it is for many Afro-Brazilians), African matrix dance provides students with valuable bodily, aesthetic, and ethical tools for perceiving their individual paths and for strengthening or changing their vital routes. For example, Candomblé dances reveal and leverage personal knowledge and contribute to overcoming genuine difficulties and existential traps. They are sources of inspiration and appreciation of one's own body and the bodies of others. They have a complex and respectful view of the natural universe and they help to integrate the dancing body, in a back-and-forth relationship between the outer world and the inner life of human beings.

African matrix dance introduces the ability to establish deep relationships by recognizing that the bodily principles that govern humankind are replicas of the universal principles that govern nature. Therefore, African matrix dance enhances understanding of the environmental surroundings as an internal principle, not simply as ambient context. It establishes an existential ecology of enjoyment and respect for the elements of nature, which are reciprocal within and among bodies.

The pedagogies developed through the analysis of African matrix dance can sensitize and educate more integrated and humanized teachers and provide tools for constant dialogue with the struggle for freedom. Teachers also contribute to building curricula that incorporate the struggle against social and racial inequality; they can more easily and empathetically teach the history and contemporary situations of African Diaspora people. Armed with bodily experiences and learned principles of African matrix dance, they can relate the strength and courage of those who maintain ancestral knowledge in harsh and inhuman conditions. Despite these conditions, Afro-Brazilians have kept body memories that are revealed in dance performance and can be understood and taught today. African matrix dance repeatedly retells the infinite remembrances, records, histories, and knowledges of the body; it consolidates history and rectifies national culture.

With such a panorama of perspectives, I turn to the challenges in teaching and learning African matrix dance. The panorama is quite complex and achievements have been noted; yet, research has shown that significant remnants of educational colonialism remain. Challenges to African matrix dance teaching and learning have been reduced or disguised. New projects for bodily emancipation via African matrix dance and education are in an experimental phase currently; they are small, isolated and have few economic resources.

While the classic discourse on the black body is rooted in the criticism of a "heavy" modernity (Bauman 2001), what the contemporary praxis of African matrix dance gives is an amorphous modernity, one whose form is changing forms, able to accommodate new global contexts. This modernity is losing (but not completely) its colonized foundation. As it adapts to new everyday circumstances, modernity criticizes this foundation, but does not erase it. From this perspective, American/Canadian scholar and social critic Henry Giroux observes that the challenges of ethnic education are much greater today because the emancipatory processes have "[…] new situations that put a wider diversity of cultures and subcultures in reciprocal dialogue, it is necessary to theorize in the plural within the antagonistic relations of domination and subordination, and not from outside of them" (Giroux 2005: 342).

The presumption is that the African matrix dance form of education faces the challenge of showing more and better results than conventional education, and the political world expects very little today. The expectations placed on ethnically oriented programs are high because they have promised a liberating restructure of education and there are different standards for measuring the liberating effects that African matrix education has achieved so far. For example, the result is the empowerment of those teachers who have been involved in the corporeal arts universe. Although this phenomenon has a measure of success, which can be seen in teachers' incomes and improvement in family economies, traveling abroad to promote their work, or even moving to a different country, it is limited to very few people and does not achieve collective emancipation.

Achievement of success within the dance universe involves only those performers/ choreographers who have contacts with collectives, projects, or jobs outside of Salvador, mainly in European countries. The fight against poverty, racial discrimination, and the lack of academic opportunities engages a complex universe of social relationships that rarely address the issue of race head-on and also rarely deal with social class and gender issues.

Many of the current challenges in education, such as multiculturalism, new actors and new ways of defining African matrix culture, new forms of political agency, etc., are relegated to future educational agenda items because, as noted, the minimum conditions for a dignified Afro-Brazilian education in Salvador do not yet exist. This makes it impossible to think of or mobilize efforts around issues that, while important, end up being evaluated as secondary.

Consequently, I now enumerate six aspects of Brazilian education that encompass challenges to the pedagogy of the body and surround educational projects in this tradition. After several decades of struggle for dignity and a new pedagogy, research and participant observation for over 3 years indicate first that African-oriented projects require improvements in infrastructure and logistical resources so that appropriate, safe, and competitive conditions can develop. Although there are challenges associated with the topic of multiculturalism, and with a long list of contemporary corporeal situations, the research emphatically highlights the very problematic situation of education projects that are based in African and African Diaspora content.

1) There is limited physical infrastructure in terms of appropriate dance spaces, classrooms, or buildings that accommodate theatrical pre-requisites and safe situations for audiences, instructors, and performers. There is a lack of professional training for teachers and prejudice galore against the inclusion of African matrix corporeal arts in the school curriculum. Additionally, there is not equal and fair financial remuneration for body-teaching. The need for further studies on the impact of African matrix education in Afro-descendent and non-African-descendent communities is great. There is also a lack of support for what is available and in place. For example, there is little support for entrepreneurial plans or corporeal arts professionals who are already trained. There is a lack of grants that provide stipends for musicians and dance specialists; and there is no consideration for transportation and supply costs, including dance rehearsal skirts, drums, bells, music recordings, etc.

   In these last respects, African matrix education shares the same problems as conventional public education. The same is true for the impact and dissemination of projects among a wider Afro-descendent population. Because educational coverage is restricted to certain urban areas, there is a limited number of specialists who are familiar with these projects and who are able to participate in education and arts circuits of the historical center or in tourist areas of the city.

2) What is called African matrix corporeal culture is constituted through a relational-tension among ancestral knowledges that originated on the African continent, the diasporic reinterpretation of exclusionary colonial teaching methods, and the economic difficulties faced by those involved with Brazilian dance education. In pedagogical terms, the preservation of an African matrix framework for teaching and learning should be emphasized. Yet, teaching in a festive atmosphere of play and games is rarely emphasized; the relationship among dance, spirituality, and educational policy is not fully supported; the development of circularity and collectivity as educational methods are not clearly understood or practiced; and there is little attention to the principle of ancestry. The challenge remains; it is a question of implementation of dance as a tool for remembering and acknowledging the past within present concrete contexts.

Daily teaching practice shows that the perspectives and principles within an African matrix dance pedagogy are in opposition to conventional discipline practices. Student ranking policies, public punishment practices, the repeated exposure to topics and images associated with modernity's sense of progress and a monolithic and Eurocentric idea of bodily perfection certainly raise suspicions about achieving effective learning. Especially, the use of pain and excessively strenuous physical effort as viable pedagogical strategies have been questioned in relation to contemporary education and achievement studies. In the testimonies of several dance masters, African matrix education introduced the principle of freedom, including the emancipation of pedagogical practice from the jowls of corporal punishment within conventional schooling; however, during the research process, their testimonies and observed practices showed that the praxis is imbued with colonial pedagogical knowledge and hierarchical paradigms.

3) With respect to cultural diversity within the classroom, the project recorded a potpourri of different ways of expressing "blackness," some of which may or may not coincide with the political dimension generally associated with African matrix dance education. This diversity includes, for example, African-descendent teachers and students who were: evangelicals, Jehovah's Witnesses, foreign-born African descendants, transvestites and members of the gay community, supporters of political struggles different from the Brazilian Black Movement of the 1970s, African descendants who were not interested in political and racial issues, African descendants who were simply unaware of the national black inclusion policies, and young African descendants who belong to new non-ethnic African matrix "urban tribes,"[10] but who have developed political strategies to fight racism through aesthetic, media, or eco-spiritual tools. With new politics of belonging and political agency, these actors challenge the concepts of the "black body" and "African culture" that previously unified African descendants in Salvador, and were affiliated with most African educational methodologies. As noted above, African matrix pedagogies are inspired by traditional concepts of "the African community" that were formulated in black political activism of the 1970s and 1980s. Albeit with difficulty, some new actors can deal with Afro-multicultural classroom environments and the current questions that this environment generates. Of considerable concern, however, are new religious groups that include a significant number of African-descendent actors. These have established an emphatic and problematic distance from issues related to Candomblé spiritual practices, from which aesthetic, pedagogical, and emancipatory principles within the African matrix dance project have evolved. These actors support the dialogue and education program that opposes racial exclusion; however, they do not accept the use of African matrix ritual or spiritual discourses. Accordingly, there are multiple, serious challenges to the paradigm of the African matrix pedagogy.

4) On the other hand, projects that aim to overcome racial exclusion through the corporeal arts are woven into Salvador's tourism economy, since most of these projects have limited government support. While the projects have the emancipation of the "black body" as a political principle, they simultaneously participate in the logic of the

tourist industry where the purchase and sale of various prejudices about "blackness" are primary. For example, the hyper-eroticization and circulation of stereotypes such as the "big black Bahian" ("*ego baiano,*" an image with erotic overtones) and "little black girl" ("*neguinha,*" which also has erotic overtones) are rampant. The essentialist relationship of "blackness" with festivity and dance is over-produced; corporeal knowledge is relegated to folklore and Afro-descendants from professions that are not arts-related are perceived as non-existent. "Non-ethnic" or "less traditional blackness" is rejected. Within a "survival economy," income-generating stereotypes continue; the professions of dance performer/choreographer, dance instructor, or *capoeira Angola* master are fastened to those lingering images. Dance professionals turn themselves into available symbols of consumption due to financial need and market demand.

As long as there is no educational policy that has assessed the causes, consequences, and alternatives to ethno-exotic consumption of Afro-Brazilian culture, Salvador's educational projects will remain in an informal and inexpensive market, providing support for limited ethno-development and contributing minimally to a solution for Salvador's structural poverty. This is a problem that affects teachers directly, because many of them participate in the "survival economy," in which corporeal-pedagogical projects are created in order to achieve economic emancipation through the tourism and foreign travel networks.

5) Regarding the encounter of pedagogical matrixes inside schools and classrooms, many of the conventional education centers in Salvador opened space for the implementation of the law mandating the teaching of African and African Diaspora history; this included African-descendent corporeal arts within the curriculum in a controlled and incomplete way (Moreira 2011). This openness represented substantial educational progress, but prejudice and discriminatory obstacles persist. The present educational syncretism does not necessarily support teachers and students who wish to deepen their work within Afro-pedagogical experiences; the syncretism still relies on conventional teaching methods for validation and legitimization. In this respect, the African matrix education system, though partially accepted within schools, lacks logistical support and space and cannot work due to censorship or control by conventional educational paradigms and values.

6) Unfortunately, physical pain is still being used as a pedagogical strategy. Although conventional schools make reference to a festive and playful learning environment, learning through pain and the image of the student as martyr, overcoming her/his own self to achieve the perfect body through physical practice, are methodologies that repeat the model of learning from the enslavement period. The later models adopted by dance schools in the 1970s and 1980s, during the military dictatorship in Brazil, coincide with the strengthening of Afro-Brazilian educational proposals; however, their adoption had to do with the process of legitimization of African matrix knowledge within the military context of productivity, progress, and science during those decades. These were implemented in schools without much reflection (Silva 2009) and surely, it is time for such values to be fully analyzed, openly and impartially critiqued, and officially changed.

In sum, Salvador has an African matrix pedagogical tradition that has been adopted officially since the first decade of the twenty-first century; it has been disseminated in everyday practice even longer, but there is a need for further reflection and heightened education regarding the historical processes that led to each of its components. With careful scrutiny, impartial critique, and fair and total assessment of educational components, improvements in student learning and achievement should persuade teachers and administrators of the benefits offered within African matrix dance and body education.

The development of the African matrix educational model, as an emancipatory tool for society and educational policy, still requires further deepening of the historical and pedagogical processes that legitimize it. In addition, African ancestral wisdom and both colonial and modern legacies need to be fathomed and clarified within the African matrix dance pedagogies of today. I remain concerned since African matrix dance and education projects do not affect significant influence on the traditional colonial educational system; they do not contribute sufficiently to the process of overcoming conventional and exclusionary representations of the body in school settings.

Conclusion

As presented, this text is a short summary of the innumerable investigative findings that were developed during my doctoral research. Here, only some general points of a theoretical and epistemological order have been discussed. Personally, I consider the African matrix dances of Salvador an immense and rich field of liberating pedagogical action. There is much yet to be done in the development of critical and historical readings. The study of the African dance matrix will expand concepts, techniques, and methodological treatments of African Diaspora culture, introducing new dynamics and definitions that daily mobilize African-descendent culture and identification.

This investigation was concluded in 2012 and thereafter, I have dedicated myself to diverse groups, especially the women of Porto Alegre in the south of Brazil. There, I have developed the pedagogical and body presumptions of the African matrix dances with positive results, providing these women with aesthetic practices, education, and subjectivity. I say "positive results" due to the fact that the pedagogical foundations of the African matrix I have worked with, which were developed through dance, could be used as didactic and epistemological tools for the body. These facilitate improved learning in a humanized and profound approach to the understanding of the body within each student, whether s/he is a professional dancer or new to the dance and its implications for the body.

The richness of knowledge about the body [gained] from the African matrix – which involves culture, art, political struggle, history, literature, and other knowledges that construct ideas about dance – is a pedagogical foundation, and in this sense, I consider it contains emancipating seeds for life. Thus, the knowledge of the African matrix avails subjects to a fuller comprehension of Brazilian society and to new forms of education that come *from* marginalized social groups. Knowledge of the African matrix avails subjects to the inclusion and break of racist readings on the spirituality of African roots, and affords access to the body practices that this knowledge includes.

As a guide to the dance, I make use of these pedagogical fundamentals, not only for specific courses on the African matrix, but within diverse dimensions of my relationships with students and educational communities, incorporating this knowledge/wisdom in daily life. I believe firmly that this epistemological field mobilizes new positions on how to teach, and for me, this is the most important awareness that I gathered from my investigations: it can be used not solely as a theoretical product, but also, and above all, as a political tool in daily life, and as a focus of social change and mobilization of new paradigms.

References

Bakhtin, Mikhail (1999), *La cultura popular en la edad media y en el renacimiento: el contexto de François Rabelais*, Madrid: Alianza Editorial.

Bauman, Zigmunt (2001), *Modernidade líquida*, Rio de Janeiro: Zahar.

Brasil Bahia (2014), "Dança Afro-brasileira com Pakito Lázaro," YouTube, https://www.youtube.com/watch?v=R3_eRaKUiSo&authuser=0. Accessed October 30, 2017.

Conrado, Amélia de Souza (2006), "Capoeira Angola e Dança Afro. Contribuições para uma política de educação multicultural na Bahia," Ph.D. dissertation, Salvador, Bahia, Brasil: Universidade Federal de Bahia.

Drumeaux, Jonathan (2012), "Tatiana Campêlo – Dança Afro-Brasileira," YouTube, https://www.youtube.com/watch?v=T13qjBZJyAU&authuser=0. Accessed October 30, 2017.

Echeverry Zambrano, Claudia Del Pilar (2011), "Pesquisas representativas dos temas corpo, dança e educação de matriz afro em Salvador, Bahia," *Entrelaçando*, 4:2, pp. 127–37.

Giroux, Henry (2005), *Estudios culturales, pedagogía crítica y democracia radical*, Madrid: Editorial Popular.

Greiner, Christine (2005), *O corpo: Pistas para estudos indisciplinares*, São Paulo: Annablume.

Instituto Brasileiro de Geografía e Estatística (Brazilian Institute of Geography and Statistics) (IGBE) (2010), "Censo Demográfico do Instituto Brasileiro de Geografia e Estatística," http://www.ebc.com.br/censo-demografico-do-instituto-brasileiro-de-geografia-e-estatistica. Accessed November 12, 2017.

Kats, Helena (2005), *Um, dois, três: a dança é o pensamento do corpo*, Belo Horizonte: FTD.

Lino Gomes, Nilma (2002), "Trajetórias escolares, corpo negro e cabelo crespo: Reprodução de estereótipos, ou resignificação cultural?," *Revista Brasileira de Educação*, 21, pp. 40–51.

Maffesoli, Michel ([1988] 1996), *The Time of the Tribes: Decline of Individualism in Mass Society*, London: Sage Publications Ltd.

MARIO SERGIO PEREIRA (2016), "FUNCEB – Escola de dança – Aula de dança afro com Vania Oliveira 19/01/2016 – MSF 7997," YouTube, https://www.youtube.com/watch?v=9BhRjkCjIWA&authuser=0. Accessed October 30, 2017.

Monteiro, Marianna Francisca Martins (2002), "Espetáculo e devoção: burlesco e teologia política nas danças populares brasileiras," Ph.D. dissertation, University of São Paulo.

Moreira, Anália and Silva, Maria Cecília de Paula (2008), "A cultura corporal e a lei nº 10639/03: Um estudo sobre os impactos da lei no ensino da educação física em Salvador," MA thesis, Federal University of Bahia.

Moreira, Anália de Jesus (2011), *Processo civilizatório da cultura africana e afrobrasileira e as concepções de corpo, cultura e educação no bloco Ilê Aiyê*, Cruz das Almas, Bahia: Entrelaçando.

Nóbrega Oliveira, Nadir (2007), *Agô Alafiju,Odara! A presença de Clyde Wesley Morgan na Escola de Dança da UFBA, 1971 a 1978*, Salvador: Fundação Pedro Calmon.

Oliveira, Eduardo (2007), *Filosofia da ancestralidade: Corpo e mito na filosofia da educação brasileira*, Curitiba: Gráfica Popular.

Raimundo Bispo dos Santos (2015), "Aula de Dança Mestre King," YouTube, https://www.youtube.com/watch?v=wHds0uPFOxg&authuser=0. Accessed October 30, 2017.

Sansone, Lívio (2007), *Negritude sem etnicidade*, Salvador: EDUFBA and Pallas.

Silva, Maria Cecília de Paula (2009), *Do Corpo Objeto ao Sujeito Histórico: Perspectivas do Corpo na História da Educação Brasileira*, Salvador: EDUFBA.

Wacquant, Loic (2002), *Corpo e alma: Notas etnográficas de um aprendiz de boxe*, Rio de Janeiro: Relume Dumara.

——— (2013), "Pedagogias do corpo na dança de matriz africana em Salvador, Bahia Brasil: perspectivas e desafios do projeto emancipatório," Ph.D. dissertation, Federal University of Bahia.

Notes

1 http://www.un.org/en/sections/observances/international-decades/.

2 This article was extracted and revised from Echeverry Zambrano's Ph.D. dissertation: "Pedagogias do corpo na educação das danças de matriz africana em Salvador, Brasil: Tensões e perspectivas do projeto emancipatório."

3 http://portal.unesco.org/geography/en/ev.php-URL_ID=12587&URL_DO=DO_TOPIC&URL_SECTION=201.html. Also, https://blackwomenofbrazil.co/2013/01/12/ten-years-of-law-10-6392003-obligating-schools-to-teach-africanafro-brazilian-history-law-yet-to-be-fully-implemented/. Accessed July 8, 2016.

4 Throughout this essay, "Candomblé movement vocabularies," "Candomblé dances," or "Candomblé ritual communities" refer only to Ketu tradition forms: "My study does not tackle the African matrix dances of Angola or Jeje [nations]… my study is concentrated on the Ketu tradition in Salvador," personal communication between the author and Lucía M. Suarez, July 7, 2016.

5 Editors' note: In English, "bodygraphy," "bodywriting," or perhaps "bodymapping." We retain the Portuguese wording throughout to honor the author's thinking and naming.

6 See *dança afro* example #1, Tatiana Compelo: https://www.youtube.com/watch?v=T13qjBZJyAU&authuser=0.

7   See *dança afro* example #2, Mestre King: https://www.youtube.com/watch?v=wHds0uPFO
    xg&authuser=0.
8   See *dança afro* example #3: Vania Oliveira, https://www.youtube.com/watch?v=9BhRjkCjI
    WA&authuser=0.
9   See *dança afro* example #4, Pakito Lázaro: https://www.youtube.com/watch?v=R3_eRaKUiSo
    &authuser=0.
10 Editors' note: "Urban tribes" here refers to small fluid groupings of young people, within
    inner cities that challenge mainstream culture (Maffesoli [1988] 1996).

Chapter 4

African Matrix Dance: Repertoire Options for Approaching Race and Ethnic Relations in Brazilian Schools

Piedade Lino Videira

Introduction

Throughout each decade of Brazilian history, people of African descent have spared no effort to claim and secure access to rights for the black population in two spheres of social life: the labor market and education. The claims of activists, educators, and researchers regarding ethnic and racial issues are not only broad in scope, given the inhuman process of enslavement suffered by Africans and their descendants in Brazil, but also they are backed by qualitative and quantitative data. Studies generated by the Anísio Teixeira Institute of Educational Studies (Instituto de Estudos e Pesquisas Educacionais Anísio Teixeira/INEP), the Institute for Applied Research (Instituto de Pesquisas Aplicadas/IPEA) and the Brazilian Institute of Geography and Statistics (Instituto Brasileiro de Geografia e Estatística/IBGE) show that racism has resulted within the processes of educational and socio-economic exclusion, which affects the majority of the African-descendent population in their daily lives. This research helps to clarify the incalculable consequences of the various faces of racism that have degraded the human condition of thousands of Afro-Brazilians, who account for more than half of the national population (IBGE 2010).

The Brazilian challenge remains: to confront and overcome ethnic-racial inequalities between blacks and whites; however, over time, there have been important achievements. One of these is Brazil's preparation for the first *World Conference against Racism, Racial Discrimination, Xenophobia and Related Intolerance* in Durban, South Africa, which took place between August 31 and September 8, 2001. At the conference, 173 countries, 4000 non-governmental organizations (NGOs), and a total of more than 16,000 participants discussed urgent and polemical issues. 42 delegates and five technical advisors represented Brazil from the government of sociologist and then-President Fernando Henrique Cardoso. Edna Roland, a black woman activist from the group Fala Preta (Black Women Speak), was the rapporteur-general who was charged with presenting the list of demands by groups representing victims of discrimination and intolerance in Brazil, mistakenly labeled "minorities." The list included, among other demands:

- A proposal to create a quota program for black students in Brazilian public universities;
- The use of the criteria of self-declaration to determine an individual's color/race in the national census conducted by the Brazilian Institute of Geography and Statistics (IBGE);
- Approval and institutionalization of the Statute of Racial Equality.

Debates in Durban showed that the world was ready to create mechanisms that would eradicate all forms of prejudice and that each nation needed to do its part.

It was in this context that Brazil created an Affirmative Action Program that was unprecedented in the nation's history and which led to the approval of other relevant laws. In particular, Law No. 10.639 was passed on January 6, 2003, establishing the *National Curricular Guidelines for Education Regarding Ethnic-Racial Relations and the Teaching of Afro-Brazilian and African History and Culture* throughout the entire school curriculum, especially in the areas of arts education, literature, and history. Individual states and municipalities were charged with enforcement of these laws and some of them have shown gradual compliance with the regulations, which are also reaffirmed in the text of the Statute of Children and Adolescents (Law No. 8.096, June 13, 1990) and in the National Education Plan (Law No. 10.172, January 9, 2001).

There is no doubt that the adoption of Law No. 10.639 is an historic achievement of organized black Brazilian social movements of the twentieth century, which always fought for recognition and action by the national government to change the social position of black men and women. Historically relegated to an inferior social status, they continue today to face the challenge of asserting their presence in a positive way, as producers of material and intangible wealth and as protagonists of Brazil's history. In the education system, and particularly in education policy, the implementation of Law No. 10.639 signifies a complete break from conventional pedagogical approaches that do not recognize, in a positive way, the ethnic-racial relations and differences resulting from Brazil's nation-building process. In addition to focusing on the black population, this law should be extended to the creation of policies aimed at improving the quality of education for all Brazilians at all stages of their lives (PNE 2014).

In creating guidelines for meeting the benchmarks set by the National Education Plan (Plano Nacional de Educação/PNE 2014: 23), the Ministry of Education and Culture (Ministério de Educação e Cultura/MEC) has defined three approaches to address diversity in educational policy:

The first is based on an inclusion/exclusion binary that seeks to incorporate the excluded through a policy based on a socioeconomic perspective, disregarding their specific identities. In this approach the ethnic-racial issue is diluted, and diversity does not result in revision of the concepts, models, and references that inform educational policies. The second approach is based on affirmative action or positive discrimination, with the understanding that the situation of poverty and/or social inequality of certain social groups such as blacks, indigenous peoples, and women cannot be attributed to isolated individuals. Thus, conditions such as ethnicity, race, sex, and the definition of belonging to a group are considered in MEC programs and policies such as the University for All Program, (ProUni). In the third approach, diversity is considered in the context of a "politics of difference," which is distinguished from social inclusion policies and affirmative action policies not by an emphasis on particularity, but by the demand for equal recognition of the rights of different cultures to express themselves in the public sphere. This approach openly challenges practices associated with the myth of racial democracy and points to changes in the ideas and forms of organization that guide education policies. This approach has not yet received due attention in the MEC agenda. It is essential to emphasize that the first and second approaches are not mutually contradictory, but can be complementary. The third approach involves firm recognition of the contribution of different peoples and cultures to the composition of the nation, in order to underscore the value of ethnic and racial pluralism.

(PNE 2014: 23)

According to the same document, effective implementation of Law No. 10.639 requires the systematic development of this third approach, which is reflected in the design of new educational policies that involve the Ministry of Education as a whole in the fight against racism and the valorization of ethnic-racial education. At the same time, clear guidelines are needed for institutions of higher learning, responsible for training professionals and teachers who work in diverse fields, and also for state and municipal systems and all others who directly or indirectly work in the field of education, so that this valid approach does not become the sole responsibility of schools.

The success of state institutional and pedagogical policies, which are directed toward reparations or recognition and valorization of black Brazilians' identity, culture, and history, necessarily depends on favorable physical, material, intellectual, and affective conditions for teaching and learning; in other words, all black and non-black students and their teachers need to feel valued and supported. Success of such policies decisively depends on re-education regarding relations between blacks and whites, which we are here designating ethnic-racial relations. And it also depends on collaborative work that brings together school educational processes, public policy, and social movements, since the ethnic, cultural, educational, and policy changes in ethnic-racial relations are not limited to schools (Brazilian National Education Plan 2008: 234).

There is no doubt that Law No. 10.639, which reflects the *National Curriculum Guidelines,* is crucial in pushing Brazilians to recognize and value what educator Petronilha Beatriz Gonçalves e Silva calls "Africanisms" (Gonçalves e Silva 1997). These are contemporary linkages in today's societies, but notably in Brazil, to African values, customs, and behaviors. The new laws encourage Brazilians to learn about the various ways that an ancestral Africa is present on Brazilian land. Therefore, everyone must learn at every stage of education and within the family that Brazil is a poly-lingual, multiethnic, and multicultural nation shaped by Indigenous, African, and European hands. However, for Law No. 10.639 to be effective, researchers, Black Movement activists, teachers, staff and directors, states and municipalities through their education councils, as well as the Federal Ministry of Education, Public Ministry, and the entire general community must do everything in their power to see that it is implemented.

As a black woman activist/educator and a *marabaixo* and *batuque* dancer, born into the Afro-Amapá culture of the far northern Amazon region, I am aware of my responsibility in this process. However, I want to first reflect on the need to broaden didactic and pedagogical repertoires in order to promote dialogue, reflection, learning, and the conditions necessary for students to incorporate knowledge about the world and distant realities into their intellectual and professional training–without forgetting themselves or those like them. That is why I have chosen, for this essay, African matrix dances, the dances of African heritage and Brazilian creativity (also called Afro-Brazilian dances). These dances demonstrate theoretical, didactic, and methodological means to address African heritage in education.

Among many diverse Afro-Brazilian dances, I focus here on one Afro-Amapá dance: *marabaixo*, although both *marabaixo* and *batuque* have been the focus of my academic research since 2004 at the Federal University of Ceará. I chose to study African matrix dances because I grew up in an area of black majority, in the Laguinho neighborhood in Macapá, Amapá, where the community dances and celebrates its faith. The Holy Spirit, the Holy Trinity, and the Trinity of the Lambs festivities are celebrations in which religion and merriment are not separated (Sabino and Lody 2011). These festivities represent a cultural uniqueness in which the Trinity and the Holy Spirit of the Catholic religion are celebrated within an African heritage context and do not involve syncretism with African religious gods. The *marabaixo* cycle starts on Holy Saturday and Easter Sunday, following the tradition of "black Catholicism"[1] (Cunha 2001). In this religious context, dance reaffirms the positive ethnic identity of Afro-Amapá people and their local cultural and social history.

My focus on dance expression is also due to my perception that dance scholars have paid scant attention to the educational value of corporeal language as a relevant mechanism for positive signification of the body and the identity of the black subject. I recognize that the history of African dance in Brazil is little studied, and the existing research focuses predominantly on folkloric dances, labeling them as spontaneous popular cultural manifestations (Santos 1996; Videira 2009). Thus, this essay describes how dance practices, in their relationship to ethnic-racial relations, can assist cultural processes in Brazilian education and consolidate full citizenship for all Brazilian people. I include the relevance of training and continuing education of teachers, administrators, and technical pedagogical staff with regard to ethnic and racial diversity and the contributions that audiovisual resources can make. For an ethnic-racial approach in education, African matrix dances, specialized teacher-training, and pertinent audio-visual access are necessary. With the direct and purposeful participation of students and teachers in its construction, this educational, pedagogical and methodological approach is extremely generative.

The Black Body as a Showcase

In Brazil, the African-descendent population suffers from racism, which is directed toward the body that marks itself as black through facial features and "afro" hair and affirms itself in its movement and gestures in traditional and religious dances and in contemporary forms created in dialogue with other cultural and ethnic roots. Above all, as Beatriz Nascimento observes:

The body is also filled with meaning. It is the body that occupies space and appropriates it. A space or an event where there is a black majority is a "black place" or a "black party." These do not merely constitute bodily encounters, but the meeting of an image with other images in a mirror: with blacks, with whites, with people of other colors and physical complexions, and with other histories.

(2007: 68)

The black body is symbolic. It is historical. It is political. It is social. It is ancestral. According to ethnomusicologists Jorge Sabino and Raul Lody, the dancing body is "a social rehearsal of the motor behavior of Africans. The body as the closest referent for activating memories – a documentary gesture versus the idealization of cultural-ethnic identity" (2011: 13). For me, the black body is not only the idealization of cultural identity, it is also the affirmation of an individual and her/his/their collective cultural identity. The body is the first site and cause of suffering for the black being, because it is the black body that reveals traces of African descent and belonging.

Thus, the black subject was and still is the victim of "attack" and attempted suppression through the discourse of miscegenation. Brazilians prefer miscegenation toward whiteness rather than blackness, confirming a Brazilian desire to become white and deny African heritage or blackness. For Sabino and Lody, "experiencing the deepest relationship of belonging with peoples and cultures of the African continent through the body" (2011: 13) reaffirms the historical role of the black body as memory that was preserved and diffused through the African Diaspora, and also as living evidence of the recreation of African cultures.

Certainly, the implementation of Law No. 10.639 helps Brazilian education professionals to wake up to the need for the establishment of:

a deep intra-body dialogue, with all its psycho-physiological characteristics and in the way that these properties and these limits express what is expected or desired of a body, which above all depicts a place, historical time, activities, professions, religiosity, playfulness, rituals of sociability, and forms of communication.

(Sabino and Lody 2011: 15)

The above-cited authors help readers understand that the black body communicates in many ways and carries innumerable historical traits, which are present in its movements and materialized in a variety of African matrix dances. In my opinion, Brazilian dances emphasize one of the most fruitful possibilities for the affirmation of the black subject. Moreover, through dance, the black body acts in a way that stands as a historical document and signature of particular ethnic identities.

According to education specialist Petronilha Beatriz Gonçalves e Silva, rapporteur of the *National Curriculum Guidelines* for the implementation of Law No. 10.639, it is necessary, above all, that educators:

[...] Rethink [education systems and their] structure and include organization perspectives taken from Afro-Brazilian history and thought. By drawing attention to black experiences, initiatives, proposals, and ideals, they aim to collaborate with efforts to create democratic education for all Brazilian citizens. These efforts are based on the experience of having a black body, of being a bearer of African heritage in Brazil, in a society that wishes to be white and especially values the European roots of their culture.

(1997: 41)

A change of perspective regarding the body as a showcase of the black human being is urgent in order to deconstruct the kind of thinking that placed black bodies on display and for sale during the long period of enslavement. These were bodies belonging "to the tribe of naked men," and thus subjected to brutal conditions and violence of all kinds that denied them their humanity, as the famous poet Castro Alves wrote in his odyssey, "The Slave Ship" ([1868] 2011). The violence that African men and women and their descendants suffered as enslaved people, which normalized the sale of "pieces" in a symbolic attempt to dehumanize the black body, marked African descendants with the stigma of being considered exotic and ugly, and relegated them to the status of "things." As "things," they could be seized and used by anyone.

The black skin that covers more than half of the Brazilian population, according to Gonçalves e Silva, does not permit forgetting that "it is with the body, first of all, not just with good intentions and perfect reasoning, that we discover the world, other people and what they think of us" (1997: 41). She emphasizes:

Black bodies make visible, through their sway, gestures, speech, dress, reasoning, emotions, and intuitions, the history of different ethnic groups, different African nations, forcibly brought together in Brazil, in the Americas, as the main instrument of the slave system. Sometimes alone, sometimes as part of their ethnic group and social class, these bodies have been, over time, marking the rhythm that society imposes on them, and they bestow to society the rhythm of their prudent, rebellious, and conscious actions.

(Gonçalves e Silva 1997: 41)

The diversity of rhythms embodied by Afro-Brazilians, in addition to substantiating sociocultural constructs of ethnic diversity present in the bodies of African descendants in Brazil, represents a broad grouping of historical-cultural African origins. This diversity needs to enter social and educational environments through the front door, and its key role in the construction and development of Brazil must be recognized. I see African matrix dances as the open door in this process, recognizing and acknowledging the black body.

Faced with existing cultural pluralism, the Afro-Brazilian body communicates through dance. It speaks through gestures that immediately touch the spectator's sensitivity. In African matrix dances, that body takes on unique attributes, because it reconnects to ancestral heritages. The human body is shaped and modified, and can be reframed, by society. So it is a social and cultural construct, and according to French anthropologist David Le Breton:

> The body, the site of privileged contact with the world, is under the spotlight. This is a coherent and even inevitable problematic in an individualistic type of society that enters a turbulent zone of confusion and blurring of undisputed referents, and thus experiences a more decisive return to individuality.
>
> (2007: 10)

To the black human being, the body also signifies:

> [...] The mark of individuality, the border, the limit that somehow distinguishes the black person from others. As the social link and web of symbols that provide meaning and value, the body is the most visible feature of the actor-person [...].
>
> (Le Breton 2007: 1)

I would like to underscore that for the African-descendent population, especially those whose skin color makes them visibly salient, who suffer the most extreme forms of racist violence in Brazil, their bodies (corporeality) function as a site of alterity, resistance, and positive affirmations. Their bodies expose history and the various forms of violence that victimize black Brazilians; their bodies also expose the politics of resistance and affirmation that they must continuously engage. I believe that if African matrix dances of Brazil are taught in schools and valued as an arena of knowledge that allows students and faculty to learn about themselves and their ethnic roots (alive and pulsating in all regions of Brazil), Brazilian educators will be forming integrated human beings. As products of this education, all Brazilians would be invited to embrace new social and ideological attitudes, and know that the value of a person is not determined by the color of the skin that covers her/his body.

Theories Surrounding African and Afro-Brazilian Matrix Dances

For the early researcher of dance forms Curt Sachs, "dance is the mother of the arts. The rhythmic patterns of movement, the plastic sense of space, the representations of a seen and imagined world are things that man creates in his own body" (1956: 7). However, Sach's perspective relates in negative ways to the black body, as is recognized by sociologist Carlos Hasenbalg:

> [Black people] were raised hearing that their bodies were ugly and grotesque, and that they could not dance classic ballet because of their wide hips and flat feet, and that their color was not appropriate for the roles of princes and princesses. Their bodies were made

for *samba, maculelê, capoeira*, the *marabaixo*, the *batuque*, the *reisado*, that is, folklore, which is easily accessed, non-technical movement "of the people." Although these cultural manifestations "have been incorporated as a legitimate part of national culture," existing folkloric groups throughout Brazil express themselves as those who do "black stuff".

(1979: 253)

I believe that African matrix dance will help build all Brazilian students' education as historical, anthropological, sociological, artistic, aesthetic, holistic, and educational material. African matrix dance will help the school community, and society in general, to understand and explain important issues in an interdisciplinary way. For example, students, teachers, and other participants in the dance event will be able to differentiate among appreciation, contextualization, and production; they will value and recognize forms of shared, intangible cultural heritage through the experience of their dancing bodies, in and outside of schools, and regardless of the amount of melanin in their skin (Barbosa 1975). In other words, African matrix dances are part of all Brazilians and, therefore, all Brazilians are carriers of an unrestricted and broad cultural continuum of African ancestry. Such a continuum is gradually being recognized as intangible national culture and heritage. Similarly, Brazilian society has already recognized *samba, frevo*, the *tambor de crioula, jongo*, among other dances as its dances of African heritage and Brazilian creativity, called African Matrix or Afro-Brazilian dances. I argue here that African matrix dances contribute to raised self-esteem and educational performance of African descendants; they also can have a direct effect on the interpersonal relationships and social life of all Brazilians.

Working with African-based culture in primary and secondary schools highlights the need for pedagogical alternatives within new educational projects. New projects should enhance the experience of students with a view toward understanding that society is not a homogeneous whole, but rather is made up of multiple subjects with diverse physiognomies and different, but equal cultural characteristics. They can entertain the notion of living without violence and suffering, and without denying themselves, as they work to overcome racism, homophobia, and sexism.

Therefore, the relevance of formal education in achieving Brazil's paradigm shift is beyond question. Schools must develop strategies to build: (1) a positive black identity, in order to educate social subjects in a society that discriminates and teaches self-denial to black children from an early age and (2) a positive Brazilian identity, in order to educate non-black children and society in general, that they should not and cannot assert themselves as heirs to all of their ancestors' worth. In order to correct these misconceptions, it is critical that teachers understand students' particularities and needs, and develop actions that enable children and young people to be fully aware and proud of their ethnicity. Considering this difficult task, I offer a pedagogical proposal for the use of African matrix dance that can, perhaps, establish the seminal place of Afro-Brazilian culture in the whole of Brazilian culture. Through the (re)construction of African-descendent ethnic identity, the body becomes an important and critical element in the knowledge of oneself and others. According to dancer and dance researcher Kiusam Regina de Oliveira:

> The body, as an object, is conditioned to act in accordance with standards imposed as true by the dominant culture model, which can trigger a process of distorted self-representation because these standards make it impossible to forge an identity grounded in culture and history and disregard the individual's own life history, which are constitutive elements of identity.
>
> (2007: 141)

Given this situation, Oliveira proposes a dialectic of resistance in which it is possible to construct an African-descendent counter-body drawn from Afro-Brazilian life histories, produced through collective experience, and taken from the contradictory experiences of black bodies. In this approach, the recognition and valorization of ethnic roots and the sense of racial belonging replace the standards imposed by the dominant culture model. In this context, Afro-Brazilian dances offer a productive component of educational reorientation. Through dance, understanding of cultural values, conceptions of the world, and particularly, the expressions of African and African-descendent culture and history can all be expanded (Videira 2009). This modality of cultural heritage opens the possibility to rediscover the world's black origins and thereby, recuperate the self-esteem of children and young people in Brazilian schools. The Guyanese historian and political activist Walter Rodney emphasized the importance of dance and music in traditional African societies and their key roles in community life: "They mark their presence at births, [...] at initiation ceremonies, marriages, and also in moments of pure fun. Africa is the continent of the drums and percussion" (1975: 51). Dance has always been present among Africans who came to Brazil, (and other parts of the Americas), exerting social and religious functions. For dancers and dance researchers Joenir A. Milan and Claudiana Soerensen:

> To dance is to unite with the divine. Everyone can dance, regardless of creed, color, race, gender, or age. One of the best opportunities for us to know our mind/body is through dance, and this implies movement, a gesture inherent to human beings.
>
> (2011: 12)

It is important to clarify definitions of African dance before I refer to any dance practice that is related to the African Diaspora over the past five centuries. As sociologist Nelson Lima has observed:

> African dance that began in Brazil with the group Brasiliana and Mercedes Baptista sought inspiration in the tradition of folkloric dance, which is performed spontaneously and without technical requirements. Unlike classical dance, African dance in Brazil did not emphasize universality, but rather particularity. It sought to essentialize not only its

African cultural origins, but the black race overall. The constitution of an African dance "artistic world" has become increasingly complex over time, as recent groups are claiming other alliances and identities. However, what characterizes African dance in Brazil is its belonging in the tradition called "Afro-Brazilian culture".

(2005: 9)

Afro-Brazilian dances are performed in both rural and urban black communities. They are present in religious communities and spaces, as they are part of ancestral African heritage that has been recreated and re-signified in the Brazilian context. Afro-Brazilian dances are also mingled within diverse forms of Brazilian movement, such as in *lundu*, which emerged from African drumming, but also in *samba, jongo, pagode, congadas, maracatu, Moçambiques, reisados, cocos de roda, marabaixo, sairé*, and also in tap dance, rap, hip-hop, and many other African Diaspora dances that have come to Brazil.

African heritage dances form an element within the cultural heritage of humanity and as such, should be recognized and experienced in schools so that future generations will appreciate and value the knowledge produced by world origin Africans and their descendants in Brazil and across the planet. Brazilians, particularly, should not forget that through dance, black people transform the experience of social exclusion, oppression, prejudice, and racial discrimination into a cultural-existential foundation geared toward positive affirmation and celebration of life (Macedo 2009). Black people express their ethnicity, life history, and relationship with ancestral memory through dance. The late dancer/choreographer/artistic director and activist within 1960s Guinea (and other newly independent African nation states) Fodéba Keïta observes that:

Dance has always been a part of African black people's lives, like clothing, music, and singing. For Africans, transmission of knowledge also occurs through dance. Our black ancestors danced to express all natural events related to their communities; they danced to give thanks for the crops, fertility, birth, health, life, and even death. One learns to dance and sing just as one learns to talk.

(1958: 3)

Brazilian history can be learned through dance as an artistic language, as well as through the songs, costumes, and instruments that are presented at traditional festivals in predominantly black areas, in schools, and in other artistic and cultural learning spaces. It is also possible for students to gain appreciation of Brazil's cultural diversity through teaching about danced cultural expressions that typically represent different regions of Brazil. I consider dance a form of expression, a communication with the world that reveals life stories through an extremely creative language. Therefore, schools should make it possible for children to experience dance and become acquainted with the history of their ancestors, the history of the community to which they belong.

According to the results of my research (Videira 2009), schools should consider dance as a core subject, as this artistic language enables students to develop psychological, social, emotional, intellectual, cultural, religious, artistic, and, above all, movement skills. In addition, the direct communication it enables between the individuals who dance and those who observe is enriching for both, as is demonstrated in the example of *marabaixo do Amapá*.

Afro-descendance and *Marabaixo do Amapá* Dance

Marabaixo is a dramatic-religious courtship dance (Videira 2009: 25), as well as a way of thinking and a social practice. I attend to the latter, less well-known understanding first to explain and develop this idea with the French philosopher and sociologist Maurice Halbwachs's theoretical conception of individual/collective memory ([1925] 1990). Halbwachs differentiates among forms of memory, moving beyond psychological concepts that are restricted to the individual, to argue for the existence of collective memory, which is constructed through social relations. Halbwachs acknowledges the existence of an autobiographical-personal memory, but explains that individual memory is founded on individual/collective historical memory. For the Brazilian case, I use "Afro-descendance" for Halbwachs's individual/collective memory, which ultimately is the recognition of the existence of an African-descent ethnicity.

This conception of Afro-descendance emerges from the controversy over the existence of black identity in Brazil (Cunha 1999). The use of the term here includes acknowledgement of various African ethnic groups as the common base of African origins and recognition of the historical development of these groups into socio-religious-political "nations" within conditions of criminal enslavement, racist capitalism, and external international power. Afro-Brazilian ethnicity is diverse, not homogeneous, and it is not concerned with degrees of inter-ethnic Brazilian mixture, but rather with history. It is also based on the concept of community dance developed by Sabino and Lody, who argue that dance is "a sign of belonging and of the construction and affirmation of ethnic references from time immemorial" (2011: 12). Lastly, Afro-descendance here assumes that African descendants construct their own spaces within the territoriality of urban development, considered as an indivisible whole in which they participate and recreate themselves as autonomous subjects, in motion within Brazilian society (Santos 1996). *Marabaixo* festivities mark Afro-descendance; they are dance events that last for approximately two months, and take place in the neighborhoods of Laguinho and Favela.[2]

Laguinho, the Site and Context of *Marabaixo do Amapá*

Let me introduce the neighborhood of Laguinho, which is part of the history of being black in Macapá, the capital city of Amapá State. Macapá is a far northern territory of Brazil with many lived black life experiences, culture, and memories, and is home to the dance

107

marabaixo (Cunha 2009). Its Laguinho neighborhood has historically developed an ethnic identity. The *marabaixo* dance in Laguinho connects generations through positive affirmation of values, morals, and human principles, from religiosity to knowledge of and about the dance community. To speak of Laguinho is, above all, to talk about *marabaixo* and therefore, to talk about the Afro-Amapaense ancestry that continues uniting generations through the safeguarding of local intangible cultural heritage. To think about *marabaixo* dance is to memorialize the black men and women who, by dancing, have transmitted to posterity an historical legacy that marked ethnic and political belonging in dialogue with society. To feel *marabaixo* is to place yourself among kinship groups with the assurance that you are an insider rooted in both urban and rural Afro-Amapá communities. To live *marabaixo* is to stretch the fabric of history, reconnecting African ancestors through an intangible cultural heritage and its symbols, mythologies, faith, and philosophies to ways of seeing and conceiving the world.

Thus, dance in black culture, and *marabaixo* as a prime example, is not a set of random gestures or body movements to pass away the time or for entertainment. African and African-descendent dances, including traditional festive and religious dances within Black Catholicism, are serious business. Their organization is a union of many elements: dance, faith, drink, festivity, litanies, masses, fireworks, parades, dramatizations, and devotional promises. Performers and participants cannot deviate from the calendar without risk of disappointing the Holy Trinity and the Holy Spirit, both revered in Amapá.

Black Catholicism identifies the diverse expressions of Afro-Brazilian culture through the singularity in a faith of "the Saints" drawn from Judeo-Christian traditions. While in many Brazilian states there is a distinct, syncretic manifestation of Catholicism and other African religions, this is not the case in Amapá. The Catholic saints are celebrated without the integration of Candomblé or Umbanda perspectives and customs. Many Catholic saints are worshiped: The Holy Spirit, The Holy Trinity, São Tiago, São Joaquim, São Pedro, São Benedito, Nossa Senhora da Conceição, Santo Expedito, among others, and songs are sung to the Virgin Mary, called *cantigas* (originally medieval manuscript music). Special prayers, called *ladainhas*, are sung by those who lived in the *quilombos* of Amapá;[3] however, these are never accompanied by drums or other instruments. Interesting also, there are no Bible readings or presiding priests beyond those in Catholic churches, but in these Afro-communities, there is much *marabaixo* dancing.

Ancestral legacies have been woven and treasured within the historical neighborhood of Laguinho in Macapá. For example, elders and seniors transmit *marabaixo* to youths through oral and bodily traditions. The dance takes shape as newcomers arrive and greet their friends. Potential performers step aside to ask about a mother, a father, aunts, or the godfathers and godmothers of community members. The nuclear family and relatives, the larger family of related family branches, and the extended family of blood and non-blood kin play important roles in the learning process of dance. Dancer and dance researcher Teodora Alves reports that African dance offers a moment of learning about African and African Diaspora culture and history (2001); she sees African dance as an historic legacy of strong and proud ethnic groups, including black royalty, not simply a history of submission.

Dance and Music Description of *Marabaixo*

Dance – a gentle back and forth, here to there rhythm, wrapped in the tenderness of female voices intoned to the sound of drumbeats – takes the shape of an acquired experience as it blends with the fiery seasoning of *gengibirra* [a typical drink made with Cachaça, which is served during Afro-Amapaense festivals]. Thus, from generation to generation, tradition follows the steps of the *marabaixo* dance.

(Cunha 2009: 17)

Marabaixo, they say, is a dance form that was inherited from African and Afro-Brazilian ancestors. Oral histories make clear that little is known about the origins of the name "*marabaixo*," although it seems to recall or relate to the slave ships that went "out to sea," which in Portuguese is "*mar abaixo*." The dance term combines the two words. Despite all uncertainties, I have no doubts about its historical heritage. Interviewees have repeatedly confirmed that *marabaixo* is an African matrix cultural manifestation that was brought to Amapá by enslaved Africans in Brazil.[4]

A *marabaixo* cycle begins immediately after Holy Week, so exact dates change year to year according to the Catholic calendar (where Easter or Holy Week is always observed, but not set to a specific day of the month). The festivities are organized and prepared at the homes of community leaders who are named as heads of the festivities, *festeiros* or *festeiras*. The first *marabaixo* takes place in the urban capital, Macapá, in the neighborhood of Favela on Holy Saturday; *marabaixo* takes place in the Laguinho neighborhood on Easter Sunday. Fireworks are set off day and night throughout the *marabaixo* cycle and when they explode, the community cheers and everyone gets caught up in celebratory energy. It is an important public celebration in which everyone is welcome to participate and share the traditional drink, *gengibirra*, which is made with ginger, cane alcohol, cloves, water, and sugar. Also *cozidão*, a special beef and vegetable stew, is available for everyone.

The festive scene shows women in characteristic costume: a petticoat, a flowered skirt, and a lace blouse. They wear flowers in their hair, and accessories such as a necklace, earrings, and multi-colored bracelets. Men wear pants, shirts, and (cowboy) hats and carry a towel over the shoulders. The towel is used to clean sweat off heated brows, since the dancing takes place in crowded sheds, where temperatures rise, especially with many people dancing.[5]

Community members dance in a circle of men, women, and children in front of a stall or *barracão* built by the *festeiro/a*. The space is completely open, offering full visibility to all participants and lined with benches on each side for spectators to be seated, if they wish, or perhaps for dancers to rest. There is no hierarchy to be followed in the scenic area; community members and their guests are free to express their emotions and feelings. *Marabaixo* rhythm is marked by snare drums, which are made by specialists in Laguinho and a few *quilombola* communities in the countryside. In the past, the snare drums were hollowed out of tree trunks and covered with sheep leather, goat leather (less expensive), or anaconda (more expensive). The drums are tied with ropes and pieces of rubber that are attached on the side and used for tuning; they are carried by a thick, colorful rope or *bandolier* worn over the shoulders. Beaded strings, called "responses" (*respostas*), are on the bottom of the drums and create the snare sound. Today, the drums are a bit more elaborate; they are painted on their sides with various colors that represent the Saint being celebrated and sometimes with the images of the Holy Spirit or the Holy Trinity.

Drums are played with two drumsticks, which form a cross on top of each *marabaixo* drum. The rhythm is marked by call and response chants, intoned by the lead female or male singer (*cantadeira, cantador*) who creates a series of verses called "thieves" (*ladrões*). The thief verses satirize, criticize, or praise community members and events that are part of everyday life or local, national, and world news. Other percussion instruments, called "boxes" (*caixas*), and a rustic bass drum called *bombo*, mark the rhythms of the dance as well.[6]

Participants engage in a spirit of confraternity, sometimes dancing with their arms around one another. What is seen most in observation is the spontaneous spinning/circling/whirling of women, alternating their turns to each side and holding their long (round/hoop) skirts. They also move about the circle in a pattern that involves side-to-side and front-to-back movement of the upper body while the feet remain on the ground in a basic pattern. The men court the ladies through corporeal movements; they say full of "swing [*catimba*], grace and attitude [*presepada*]." They sometimes swagger/lean as though they are going to fall over; sometimes they shimmy their shoulders; and sometimes they spread their legs, leaning forward and marking the cadence/rhythm of the verse with their feet. The main locomotor step of *marabaixo,* for women or men, is danced by dragging/shuffling/shifting (*arrastando*) the feet, one after the other or close-to-the-ground walking-like steps, performed in time to the basic rhythm. Dancers occasionally move their arms up and down and sometimes raise them as they spin.

Thus, dancers are not tied to any rules, patterns, or models. That is, everyone dances, and each dancer develops his, her, or their singularity and expresses his, her, or their feelings through dance. Freedom, creativity, and individual development through dance allow the *brincantes* or playful participants autonomy in relation to their bodies. During breaks between songs, participants linger around the *barracão*, but when the singer throws out new improvised verses again, participants all move in one circle, in a counterclockwise direction.

Marabaixo dances and the festival are especially significant for older people of African descent, especially those who are between 50 and 85. The oldest person I met was Tereza Rosa dos Santos, ("*Tia Teresa*" or Aunt Teresa), who reached the age of 103 in 2004; thus she shares a century of local and inherited knowledge with several generations. Women form the majority of dancers and singers and are also responsible for preparing the food. Men play drums, but there are a few women who are breaking that hegemony. Men also sing, prepare the traditional drink, and launch fireworks.[7]

Marabaixo in Laguinho neighborhoods signals African ancestry, memory, tradition, and ethnic history. Afro-Amapaense participants are well aware of the African origins of their intangible cultural heritage; they have tremendous pride, which can be seen by Brazilian and foreign others–even on the Internet, my next topic.

The Relevance of Video for Teaching Afro-Brazilian Dance

Brazil is geographically huge; consequently, Brazilians do not know one another completely. Many lack an understanding of the social, cultural, geographical, and unique aspects that differentiate regional and ethnic identities. In addition, like many other countries around the world, Brazil's education system focuses only on select portions of Brazilian history, mainly excluding the pivotal significance of African Diaspora histories. Law No. 10.639, which amended the previous Lei de Diretrizes e Bases da Educação Nacional (Law to Set Guidelines and Foundations of National Education) and included the teaching of African and African-descendent cultures as part of the regular curriculum in schools, aimed to fix previous deficiencies, and promoted the appreciation and public recognition of the varied African-descendent contributions and influences within Brazil. These legal changes have furthered Brazilian educational development at all levels and have helped Brazilian society in the recognition of its Africanisms (African plurality and diversity). Africanisms are alive in all of Brazil's states and regions and if the education system would integrate the use of videos for teaching, Brazilian students could literally see how much their country has gained from the African continent.

I consider the use of video as an educational resource and as an effective and appropriate pedagogical methodology. Most Brazilian schools do not have equal access to all of Brazil's diverse cultural expressions through the institutions that promote national culture; therefore, collection of visual cultural materials from different state departments of culture and tourism websites could remedy this situation. Videotapes, which have been used previously to promote the local resources, beautiful landscapes, and unique regional features, could be used also as representations of Brazilian ethnicities and histories. Brazilian dances are among these resources and can prove to be advantageous, since learning from visual cues is sensitizing and long-lasting.

The process of collecting various videos from Internet offerings is a common practice of many contemporary students. Teachers can initiate student research and classroom projects on different Brazilian regions with intent to examine Brazilian dances and analyze and contextualize them in terms of ancestral heritages, especially previously marginalized black and indigenous ancestries. After analyses that generate geographical, historical, and ethnic understandings, an anthropological or cultural study of Brazilian religions could logically follow, so that students could come to appreciate how dance and religion are related in many cultures, and that culture is the result of the history, territory, and the social and religious context of each place.

Next, in a proposed sequence, is a concentration on the gestures that are seen repeatedly among Brazilians in ordinary life and, importantly, in Brazilian dancing. In another context, Le Breton suggested that the gesture:

> ...Refers to the actions of the body when the actors [people] meet: greeting or farewell rituals (hand signal, nod, handshake, hugs, kisses on the cheek, mouth, mimicry, etc.), the ways we consent or reject something, facial and body movements that accompany words, the direction of the gaze, the variation of the distance between the actors/people, the forms of touching or avoiding contact ....
>
> ([1953] 2007: 44)

In African and African-descendent history, gestures give life to a corporeal/poetic text; they often act as the documentary record of ancestral thought and contemporary meaning. Video is a tremendous asset in learning this important part of Brazil – in recognizing and valuing different communities within Brazilian society.

Additionally, the possibility of contemporary recreation of historical, traditional, and cultural dance forms allows for the expression of creativity within other forms of learning (e.g., research, analysis, creative production, etc.). The creative and thereby, holistic measures taken provide learners with both understanding of the dances and understanding of the values, rules, and concerns of the ethnic groups who dance. In trying to recreate or innovate within the same values and traditional boundaries, students become sensitized to differences.

My experience as an educator has demonstrated the importance of teacher participation in practical classroom activities. It makes an incomparable difference when teachers have students engage in an artistic activity that uses the body, and when teachers get involved along with students, in both study and practical activities, including dance. Good teaching is by example, as noted Brazilian education historian and philosopher, Paulo Freire, has shown, and teachers and other educators should be involved in corporeal practices inside the classroom. At times, historical (and sometimes religious) challenges enter the education atmosphere and restrict the body; however, the first step is to enter in harmony with the body's natural anatomy, through self-acceptance and respect for the body that everyone has been given.

Reflections

Brazil is the nation with the largest black population outside of the continent of Africa, and Brazilians can no longer deny belonging to or inheriting African-descendent material and immaterial cultural legacies or "Africanisms." Law No. 10.639 will help citizens in Brazilian society learn that Africanisms pulsate throughout most, if not all of Brazil's regions; those pulses are most visible in traditional and contemporary dances, displaying a rich variety of rhythms, gestures, music, drama, and historical and spiritual content. Such cultural manifestations make Brazil unique in the eyes of the world. Therefore, Afro-Brazilian dances must be recognized in Brazilian schools, along with the bodies that recreate African heritages through dance. Dance is a valid field of study as a carrier of memory (Nascimento 2007), and as a product of African and African-descendent heritage.

In writing this essay on Afro-Brazilian dance, I have sought to remove the arts from their association with entertainment and leisure pastime activities, as they have been traditionally introduced in Brazilian school curricula. I have argued that through dance, teachers can address historical, social, geographical, anthropological/cultural, philosophical, artistic, and aesthetic aspects of Brazilian society that are relevant to the many ethnic heritages. I have written in light of the application of Law No. 10.639 in schools, which can be accomplished through dances that are within national intangible cultural heritage. African matrix, or what some call Afro-Brazilian, dances need to be understood by the education community as methods or types of documents that allow teachers and students access to wide-ranging and relevant information. These dances enhance knowledge and give value to the African and African-descendent ancestors of all Brazilians.

References

Alves, Teodora de Araújo (2001), "*Coco de Zambê*: Práticas de saberes da cultura negra," in Iolanda de Oliveira and Petronilha Beatriz Gonçalves e Silva (eds), *Negro e educação: Identidade negra, pesquisas sobre o negro e a educação no Brasil*, São Paulo: Ação Educativa, pp. 259–303.

Barbosa, A. M. (1975), *Teoria e prática da educação artística*, São Paulo: Cultrix.

Benevides, Alexia (2011), "Dança típica de Amapá – Dança de Marabaixo," YouTube, https://www.youtube.com/watch?v=6kOdfcvMvNI. Accessed March 21, 2018.

Brazilian Government (2010), *Senso do Instituto Brasileiro de Geografia e Estatística*, Brasília: DF.

Brazilian Ministry of Education, National Council of Education (2004), *Diretrizes Curriculares Nacional para a Educação das Relações Étnicorraciais e para o Ensino de História e Cultura Afro – Brasileira*, Brasília: DF.

Brazilian National Education Plan (2008), *Proposta de Plano Nacional de Implementação das Diretrizes Curriculares Nacionais da Educação das Relações étnico-Raciais e para o Ensino de história e Cultura Afro-Brasileira e Africana – Lei 10.639/2003*, Brasilia: Ministry of Education.

Breton, David Lê ([1953] 2007), *A sociologia do corpo* (trans. Sônia M.S. Fuhrmann), 2nd ed., Petrópolis, RJ: Vozes.

Câmara dos Deputados (2014), *Plano Nacional de Educação 2014-2024*, Centro de Documentação e Informação Coordenação Edições Câmara, http://www.observatoriodopne.org.br/uploads/reference/file/439/documento-referencia.pdf. Accessed September 28, 2017.

Castro Alves, Jose Cassais ([1868] 2011), *The Slave Ship*, Rio Grande do Sul: Enigmax Editora.

Cunha Jr., Henrique (1999), "Pesquisas educacionais em temas de interesse dos afrodescendentes," in I. Costa, J. Romão and S. M. Silveira (eds), *Os negros e a escola brasileira*, Florianópolis: NEN, pp. 13–25.

—— (2001), "Africanidade, Afrodescendência e educação," *Educação em Debate*, 2:42, pp. 5–15.

Etetuba Etetuba (2015), "Marabaixo do Languinho," YouTube, https://www.youtube.com/watch?v=0Ya3LAlJhOs. Accessed March 21, 2018.

Gonçalves e Silva, Petronilha Beatriz (1997), "Vamos acertar os passos?," in *As Ideias Racistas, os Negros e a Educação*, Série Pensamento Negro em Educação, Florianópolis: Atilénde Editora-Apoio Fundação Ford, pp. 39–59.

Halbwach, Maurice ([1925] 1990), *A Memória Coletiva* (trans. Laurent Léon Schaffter), São Paulo: Edições Vertice.

Hasenbalg, Carlos A. (1979), *Discriminação e Desigualdades Raciais no Brasil*, Belo Horizonte: Edições Graal.

Instituto Brasileiro de Geografía e Estatística (Brazilian Institute of Geography and Statistics) (2010), "Instituto Brasileiro de Geografia e Estatística – 2015," http://www.planejamento.gov.br/acesso-a-informacao/auditorias/instituto-brasileiro-de-geografia-e-estatistica-ibge/instituto-brasileiro-de-geografia-e-estatistica-2015. Accessed November 12, 2017.

Keïta, Fodéba (1958), *Afrikan dance and stage in the theatre dans le world* (xeroxed excerpt), pp. 1–15.

Le Breton, David (2007), *A sociologie do corpo*, (trans. Sônia M. S. Fuhrmann), Petrópolis, Rio de Janeiro: Vozes.

Lima, Nelson (2005), *Dando conta do recado: a dança afro no Rio de Janeiro e as suas influências*, Rio de Janeiro: Brasil Lincense.

Macedo, Marluce de Lima (2009), "Tradição oral afro-brasileira e escola: Diálogos possíveis para a implantação da Lei 10.639/03," in Márcia Ângela da Silva Aguiar, Ahyas Siss, Iolanda de Oliveira, Janete Maria L. de Oliveira, Marcia Soares de Alvarenga, Petronilha Beatriz G. e Silva and Raquel de Oliveira (eds), *Educação e diversidade: Estudos e pesquisas*, Recife: Gráfica J. Luiz Vasconcelos, pp. 1–263.

Milan, Joenir Antônio and Soerensen, Claudiana (2011), "A dança negra/afro-brasileira como fator educacional," *Revista África e Africanidades*, 3:12, pp. 1–14.

Nascimento, Beatriz de (2007), *Eu sou atlântica: Sobre a trajetória de vida de Beatriz Nascimento*, Sao Paulo: Alex Ratts, Imprensa Oficial do Estado de São Paulo, Instituto Kuanza.

Oliveira, Kiusam Regina de (2007), "O papel da consciência sociorracial na luta contra o racismo," in Cynthia Pereira de Sousa and Denice Barbara Catani (eds), *Multiplicidades culturais: Projetos de formação e trabalho escolar*, São Paulo: Escrituras Editora, pp. 133–52.

Plano Nacional de Educação (PNE) (2014), *Câmara dos Deputados, Edições Câmara, Série legislação*, p. 125.

Rodney, Walter (1975), *Como a Europa sub-desenvolveu a África*, Lisboa: Bogle and L'Ouverture Publications.

Sabino, Jorge and Lody, Raul (2011), *Danças de matriz africana: Antropologia do movimento*, Rio de Janeiro: Pallas.

Sachs, Curt (1956), "Apostila apresentada na Disciplina História da Dança," in *O que é a dança*, Bahia: Universidade Federal da Bahia, pp. 1–12.

Santos, M. (1996), *Metamorfoses do espaço habitado: Fundamentos teóricos e metodológicos da geografia*, 4th ed., São Paulo: Hucitec.

Som do Norte (2015), "Natalina (As Tias do Marabaixo 4)," YouTube, https://www.youtube.com/watch?v=kOWzcayoSkY. Accessed March 21, 2018.

Videira, Piedade Lino (2009), *Marabaixo, dança afrodescendente: ressignificando a identidade étnica do negro amapaense*, Fortaleza: Edições UFC.

Notes

1 "Black Catholicism" is a term coined by Henrique Cunha, Jr. (professor of electrical engineering at the Federal University of Ceará). In Amapá, specifically, it means the celebration of the Catholic saints (each black community has its own specific saints) through local and African-descendent festival celebrations that include African heritage dancing, Afro-Brazilian food and drink, but not the African spiritual entities that are common in other Brazilian states.

2 For *marabaixo* calendars, see Videira (2009: 135–37).

3 *Quilombos* are communities of Afro-Brazilians who have descended from maroon or "runaway slave" communities in the colonial era.

4 Author's field notes, 2003–05.

5 See video examples: https://www.youtube.com/watch?v=xxhu6RIwmcw, and https://www.youtube.com/watch?v=BgcAw0ndwzw.

6 https://www.youtube.com/watch?v=kOWzcayoSkY. Accessed March 21, 2018.

7 https://www.youtube.com/watch?v=6kOdfcvMvNI; https://www.youtube.com/watch?v=0Ya3LAlJhOs. Both accessed March 21, 2018.

Chapter 5

After-School *Samba*: Cultural Memory and Ownership in the Wake of UNESCO Recognition as Intangible Heritage of Humanity

Danielle Robinson and Jeff Packman

Introduction

For almost 100 years, images, recordings, and performers of *samba* have traveled the world. Lightning fast feet, reverberating hips, and feathered headdresses (not to mention scantily clad women) have become recognizable globally as signifiers of Brazil (Vianna 1999). Over time, *samba* musicians and dancers have come to serve as unofficial ambassadors for the Brazilian nation as they showcase *samba*'s beauty, spectacle, and cultural richness. Yet the national music and dance that have become so visible internationally are from a very particular city, Rio de Janeiro. There are other *sambas* in Brazil, though, and this essay focuses on a less globally recognized manifestation from the other end of the country, the northeastern state of Bahia – where most of the nation's enslaved peoples once lived and where their descendants live on today.

The Bahian music and dance practice, known as *samba de roda*, is often considered the roots of Rio *samba*. Most historians acknowledge that *samba de roda* was brought to Rio by Bahians who migrated south at the end of the nineteenth century. In its new context, the sounds and movements were altered, adapted, and shifted into a distinct music and dance genre that eventually became central to Carnival celebrations and, shortly thereafter, an emblem of the Brazilian nation-state. The significance of *samba de roda*, however, hardly ends with being the raw material of Brazil's nationalized *samba*. Rather, *samba de roda* has been practiced continuously in Bahia since its inception on plantations centuries ago, albeit out of the view of most scholars and far from the concerns of most urban, middle-class Brazilians, let alone international audiences.

In the shadow of its glamorous urban progeny, *samba de roda* has led a comparatively quiet life in rural Bahia, where it still knits communities and families together. It has been the music and dancing that accompanies birthday parties and helps fans celebrate *futbol* victories. It can close a game of *capoeira* (a music, dance, and martial art), or enliven an Afro-Diasporic religious event (Chada 2006); in rural Bahia in particular, it has been an alternative to the *forró* and *quadrilhas* used to commemorate the harvest-focused June Festivals that celebrate São João, São Pedro, and Santo Antônio. All generations, genders, and abilities can participate in *samba de roda* as musicians, dancers, or active audience members.[1]

Samba de roda's dance movements differ from Rio *samba* in several key ways. *Samba de roda* is danced exclusively in a ring or circle formation with dancers taking turns entering the center, one or two at a time, in relation to the musical accompaniment. Dancers' feet pulse swiftly and flatly into the ground in accented triplet-rhythm, while languid arms and skirts arc and sway above. Hips reverberate constantly but remain obscured from view, usually beneath voluminous skirts.

In terms of musical sound, *samba de roda* tends to be rather harmonically simple – that is, if it includes harmonic accompaniment at all. In fact, many *sambadores* or *sambadeiras* (local terms for *samba* practitioners) will say that all that is really needed for a Bahian *samba roda* or *samba* circle is people to sing, dance, and clap their hands in *samba's* distinctive rhythm. However, ensembles are often augmented with *pandeiros* (a Brazilian tambourine), other types of percussion, and plucked string instruments, such as guitars, *cavaquinhos* (a four-stringed ukulele-like instrument) and the *samba de roda* instrument par excellence, the *viola machete*, a small ten-stringed lute.

Despite being foundational to Brazil's national *samba*, Bahian *samba de roda* has never attained the fame or fortune of its offspring. Rio *samba* is typically considered the benchmark for *samba* authenticity and is revered nationally and internationally for its glamour, cosmopolitan-ness, and artistic brilliance. In contrast, if noticed at all, *samba de roda* has often been treated as a dusty relic – literally and figuratively. Even in Bahia, *samba de roda* is widely viewed as a repository for vanishing local cultural memories of slavery, since it developed on plantations in Bahia during the period of colonization.[2]

This all dramatically changed in 2005, however, when *samba de roda* burst into the national and international spotlight with recognition by UNESCO (the United Nations Educational, Scientific, and Cultural Organization) as a masterpiece of the oral and intangible heritage of humanity. It was nominated instead of Rio *samba* – after much debate according to Carlos Sandroni, the ethnomusicologist who coordinated the candidacy dossier on behalf of IPHAN (Institute for National Artistic and Historical Heritage) (Brazil's national heritage organization) – because of the UNESCO requirement that the "masterpiece" be in need of safeguarding; it had to be at "risk of extinction" (Sandroni 2010; Samson and Sandroni 2013). As much as Brazilians might have wanted to see the national *samba*, or even *capoeira*, awarded this international distinction, neither could remotely be considered dying or vulnerable practices and so they had to be passed up for the nomination.[3]

One result, however, was that *samba de roda*, in its mass media debut, became strongly connected with images of precarious, indigent, and elderly people in many of UNESCO's public representations. Weathered hands slapping *pandeiros* and knees; swirling old-fashioned skirts in bright tropical shades; wrinkled dark grinning faces with sparkling eyes; broken down rubber sandals – or, better yet, bare feet – stirring up dirt and sand; wide open mouths (at times with missing teeth) singing in full-throated joy; rhythmically vibrating and quivering rolls of soft flesh – such are images of participants in Bahian *samba de roda* that circulate nationally and internationally today (Sandroni and Sant'Anna 2007). Consequently, authenticity within this practice has come to be aligned with age, poverty, and rurality – not to mention African heritage. While it is true that today *samba de roda* draws to it older Bahians more so than younger ones, it is far from dying as a practice. Overlooked is not the same as dying. Non-commercialized is not the same as in danger. And, having a strong sense of the past is not the same as being a relic.

As researchers, we first encountered *samba de roda* shortly before UNESCO recognition, while living in Bahia's capital, Salvador, between 2004 and 2005. We have been researching this dance/music form intermittently together – in partnership with Brazilian colleagues (Eloisa Domenici and Luciano Carôso) – ever since. Between the two of us, we have spent over five years in Bahia since our first visit in 2002. Our ethnographic fieldwork includes participant observation, music and dance lessons, formal and informal interviews, archival research, and lots of dancing and music-making. Our larger collaborative research project focuses on variations of *samba de roda* across urban and rural Bahia.

This essay, which is an off-shoot of the larger collaborative project, illuminates how a few Bahian *samba* artists from a small city in the state's rural interior, known as the Recôncavo, are addressing concerns over cultural ownership and stewardship of *samba de roda* in the wake of their practice being claimed by UNESCO on behalf of "humanity."[4] One manifestation of this impulse – and there were several – was the creation of after-school arts programs that offer local children opportunities to learn and practice *samba de roda* together. All these programs involve local practitioners to varying degrees, although some were spearheaded by non-artists. The programs are funded by both government and corporate sources.

After observing several different after-school sessions and speaking with the teachers and organizers, on and off between 2007 and 2011, we have taken notice of how these community leaders are mobilizing a multilayered strategy that helps negotiate complex, post-plantation politics and histories, and affirms an alternative model for cultural authority rooted in embodied experience. In particular, the teachers' corporeal epistemology promises to empower children from the Bahian Recôncavo as knowledge and culture bearers of an important practice. Additionally, however, following UNESCO's recognition, they have seen their *samba* practice turned into a commodity and even a scholarly artifact that does not necessarily bring them any increased benefit. As João, one of the teachers, told us, he wants to make sure the next generation of Recôncavo residents is invested in *samba de roda*'s future, not just its past.[5]

In the following section, we explore rural Bahia's complex relationship with *samba de roda* and how this has impacted the practice's reception among youth who live there. Next, we describe the after-school programs, since there is no known scholarship on this specific topic in print at this time. Finally, we analyze and interpret the significance of these programs, considering Bahia's distant and recent past and especially *samba de roda*'s 2005 UNESCO recognition.

Samba de Roda in Bahia

In the decades before UNESCO recognition drew worldwide attention to rural Bahia, people from the Recôncavo still grew up seeing and hearing *samba de roda*. However, as a local practice with strong associations with their parents' and grandparents' generations, and indeed the past in general, this dance form, its associated style, and the accompanying musical sounds were not especially popular with young people. *Samba de roda* lacked the glamour and contemporary allure of the numerous music and dance practices from afar that saturate, and indeed dominate, their local sound and movement spaces. Such attraction to non-local culture is not unique among these children or Bahians in general; rather the tendency to look outward and valorize non-local culture has been cited by Brazilian ethnomusicologist Martha de Ulhôa Carvalho as a characteristic of many, if not most Brazilians.[6] Consistent with Ulhôa's claims, we continually saw (and heard about) young people in rural Bahia who were and are more excited about *urban* Bahian music and dance forms such as *pagode* (see Leme 2003 and Lima 2011), national ones like Rio *samba* (Vianna 1999), and even international practices such as hip-hop, pop, and rock, in part because of their strong presence in nationalized television and radio.[7]

These outside practices have the allure of the city and cosmopolitan-ness, which stands in stark contrast with the rural poverty that typifies everyday life for most Recôncavo residents. Moreover, urban and foreign music/dance genres are easily associated with the future, instead of the past. In comparison, *samba de roda* can seem old and crude; moreover, it can seem so rooted in the past that it becomes foreign, albeit in an undesirable way. Indeed, *samba de roda* stands as a type of temporal other, preserving and conveying memories of a violent past – a past that is ever-present in the Recôncavo's plantation ruins, decrepit sugar mills, and crumbling colonial architecture, not to mention its rigid social hierarchies. It is not hard to understand why Bahia's rural youth might seek distance from *samba de roda* and instead embrace a slick form of expressive culture from afar.

The challenge, then, for *samba de roda* leaders is to help Bahian children create their own positive embodied memories of *samba de roda* that can withstand the distraction, escapism, and allure of national and international popular practices. But how can a practice that is so strongly associated with old, indigent, and even dominated people be made relevant and more attractive to outward-looking young people?

After-school *Samba*

Since 2007, we have visited three after-school arts programs in the Bahian Recôncavo that are part of residents' efforts to counter the strong pull of non-local, heavily mediatized music and dance, as well as other threats such as an encroaching drug trade, through the teaching of local forms of expressive culture, including *samba de roda*. These programs can also be viewed as a strategic community response to the UNESCO recognition and its perceived threat to local control of the practice, as will be discussed in the next section. While in some ways these goals might seem parochial or rooted in a somewhat problematic premise – the old ways are good for you – as we will argue, the timing of any re-introduction is crucial; the stakes are high; the methods are compelling; and the outcomes, at least for now, seem promising.

Organizations that conduct public outreach through expressive culture are fairly common in Bahia. During an early fieldwork stay in Salvador in 2004, before we embarked on this particular research project, we visited rehearsals and performances of a youth chorale program sponsored by the city government. Through this program, public school children from poor neighborhoods received free music lessons and health care. In addition, a number of secular organizations such as Salvador's famous *blocos afros* – Afrocentric Carnival groups (for example: Olodum, Ilê Aiyê, and Timbalada) – offer classes to local children in music and dance (King-Calnek 2006; Lima 1998). Finally, various other NGOs, including Projeto Axé and the Fundação Steve Biko, are also notable for their work supporting the education and general well-being of poor children in Salvador, for example, through tutoring programs in basic academic skills and preparation for university entrance exams.

The after-school *samba* programs, which we visited between 2007 and 2011, all had some degree of government subsidization, but were typically spearheaded by respected community leaders and operated in an array of public and private spaces. The first one we visited was housed at a private local history museum and run by a community leader, Dinha, who loved *samba* but does not see herself as a *samba* artist. She hired a local practitioner, Mestre Ratinho, to teach *samba de roda* as well as other local expressive culture forms like *capoeira*. In addition to these embodied practices, children also participated in a large-scale drama production led by a theater director brought in from the capital city of Salvador. In between these creative activities, the youngsters received training in personal hygiene and healthcare as well as a free meal.

The second program was situated at a public elementary school and was paid for by the local city government. Two highly respected professional *sambadores* were hired twice a week to teach dozens of children three practices – *capoeira*, *maculelê* (a stylized stick fight accompanied by drumming and singing), and *samba de roda*. While the older children, both boys and girls, were given opportunities to learn drumming, all were expected to enter the *roda* or circle at some point. These three practices form the core of the program, with *samba de roda* at the center. In between activities there is also informal mentoring between the artists and children, in a fatherly or grandfatherly sort of way, but no direct health instruction that we observed. We visited this program several times and everyone involved eventually felt comfortable with our photographing and videotaping their music and dance practices. In fact, they asked us to do so, which facilitated documentation of their program for themselves.

The largest of these programs, which is the focus of our analysis here, is housed at a community center not far from the Recôncavo city's main plaza. It is primarily funded by one of Brazil's largest banks and run by a professional administrator, who has hired the two *sambadores* who taught at the public school mentioned above as instructors. As they do in other contexts, these two men teach elementary and middle school children *capoeira*, *maculelê*, and *samba de roda* as well as basic life lessons. The teachers, João and Seu Pingo, are core members of one of the region's most lauded *samba de roda* ensembles and, as part of that group, have performed throughout Brazil and even internationally. At the same time, however, both are heavily invested in supporting *samba* on a local scale, maintaining local stewardship in the face of non-local attention, and harnessing the music and movement's potential for the benefit of local children.

João and Seu Pingo have taught a variety of students, but much of their work is with children from the region, most of whom are from very poor families. In many ways, their work at the community center resembles the other settings in which we have observed them teach. However, there are some differences. For example, at the community center, the children's matching t-shirts are emblazoned with the logo of the bank that funds the activities, rather than the name of the public school they attend. Another difference is that the community center can offer a wider variety of activities to an even greater number of students, thanks also to that bank's support. This is all possible because the funded community center has a dedicated performance space for the *samba* class, which can also permit art classes and academic tutoring to take place simultaneously.

The dozens of students, aged 5–15, who participate in the program, are brought to the facility from multiple schools in the area after regular instruction ends. While few, if any of the students attending local public schools, can be considered to be from wealthy or even middle-class families, those selected to be part of the after-school arts program are considered by their teachers to be especially "at risk" because of their dire family circumstances or proximity to dangerous, even lethal, circumstances in their neighborhoods.

Faced with these conditions, João and Seu Pingo are charged with doing much more than just teaching lessons in expressive culture. Over the course of each class, they alternate between playing instruments; directing children's behavior with words and, more often, gestures and touch; and occasionally speaking to the students about the practices in which they were engaged – situating them historically, but also in their present. Between songs the two men also dispense various life lessons through stories and sayings. In fact, in interviews with us, João, Seu Pingo, and administrators of this program all stressed the need for practical instruction on matters as basic as personal hygiene, although we did not witness these kinds of lessons ourselves.

On the days we observed classes, there was relatively little direct instruction about how to do *samba de roda*, *capoeira*, and *maculelê*. Students simply went from one practice to another with only a short break to pick up or put down instruments. If the activities were not going smoothly, sometimes Seu Pingo would stop the music and briefly address the problems he was seeing, but this was infrequent. Much more common were small gestures and looks given to students in the course of performance, which told them whether their teachers approved of their behavior. Overall, there was a gentleness to the teacher-student interactions throughout, perhaps predicated on the teachers' knowledge that most participating students came from broken homes of some kind and thus need encouragement more than stern correction.

This and other after-school *samba* programs we visited, thus attempt to serve a number of important aims – cultural, personal, and social. In fact, Tais, director of the community center, was less interested in matters of cultural "roots" and more focused on how the program was keeping children off the streets. She emphasized that as pressing as cultural heritage or hygiene might be, in her mind, both were secondary to the rapidly increasing risks of the drug trade, which was progressively infiltrating local communities from the capital, some 70 kilometers away. Still, she noted that the children's learning of *samba de roda* was able to address some of her concerns indirectly: children experienced a highlighting of community values and even pleasure in cooperation, adhering to rules, paying attention to instructions, and waiting one's turn.

Indeed, participation in each practice was contingent on careful listening and observation. For example, in order to know when it is one's turn to enter the circle that surrounds *samba* dancers or in the "fighting pairs" when playing *capoeira* and *maculelê*, students must listen closely to the song lyrics and drum rhythms, as well as watch carefully for non-verbal signals by those already within the circle. Thus (perhaps surprisingly for children of this age), participants rarely chatted among themselves. Patience was required, as was self-control; and both were readily evident.

Participation in the class was also dependent on learning and following implicit directives. There are layers of rules governing all the practices, which they worked on – from what to do with your hands, what sounds you can make, where to stand, where to look, and whose turn it is. In order to take part at all, a student had to learn and then obey these conventions. In all the sessions that we watched, over a four-year span, we never saw a student deliberately break a rule or disobey a teacher's instructions.

Finally, cooperation is at the heart of all three bodily practices: *samba, capoeira,* and *maculelê*; none of them are solo activities. Instead, they are built around complex interactions between dance movers and music makers. Multiple drum rhythms fit within one another by means of a guiding and enlivening *agogô* (double bell) timeline – for example. Movers in the circle entered and left seamlessly, one at a time (or in the case of *capoeira*, in pairs), with few if any instances of incorrect numbers of players or dancers accidently stepping in at the same time. Any transgressions were immediately resolved. We had no sense that the children felt they were fighting over scarce resources; all of them knew their turn would likely come before the song was over, and if not, in the next song. To our eyes, they seemed united in a shared sense of purpose.

Staking Claims, Normalizing Blackness, and Resignifying History

Tais (the program administrator referred to above) claimed that any success the program had in keeping children off the streets can be attributed to improved self-esteem imparted by learning these practices, including *samba de roda*. Since we did not interview the children, for ethical and practical reasons, it was hard for us to assess directly the enhanced self-esteem that she mentioned. How might these psychological or developmental steps be linked to *samba de roda*? Did the dance classes somehow buffer local children from exposure to drugs and related violence in their communities?

João explicitly told us that engendering pride in local culture – which is surely connected to self-esteem – was central to his and Seu Pingo's efforts in the schools. While perhaps not as dramatic as directly saving children from drug violence, local pride is also key for Recôncavo *sambadores* seeking to reclaim their sense of ownership and place of stewardship of *samba de roda*, post-UNESCO recognition – for themselves and, by extension, their communities and children. Evidence that this might be working lies in Tais's assertion that there is an (unfortunately) large list of children waiting for a space in the community center program and the fact that João, Seu Pingo, and other local *sambadores* are filling their daytime schedules teaching at similar programs.

Local pride in and authority over Recôncavo expressive culture, especially *samba de roda*, was expressed and inculcated in numerous ways during our visits to the various after-school *samba* programs. For example, at our first visit to the community center, Tais formally welcomed us with a brief speech before the beginning of the music and movement class. In addition to the usual niceties, she directed the children to demonstrate to us their unique hometown culture with "respect and unity."[8] This theme was further developed when Seu Pingo gave a speech of his own. He reminded the students, who were getting a little restless, that we had come from thousands of miles away to learn from them about their culture; that they deserved such attention because of the richness of their cultural inheritances; and that this heritage was theirs to protect for the future.

Tais and Seu Pingo's words offer a window into the logic behind the after-school *samba* programs from the perspective of the people implementing them. Their emphasis on local practices, for example, distinguishes what they do from similar, but more famous, projects in the capital city of Salvador. Such distinction occurs through discourse, as just mentioned and also through curricular design. At the community center, *capoeira*, *maculelê*, and *samba de roda* are all represented to the children as distinctly local dance/music practices. Yet situating *samba de roda* between *capoeira* (which despite its strong local roots is now practiced and stewarded more globally) and *maculelê* (which is very localized and much less well-known) emphasizes Bahian *samba*'s current transitional situation and the possible consequences of ceding stewardship and local association, on the one hand, or of asserting local authority with too heavy a hand, on the other.

Further, rather than celebrating Africa or African culture in their discussions with the children, as is often the case with globally known Salvador-based organizations such as Olodum and Ilê Aiyê, the after-school arts teachers emphasize the contributions of Afro-Brazilians or African-descended peoples in Bahia. This subtle distinction supports discourse that valorizes the particularities of the Recôncavo as a cultural space inseparable from the African Diaspora (see Gilroy 1998), but not limited to it.

At the same time, however, it is vital to remember that the clear majority of participants in the after-school program (and in *samba de roda* more generally) are of visible African descent and that their economic and educational circumstances are deeply entangled within Bahia's racial history, which includes colonization, slavery, plantation servitude, and maroon-age – not to mention the systematic erasure and marginalization of African cultures. Thus, the *samba* programs are certainly attentive to the issues and implications of race, but they do not dwell on the violence of the past and instead, focus on the potential of the present and the future.

Navigating this fine line means that the leaders' didactic and ideological foci take aim specifically at local concerns and populations, which are racially and culturally mixed, but deeply impacted by racial thinking (Gilroy 1998; Goldberg 2006). Thus, while notions of blackness and discourses of Afro-Brazilian history are addressed during classes, an emphasis on the contemporary makes *samba de roda* appear to be less a relic of a troubled past and more something of meaning and value in the now. Further, since the only requirement for involvement is attendance at a public school in the region, along with "at-risk" status, the scope of these programs becomes more concentrated on the teaching of local citizenship and valorization of Recôncavo culture and identity. Race politics are less foregrounded, but since their implications are omnipresent, they are never erased.

Rather, the Recôncavo after-school programs normalize blackness in important and potentially empowering ways. They bring it to the center of local history and perhaps more importantly, the contemporary quotidian and thus avoid marginalizing it on one hand or fetishizing it on the other. This careful positioning helps dodge highly charged Brazilian and Bahian racial politics, which are embedded in histories of official and unofficial racial subjugation; this positioning also promises to maximize the participation of young people from various racial backgrounds without erasing the region's culture or ignoring *samba de roda*'s racial history.

Looked at from a cultural memory perspective, we can also appreciate how these programs transform negative memories of slavery and its associated tortures into positive memories of survival and strength. In this way, references to slavery's lingering racial hegemony are avoided. Furthermore, cultural memories that might be linked elsewhere via nationalist discourses (i.e., Brazilian nationalism or African nationalism) are deftly redirected towards the Bahian Recôncavo and its rich past. Here we see a resignifying of official histories through cultural memory in order to appeal to contemporary youth participants, who might be especially sensitive to feeling inferior to externally or internally positioned dominating forces.

Teaching *Samba* in the Wake of UNESCO

In many ways, these after-school *samba* programs are part of broader efforts to assert stewardship of, and benefit from, *samba de roda* in the wake of UNESCO recognition and the ensuing international interest. In conversations and interviews, Recôncavo residents mentioned time and time again how much they resented having outsiders come in to "document" their practice, both as part of preparing the UNESCO dossier and especially following its designation as a masterpiece of humanity. The phrase "and they left nothing behind" was uttered to us repeatedly. It was clear that they felt as if *samba de roda* – and the cultural memory embedded within it – had been appropriated from them, along with their authority as experts, as stewards of meaning, and as benefactors of what George Yudice might call its "expediency" (2003).

Similarly, even as some *sambadores* look to the example of *capoeira* as an instance of such expediency – its capacity as a political, social, and economic resource – it also provides a cautionary tale. Many *sambadores* and *sambadeiras* voiced concerns to us about the commercializing, nationalizing, and indeed, globalizing of *capoeira* since the 1930s. These changes eventually led to local *capoeira* practitioners being marginalized and a degree of control over the tradition being lost as it shifted to external governing bodies and organizations.

These situations are very familiar to the *sambadores* of the Recôncavo. All have seen stylized presentations of *capoeira*, *maculelê*, *samba de roda*, as well as Candomblé (*Orixá*) dances presented theatrically for tourists. Moreover, between 2007 and 2014 we have encountered numerous "producers" scouting and trying to bond with local artists, while looking for ways to globally capitalize on the recent interest in *samba de roda* – much like the Buena Vista Social Club project in Cuba.[9] Whether *samba de roda*'s artists will be rewarded with the same fame and fortune of a handful of Cuban artists is, however, yet to be seen.

As a point of comparison, the histories of the *blocos afros* and *capoeira* – despite their unquestionable notoriety and successes – are also punctuated with various debates, instances of appropriation, and interference by outsiders, elites, foreigners, and the like. For example, the *samba reggae* rhythm pioneered by the politically focused *blocos afros* during the 1980s has become foundational to Bahian commercial music known as "*Axé*" music. Thirty years later, there is still discussion in Bahia, and amongst scholars, over the incorporation of politically activist musical practices into what has become a type of party music for all of Brazil (Crook 1993). At issue is that *Axé* music generates income for those already economically and racially privileged (lighter-skinned Brazilians), while also trafficking in (and sometimes exoticizing) African and Afro-Bahian imagery.[10]

Surprisingly, none of our collaborators expressed concern over commodification in and of itself. In fact, many, if not most of them, wanted very much to earn money from *samba*. Thus, their concern lies with who benefits and, importantly, who is representing the practice, its practitioners, and the region from which it comes. Thus, while we occasionally heard disagreements and tensions over the "authenticity" of certain aspects of particular groups' performances – usually expressed by members of a competing *samba* group – we also heard unified concern about public performances that violated certain basic and fundamental conventions, procedures, and values in *samba de roda*. No one wants Bahian *samba* radically diluted, distorted, or simplified. Yet change alone is not the issue, nor is its variation. The concern is transformation that neglects what local culture bearers value about *samba de roda* and its defining features, although they do not always agree on what those features are. Ultimately, the kind of transformation that concerns them most is that which would render local artists' unique contributions less valuable and thus threaten the future of *samba de roda* as it is practiced, understood, and made meaningful in its home context.

Strategic Authority and Authenticity

Here is where the after-school *samba* programs promise to intervene perhaps most significantly. In addition to transmitting and simply valorizing the practice, local artists are actively teaching children to participate in *samba de roda* in a manner consistent with what they, as long-time culture bearers, value in movement and sonic practices. Key is that they are not constructing a codified notion of "the authentic" *samba de roda* even as they instill "correct" techniques in their students.

A productive rubric for thinking through this subtle negotiation has been theorized by anthropologist Michelle Bigenho (2002) in her writing about Bolivian indigenous music (see also Handler and Saxton 1988; Daniel 1996). In exploring the tensions over various notions of authenticity deployed in differing contexts, Bigenho teases out three interrelated but ultimately distinct conceptualizations: cultural-historical authenticity, experiential authenticity, and unique authenticity (2002: 16–19).

Applied to this situation, representations, commodifications, and valorizations of *samba de roda* by outside interests such as visitors, scholars, NGOs, and other institutions tend to emphasize what Bigenho calls "cultural-historical authenticity." She associates this with asserting "[…] a continuity with an imagined point of origin, situated in a historical or mythical past" (2002: 18). This is exemplified in the abundance of images of aged black bodies, references to the pastoral Bahian Recôncavo, and concerns over the loss of humanity's (and the Brazilian nation-state's) treasured heritage in so much recent discourse about *samba de roda*.

By contrast, in their emphasis on practice during the after-school sessions, artists privilege the embodied-ness of local culture, which is a key aspect of Bigenho's formulation of "experiential authenticity"[11] (2002: 17). She connects this particular type of authenticity with practice and embodied knowledge – precisely the approach to conveying an understanding and appreciation of local culture taken by João and Seu Pingo during their after-school sessions. The corporeal dispositions and experientially engendered local pride that results are, furthermore, not merely rooted in the doing, but also in doing with and in a manner approved by recognized and respected local practitioners. In this context, local artists are not relying on associations with prescribed cultural memories as much as lived experience. In a sense, they are constructing new cultural memories with these children as a way of focusing on the future and moving forward.

Likewise, the manner that the programs address more quotidian concerns – hygiene, staying in school, good citizenship – also situates such knowing at home. Indeed, as identified by Brazilian educational theorist Paulo Freire, whereas outsiders inform so much of the educational experiences of Brazilian children (university educated teachers, government officials, and directors of NGOs), through these arts programs, Bahian children are now receiving information from "one(s) of their own" (1993). Moreover, through their participation and coming to know the very practices that grant authority to their teachers, they are empowered to take control over their own knowing, wresting it from the threat of outside and elite interest as has been the case in Brazil for so long. Though implemented in small-scale after-school *samba* programs, in a little city within an impoverished region, this vision for locally focused arts education and grass-roots community uplift provides a methodology for disarming some of Brazil's most longstanding and disempowering colonial legacies – especially entrenched social hierarchies – while at the same time helping secure the future of one of its most unique performance traditions.

These after-school *samba* programs are doing much more than just transmitting music and dance skills; in a sense, they are passing on the responsibility of stewardship to the next generation. To do so, they put far less emphasis on the past and its complex and often painful cultural memories and more on the future and its possibilities. In this way, the artists involved subtly contest the impact of UNESCO recognition as well as the dominance of Rio de Janeiro's *samba* legacies. This allows them to re-establish and indeed assert their region's *samba* authority, not just authenticity, in order to maintain control over their own practices, in the wake of national and international interest. In this case, cultural memory is not just about the past, but is also about the future.

References

Allen, Roger M. (1999), "Cultural imperialism at its most fashionable," in Robert M. Levine and John Crocitti (eds), *The Brazil Reader: History, Culture, Politics*, Durham: Duke University Press, pp. 447–53.

Araújo, Samuel Mello Junior (1988), "*Brega*: Music and Conflict in Urban Brazil," *Latin American Music Review*, 9:1, pp. 50–89.

Azevedo, Ricardo (2007), *Axé-Music: O Verso e o Reverso da Música que Conquistou o Planeta* (*Axé-Music: The Verse and Reverse of the Music that Conquered the Planet*), Salvador: Alpha Co.

Bacelar, Jefferson (1999), "Blacks in Salvador: Racial paths," in Larry Crook and Randall Johnson (eds), *Black Brazil: Culture, Identity, and Social Mobilization*, Los Angeles: UCLA Latin American Center Publications, pp. 85–101.

Bigenho, Michelle (2002), *Sounding Indigenous: Authenticity in Bolivian Music Performance*, New York: Palgrave Macmillan.

Bourdieu, Pierre (1984), *Distinction: A Social Critique of the Judgment of Taste* (trans. Richard Nice), Cambridge: Harvard University Press.

Butler, Kim D. (1998), *Freedoms Given Freedoms Won: Afro Brazilians in Post-abolition São Paulo and Salvador*, New Brunswick: Rutgers University Press.

Carvalho, José Jorge de (1999), "The multiplicity of Black identities in Brazilian popular music," in Larry Crook and Randall Johnson (eds), *Black Brazil: Culture, Identity and Social Mobilization*, Los Angeles: UCLA Latin American Center Publications, pp. 261–95.

Carvalho, Martha de Ulhôa (1995), "Tupi or not Tupi MPB: Popular music and identity in Brazil," in David J. Hess and Roberto DaMatta (eds), *The Brazilian Puzzle: Culture on the Borderlands of the Western World*, New York: Columbia University Press, pp. 159–79.

de Certeau, Michel (1984), *The Practice of Everyday Life* (trans. by Steven Rendell), Berkeley: University of California Press.

Chada, Sonia (2006), *A Música dos Caboclos nos Candomblés Baianos*, Salvador: Fundação Gregório de Mattos.

Crook, Larry N. (1993), "Black consciousness, *samba-reggae*, and the re-Africanization of Bahian carnival music in Brazil," *The World of Music*, 35:2, pp. 90–108.

——— (2009), *Focus: Music of Northeast Brazil*, New York: Routledge.

Crowley, Daniel J. (1984), *African Myth and Black Reality in Bahian Carnaval*, Los Angeles: UCLA Museum of Cultural History.

DaMatta, Roberto ([1979] 1991), *Carnivals, Rogues, and Heroes: An Interpretation of the Brazilian Dilemma*, Notre Dame: University of Notre Dame Press.

Daniel, Yvonne Payne (1996), "Tourism dance performances: Authenticity and creativity," *Annals of Tourism Research*, 23:4, pp. 780–97.

Dent, Alexander Sebastian (2009), *River of Tears: Country Music, Memory, and Modernity in Brazil*, Durham: Duke University Press.

Draper, Jack A. III. (2010), *Forró and Redemptive Regionalism from the Brazilian Northeast*, New York: Peter Lang.

Dunn, Christopher (1992), "Afro-Bahian carnival: A stage for protest," *Afro-Hispanic Review*, 11:1–3, pp. 11–20.

Ernst and Young Terco (2011), *Doing Business in Brazil*, http://www.ey.com/Publication/vwLUAssets/Doing_business_in_Brazil_2011/$FILE/Doing%20Business%20in%20Brazil%202011.pdf. Accessed May 27, 2013.

Foucault, Michel (1972), *The Archaeology of Knowledge and the Discourse on Language* (trans. A. M. Sheridan Smith), New York: Pantheon Books.

——— (1988), "Technologies of the self," in Luther Martin, Huck Gutman, and Patrick H. Hutton (eds), *Technologies of the Self: A Seminar with Michel Foucault*, Amherst: University of Massachusetts Press, pp. 16–49.

Freire, Paulo (1993), *Pedagogy of the Oppressed*, 20th anniversary ed., New York: Continuum.

Freyre, Gilberto ([[1933] 1964), *The Masters and the Slaves: A Study in the Development of Brazilian Civilization* (trans. Samuel Putnam), New York: Knopf.

Galinsky, Philip (1996), "Co-option, cultural resistance, and Afro-Brazilian identity: A history of the *Pagode Samba* movement in Rio de Janeiro," *Latin American Music Review*, 17:2, pp. 120–49.

Garcia Canclini, Nestor (1995), *Hybrid Cultures: Strategies for Entering and Leaving Modernity* (trans. Christopher Chiappari and Silvia Lopez), Minneapolis: University of Minnesota Press.

Giesbrecht, Érica (2011), "O passado Negro: A incorporação da memória Negra da cidade campinas através das performances de legados Musicais" ("The Black past: The embodiment of Black memory in campinas through the performance of musical legacies"), Ph.D. dissertation, São Paulo: Universidade Estadual de Campinas.

Gilroy, Paul (1993), *The Black Atlantic: Modernity and Double Consciousness*, Cambridge: Harvard University Press.

——— (1998), "Race ends here," *Ethnic and Racial Studies*, 21:5, pp. 838–47.

Goldberg, David Theo (2002), *The Racial State*, Malden: Blackwell Publishers.

—— (2006), "Racial Europeanization," *Ethnic and Racial Studies*, 29:2, pp. 331–64.

Guerreiro, Goli (2000), *A Trama dos Tambores: A Música Afro-Pop de Salvador* (*The Trauma of the Drums: Salvador's Afro-Pop Music*), São Paulo: Editora 34.

Guss, David M. (2000), *The Festive State: Race, Ethnicity, and Nationalism as Cultural Performance*, Berkeley: University of California Press.

Hall, Anthony (2006), "From *Fome Zero* to *Bolsa Família*: Social policies and poverty alleviation under Lula," *Journal of Latin American Studies*, 38, pp. 689–709.

Hall, Stuart ([1980] 1996), "Race, articulation, and societies structured in dominance," in Houston A. Baker Jr., Manthia Diawara, and Ruth H. Lindeborg (eds), *Black British Cultural Studies: A Reader*, Chicago: University of Chicago Press, pp. 17–60.

Halsenbalg, Carlos (1999), "Perspectives on race and class in Brazil," in Larry Crook and Randall Johnson (eds), *Black Brazil: Culture, Identity, and Social Mobilization*, Los Angeles: UCLA Latin American Center Publications, pp. 61–84.

Hanchard, Michael George (1994), *Orpheus and Power: The Movimento Negro of Rio de Janeiro and São Paulo, Brazil, 1945–1988*, Princeton: Princeton University Press.

Handler, Richard and Saxton, William (1988), "Dyssimulation: Reflexivity, narrative, and the quest for authenticity in 'living history'," *Cultural Anthropology*, 3, pp. 242–60.

Henry, Clarence Bernard (2008), *Let's Make Some Noise: Axé and the African Roots of Brazilian Popular Music*, Jackson: University Press of Mississippi.

Jones de Almeida, Adjoa Florência (2003), "Unveiling the mirror: Afro-Brazilian identity and the emergence of a community school movement," *Comparative Education Review*, 41:1, pp. 41–63.

King-Calnek, Judith E. (2006), "Education for citizenship: Interethnic pedagogy and formal education at *Escola Ciativa Olodum*," *The Urban Review*, 38:2, pp. 145–64.

Kondo, Dorinne K. (1990), *Crafting Selves: Power, Gender, and Discourses of Identity in a Japanese Workplace*, Chicago: The University of Chicago Press.

Leme, Mônica Neves (2003), *Que Tchan é Esse? Indústria e Produção Musical no Brasil dos Anos 90* (*What Tchan is This? Industry and Musical Production in Brazil in the 1990s*), São Paulo: Anna Blume.

Levy, Janet M. (1987), "Covert and casual values in recent writings about music," *The Journal of Musicology*, 5:1, pp. 3–27.

Lima, Ari (1998), "O Fenômeno Timbalada: Cultura Musical Afro-Pop e juventude Baiana Negro-mestiça," in Livio Sansone and Jocélio Teles dos Santos (eds), *Ritmos em Trânsito: Sócio-Antropologia da Música Baiano*, São Paulo: Dynamis Editorial, pp. 161–80.

—— (2002), "Funkeiros, Timbaleiros, e Pagodeiros: Notas Sobre juventude e música Negra na cidade de Salvador" ("Funkeiros, Timbaleros, and Pagodeiros: Notes on Black music and youth in the city of Salvador"), *Cadernos CEDES*, 22:57, pp. 77–96.

—— (2011), "Modernity, agency, and sexuality in the *Pagode Baiano*," in Idelber Avelar and Christopher Dunn (eds), *Brazilian Popular Music and Citizenship*, Durham: Duke University Press, pp. 267–77.

Magaldi, Christina (1999), "Adopting imports: New images and alliances in Brazilian popular music in the 1990s," *Popular Music*, 18:3, pp. 309–29.

Marx, Anthony W. (1998), *Making Race and Nation: A Comparison of the United States, South Africa, and Brazil*, New York: Cambridge University Press.

McLaren, Peter (1995), "White terror and oppositional agency: Towards a critical multiculturalism," in Christine Sleeter and Peter McLaren (eds), *Multicultural Education, Critical Pedagogy, and the Politics of Difference*, Albany: State University of New York Press, pp. 33–70.

Meintjes, Louise (1990), "Paul Simon's 'Graceland, South Africa,' and the Mediation of Musical Meaning," *Ethnomusicology*, 34: 1, pp. 37–73.

Moehn, Frederick (2013), *Contemporary Carioca: Technologies of Mixing in a Brazilian Music Scene*, Durham: Duke University Press.

Omi, Michael and Winant, Howard (1994), *Racial Formation in the United States: From the 1960s to the 1990s*, New York: Routledge.

Packman, Jeff (2011), "Musicians' performances and performances of 'musician' in Salvador da Bahia, Brazil," *Ethnomusicology*, 55:3, pp. 414–44.

Pena, Felipe (2013), "Religion: Evangelicism in Brazil," *Americas Quarterly*, http://www.americasquarterly.org/node/3823. Accessed May 27, 2013.

Perrone, Charles (1989), *Masters of Contemporary Brazilian Song: MPB, 1965–1985*, Summer, Austin: University of Texas Press.

———— (1992), "*Axé, Ijexá, Olodum*: The rise of Afro and African currents in Brazilian popular music," *Afro-Hispanic Review*, 11:1–3, pp. 42–50.

Pinto, Tiago de Oliveira (1991), *Capoeira, Samba, Candomble: Afro-brasilianische Musik im Reconcavo, Bahia* (*Capoeira, Samba, Condomble: Afro-Brazilian music in the Reconcavo, Bahia*), Berlin: Museum fur Volkerkunde.

Risério, Antonio (1981), *Carnaval Ijexá: Notas sobre a Afoxés e Blocos de novo Carnaval Afro-Baiano* (*Carnival Ijexá: Notes on the Afoxés and Blocos of the new Afro-Bahian Carnival*), Salvador: Corrupio.

Robinson, Danielle (2010), "The ugly duckling: Race, refinement, and the birth of the modern dance industry," *Dance Research*, 28:2, pp. 179–99.

Samson, Guillaume and Sandroni, Carlos (2013), "The recognition of Brazilian *samba de roda* and *reunion maloya* as intangible cultural heritage of humanity," *Vibrant: Virtual Brazilian Anthropology*, 10:1, pp. 530–51.

Sandroni, Carlos (2010), "Samba de roda, patrimônio imaterial da humanidade," *Estudos avançados*, 24:69, p. 373.

Sandroni, Carlos and Sant'Anna, Marcia (eds) (2007), *Samba de Roda do Recôncavo Baiano*, Bahia: Dossiê IPHAN 4.

Selka, Steven L. (2005), "Ethnoreligious identity politics in Bahia," *Latin American Perspectives*, 32:1, pp. 72–94.

Sheriff, Robin (2001), *Dreaming Equality: Color, Race, and Racism in Urban Brazil*, New Brunswick: Rutgers University Press.

Skidmore, Thomas E. (1998), *Black into White: Race and Nationality in Brazilian Thought*, Durham: Duke University Press.

Stroud, Sean (2008), *The Defense of Tradition in Brazilian Popular Music: Politics, Culture, and the Creation of Música Popular Brasileira*, Aldershot: Ashgate.

United Nations Educational, Scientific, and Cultural Organization (UNESCO) (2005), "The *Samba de roda* of Recôncavo of Bahia," (sic), Third Proclamation of Masterpieces of the Oral and Intangible Heritage of Humanity, http://www.unesco.org/culture/intangible-heritage/07lac_uk.htm. Accessed May 27, 2013.

Tinhorão, José Ramos (1998), *História Social da Música Popular Brasileira* (*Social History of Brazilian Popular Music*), São Paulo: Editora 34.

Twine, Francis Winddance (2001), *Racism in a Racial Democracy: The Maintenance of White Supremacy in Brazil*, New Brunswick: Rutgers University Press.

Ulhôa, Marta Tupinambá de (2007), "Categorias de avaliação da MPB: Lidando com a recepção da música Brasileira popular" ("Categories of evaluation in MPB: Addressing the reception of Brazilian popular music"), www.hist.puc.ci/historia/iaspm/mexico/articulos/ulhoa.pdf. Accessed January 31, 2009.

Vianna, Hermano (1999), *The Mystery of Samba: Popular Music and National Identity in Brazil* (ed. and trans. John Charles Chasteen), Chapel Hill: The University of North Carolina Press.

Waddey, Ralph (1980, 1981), "*Samba da Viola, Viola de Samba*," *Latin American Music Review*, 1:2 and 2:2, pp. 196–212 and pp. 252–79.

Winant, Howard (2001), *The World is a Ghetto: Race and Democracy since WWII*, New York: Basic Books.

Yudice, George (2003), "The expediency of culture," in *The Expediency of Culture: Uses of Culture in the Global Era*, Durham: Duke University Press.

Notes

1 For videos of *samba de roda*, see: http://www.unesco.org/culture/ich/en/RL/samba-de-roda-of-the-reconcavo-of-bahia-00101; http://www.unesco.org/culture/intangible-heritage/07lac_uk.htm; and http://www.unesco.org/archives/multimedia/?s=films_details&pg=33&id=615. Accessed May 22, 2018.

2 For example, ethnomusicologist Ralph Waddey (1980), in one of the first English language studies of *samba de roda*, notes that several of his middle-class friends in Bahia expressed (perhaps quaint) nostalgia for *samba de roda* and a certain fondness for it. Nevertheless, the introductory paragraph to the first of his two articles illustrates in a disturbing way the disparaging attitude of many middle- and upper-class Bahians toward local *samba* – one that we have also experienced on various, more recent occasions.

3 Brazil's Minister of Culture, at the time, was Gilberto Gil, a famous Bahian musician, which might help explain why *samba de roda* was considered after it was clear that Rio *samba* and *capoeira* could not be chosen.

4 The Recôncavo is the rural area to the west of Bahia's capital, Salvador. It was the site of numerous sugar plantations and maroon societies called *quilombos*, where *samba de roda*, *maculelê*, and arguably, *capoeira*, coalesced.

5 The names of all participants in the after-school *samba* program have been changed.

6 See Allen (1999) for a brief but provocative article on the fashion of consuming foreign consumer goods in Brazil.

7 The negative associations with *samba de roda* held by Bahian children – in contrast with outsiders' fascination with the practice – is noted by Waddey (1980: 269–70). Particularly notable is his assertion of a linkage between the practice and "rural poverty and social immobility." While we never heard such language used ourselves when discussing *samba de roda* in Bahia, it is certainly possible that such associations continue today. Interestingly, since Waddey's article was published in 1980, it is entirely possible that some of the young people he mentions are now active as *samba* practitioners. In fact, in 2010, the outgoing president of the Bahian Association of *Sambadores* and *Sambadeiras*, Nando, remembers Waddey staying with his family when he was young.

8 All translation of interviews was made by the authors.

9 The following is a link to the official trailer for the movie associated with this project: https://www.youtube.com/watch?v=mwyGPg8cYvY. Accessed May 22, 2018

10 See Crook (1993) for a discussion of concerns related to the prominence of Olodum. See also Perrone (1992) on issues of African and Afro-Diasporic influences in contemporary Brazilian popular music. Finally, see Meintjes (1990) regarding Paul Simon's collaborations with South African musicians for his album *Graceland*. Notably, Simon's subsequent "collaborative" album, *Rhythm of the Saints* featured Olodum along with various other artists from Brazil. Many of the issues raised by Meintjes apropos of the power imbalances, representations, and implications for discourses of cross-cultural collaboration are, we suggest, relevant here as well.

11 Certainly, they also build on narratives of history and infuse their teaching with a discourse resonant with cultural-historical authenticity. But this is secondary to their primary mode of asserting authenticity through practice.

Part III

Reflections: Paths of Courage and Connections

Chapter 6

Why Not Me? Reflections on Afro-Dance and Law No. 10.639

Nadir Nóbrega Oliveira

Introduction

This essay is the result of my attempt to contextualize specific aspects of African and Afro-Brazilian culture, especially black dances. It also reflects part of my life, both professional and personal, the fight against disparagement, repression, and the negative image of black people that has been imposed on us over the centuries.

From the time of European colonization of Brazil, the color white and the attributes held to accompany whiteness have never ceased to be associated with "beauty" and human "intelligence." The absence of black people is notable in general advertisements, women's fashion, and other popular magazine covers in Brazil, a country where the white population is smaller than the sum of the black and brown (two census categories that together form the broader social category of *negra*), "yellow" (Asian), and indigenous populations, according to the 2010 census by the Brazilian Institute of Geography and Statistics (IBGE).

My city, Salvador, the capital of the state of Bahia, is overflowing with social or festive gatherings, dances, bodily gestures, and movement. I am part of this, and as much as possible, I try to keep up with cultural changes brought by new technology and contemporary commercial and educational relationships. My involvement in Bahian artistic and religious manifestations, especially, began in the neighborhood where I was born and raised, Uruguay, a neighborhood in the outskirts of Salvador. Uruguay was created in the mid-twentieth century by workers who migrated from the interior of the State of Bahia in search of work. It was an area between a swamp and the sea, and the first structures were built on stilts. It was exciting to walk through Uruguay, for example, to look at the creative ways St. Anthony's altars were put together with laminated crêpe paper and to smell the incense that was burned during the month of June.

It was there that I grew up participating in popular festivals, *samba* dances, *Carnaval* masquerade groups, and religious festivities dedicated to Santo Antônio, Senhor do Bonfim, and Nossa Senhora dos Mares. I joined festivals in nearby neighborhoods, such as Ribeira and Bonfim, and the *ternos de Reis* in the neighborhood of Lapinha, which celebrated the visit by the three kings to baby Jesus on January 6. I danced in *quadrilha* contests – traditional dance groups that are specifically part of the São João (St. John) festivals; for clam digs on the beach at low tide; for the *carurus de Cosme*,[1] and in the *twist* contests, which were very popular in the 1960s. I think that from childhood, encouraged by my family, I had

Figure 6: Nadir Nóbrega Oliveira. Courtesy of Nadir Nóbrega Oliveira.

a sensibility for the arts. My grandfather liked to play guitar and my grandmother liked to dance *samba* and frequent parties and local processions.

In the public school I attended, I actively participated in poetry recitals, choral music classes, and in making artistic panels, especially for geography, history, and Portuguese classes. Amid the poverty in which my family and I lived, I was always interested in black culture and Brazilian black people. In my youth, I was surrounded by colors, smells, and rhythms, not only in religious rituals but also in my day-to-day home life. From an early age I learned various dance styles: *bolero*, *lambada*, *samba*, and the *twist*. Everything was fun and playful. Everything was informal.

At the age of sixteen, I started my professional dance career in the folkloric dance/music group, Brasil Tropical, with tours throughout Brazil and to several European countries: Hungary, East and West Germany, Poland, Yugoslavia, and others. I sought to improve professionally by studying modern concert and African dance techniques and even dance for television studios. In 1975, I entered the Federal University of Bahia School of Dance and began a new stage of theoretical and practical learning, in a more conscious and professional learning environment. The dance school gave me "ruler and compass"[2] to trace the lines of my paths and horizons.

Under the direction of Clyde Wesley Morgan, I performed in the second Black Arts Festival in Nigeria (1977), with the show *Oxossi N'Aruanda*. I acquired extensive experience in art education and choreography by working in public schools, theaters, Candomblé spaces,[3] and Afro-Carnival dance/music groups or *blocos afro*. In Salvador, 1991, I coordinated seminars at the State Public Library, with guests who work in what is conventionally called "Afro-Dance" (*dança afro*) within their respective sociocultural spaces, for example, Vera Lacerda, from the carnival *blocos afro* Araketu, Edileusa Santos, one of the most respected masters of black dance in Salvador, Dimi Ferreira, from the Conservatoire Charles Münch in Paris, and other professionals who also work with dance and black culture, such as Marcos Rodrigues, Conceição Castro, Emília Biancardi, Guilherme Santos Barbosa, and Carlos Moraes. Through this professional trajectory, I learned that human beings dance in order to express their feelings, anxieties, and cultural values and that dance involves ritual, entertainment, and more than artistic functions.

Dance and Afro-Brazilian Heritage

Dance has always been part of varied human cultures, and is especially important for Africans, from whom we directly, and everyone indirectly, descends. For African descendants, the transmission of knowledge takes place through dance, costumes, music that is played and sung, and also through cuisine. I agree with those dance scholars who observe that dance is a cultural representation of all peoples and it is always present in all periods from birth to death (Welsh Asante 2004).[4] This representation – dance – is present in the Indigenous-, African-, and European-descendant communities of Brazil, and it is always seen in rituals honoring ancestors.

Learning to dance and sing in the same way we learn to speak is something African descendants, in particular, have inherited from our ancestors; for us, parties are spaces in which we relive and renew ancestral knowledge. The Luso-Bantu-Sudanese encounter with Iberians and Indigenous peoples in the Americas, despite its asymmetries, predominated in the constitution of northeastern Brazilian cultural production especially. In Bahia, this mixture is especially visible, thanks to our African ancestors. Our mixture of the Catholic religion with traditions of African origin is also well documented by many intellectuals of the past and present, such as Arthur Ramos, Edison Carneiro, Gilberto Freyre, José Ramos Tinhorão, Leda Maria Martins, Luiz da Câmara Cascudo, Pierre Verger Fatumbi, and Suzana Martins, among others. Despite police harassment of such religions, from the colonial period to the beginning of this century, the religious spirit that sustains black art forms persists. For example, Afro-Brazilian processions have lit Brazilian Carnival up to the present, especially in Pernambuco, where parading to the sounds of drums (*alfaias*, *xequerés* or *agbês* and *agogôs* creating a unique percussive beat[5]), colorful clothes, including embroidered hoop skirts, a standard-bearer, and the Calunga[6] doll, believed to carry magical powers, all reign triumphant.

Afro-Dance, heir to traditional African social activities in Bahia, bears the weight of historic racial segregation. In public and private dance schools in Salvador, most white dancers enjoy fairly good living conditions, while black dancers deal with difficulties in housing, health, work, and their dance education. Discrimination and disdain for the folk dances that were created and preserved by blacks, which are present in public elementary and secondary schools, as well as private dance schools, also exists in the Federal University of Bahia, where forms of popular and black dance are excluded from the academic curriculum. Many dancers of African origin – black and poor, slum dwellers, victims of the manipulation of black culture, who compete on unequal terms with other dancers and dream of living in Europe or the United States (sometimes having to prostitute themselves) – are professionals who engaged in various expressions of African-influenced culture, such as reggae, the *congada*, *maculelê*, *samba*, *capoeira*, dances of the *Orixás* (Candomblé deities), the *coco* of Alagoas, and the *frevo*.[7] Just like the *maracatu* in Recife, which is another example of Africa Diaspora cultural expression and a festive version of the Congolese kings and queens who used to parade in the city streets, there are similar festivals in Bahia. Candomblé scholar Pierre Verger reports:

> [...] on the eve of the Feast of the Three Kings...[King Balthasar, the black king, arrives]... in Bethlehem. [He]... had come to worship baby Jesus. Religious authorities then transferred the realization of this sumptuous event and unrestrained parade to coincide with Carnival, turning an act of faith into a more frivolous celebration.
>
> (Verger 1987: 10)[8]

The referenced festivals are manifestations originating from the African continent with coded movements quite different from the techniques of Europeans within dances of European origins. These expressions of knowledge are still present and meaningful in the Candomblé communities, *capoeira* circles, and black religious brotherhoods and sisterhoods of Bahia, Pernambuco, and other Brazilian states. In these communities, the events and celebrations are performed with dancing, singing, praise, and vivacious flavor. Some dancers combine these manifestations with varied dance styles (modern concert dance, African traditional dances, and ballet[9]), using black casts and percussive music as background, creating a choreography of dance syncretism.

Yet, here in Brazil, racial and cultural separation is still reinforced by the "apparatus of ideological reproduction and institutions such as school, church, and even the family, which reproduce the dominant ideology" (Silva 1989: 56).

Education, the Black Aesthetic, and Dance

It is well known that art is one of the languages of communication, and there is no common definition of art across all societies and civilizations because its aesthetic varies according to geographical regions, ethnic groups, and time periods. Schools do not often teach students to recognize the work of anonymous African artists or what these artists have wanted to express. For example, Bahian children and youths do not learn about the importance of ancestry, the founding myths of their cultures, the place of fertility and prosperity in culture.

By European standards, these features are the opposite of what a work of art must contain; in order to be accepted in European art fields, an artwork should demonstrate a technical framework, a signature, and references that make it comprehensible to a general public.

For a long time, African art was excluded from the history of so-called "Western" art and attempts to define it considered it ritual or religion, thus disregarding the civilized expressions of values in objects, sculptures, various materials and paintings that were produced by African peoples for centuries. Values that are transmitted through oral tradition were neglected, even though the oral tradition also transmits the importance of dance, music, and the black aesthetic, as well as the value of the words (oral tradition) themselves.

In Afro-dance classes of Bahia, the aesthetic that is predominant is a synthesis of the culture, politics, and art of black Africans who were captured and transported involuntarily during the late fifteenth century until the nineteenth century or who migrated more voluntarily after the end of the nineteenth century. Over time in Brazil, these African descendants (re)created Candomblé, braided hair and dreadlocks, black cuisine, and *samba*. They are responsible for Afro-dance, which can be characterized by its spiral discursive practices and the use of black Brazilian experiences as suitable material for making art. Their practices have been guided by the values of Afro-Brazilian civilization: ancestry, memory, vital energy/*axé*, playfulness, orality, circularity, religiosity, physicality, musicality, generosity, and cooperation.

The African American feminist bell hooks indicates that the black aesthetic is inherently political, as it has challenged white racist notions about black people's capacities – to produce art in any context, whether in written texts, music, visual arts, or dance.[10] This emphasis on political-racial opposition to white society resonates not only in hooks' work, but also in the works of other activists who are involved in producing a revolutionary artistic culture, such as those in the Black Power and the black art movements of the 1960s and 1970s forward. Similarly, and since their foundations, Bahian Afro-dance groups question the white hegemony that is represented and sustained by various segments of Bahian society, including schools and the media. We, choreographers, problematize these issues through our practices and affirmative action, and not in a superficial way, but as issues of respect for diversity and tolerance for multiculturalism.

In my book *Dança afro: sincretismo de movimentos (African Dance: Syncretism of Movement)* (1992), I discuss the didactic and pedagogical actions of women and men who work with Afro-dance, recognizing them as active subjects in Bahia's social fabric. In the book, I also discuss the three energy channels of Afro-dance: (1) the head and upper body, which, in reference to nature, represent the sky; (2) the trunk, the mid-section of the body, in reference to nature, represents the sea and is important in reproduction and helping the body swing while walking and dancing; and (3) the feet and lower body, in reference to nature, represent the ground or the earth, transmitting sensations of the earth to the rest of the body through the soles of the feet and are important in getting out to work, to a party, or to war. My research concludes that while the feet, the trunk, and the head are interrelated and interconnected, they also structure dance.

The teaching methodologies and choreographic conception of Afro-dance use quite a few dynamic verbs, for example, "hold," "cross," "shake," "run," "fall," "rotate," "tremble," etc. These verbs support the movements of dancing bodies, whose basic principles are parallel feet (front-to-back), loose and independent hip movement, and the leaning forward of the upper body into the "get down" position, the phrase used pointedly by Robert Farris Thompson (1974: 1–25). This is the stance of the *Orixá* (deity) Oxalá and of the *Orixá* Oxum's descent to the ground. In Salvador, Bahia, there is noticeable movement inspired by one or another *Orixá*'s dance, and this dance is inseparable from the religious phenomenon itself. Dance is an integral part of Candomblé ritual, representing the direct worship of the deities.

Dance plays a key role in African descendants' lives, in their respective cultures, where every important social event is marked by the celebration of a particular ritual and bodily expression through movement. In African people's worldview, the world of nature is permeated by the vital and dynamic force that exists both in living beings and in objects. This profound understanding of nature communicates within the deep essence of human beings, and even "in an adverse context of colonialism and neo-colonialism, we [have] inherited the vigor of our commonalities from...[our] black ancestors" (Luz 2005: 52).

To do my dance work, I reference the study of the body, society, and the black presence in dance, highlighting in particular the value of African heritage in Brazilian dance. To do so, I observe the symbolic relationships that are relevant to demonstrations of Brazilian-ness, religion, and sexuality in performance. In my view, songs and vocal selections are the verbal protest, and the presence of Afro-descendants on stage, with their energetic motor activity, is the bodily statement: black music and dances provide politico-aesthetic sustenance to performances.

These are bodies/subjects that tell their own stories, creating forms – rippling, sliding, jumping, spinning, energizing, cutting, and demonstrating their ancestry at the same time. These bodies/dancers/subjects are able to perform so many movements, as many as needed! They perform from the standpoint of cultural and racial consciousness with markers of domination that are soldered, tattooed on bodies, as signs of an imposed subalternity. I conclude that this body, believed to be suitable only for Candomblé and *capoeira*, does not render itself banal, lend itself to stereotype, or subjugate itself, but rather it proposes an autonomy, which I call the "subject body." That body performs its dance as an expression of its own self, its desires, and its ancestry.

Conclusion

To speak of Afro-dance requires an understanding of the behavior of an African Diaspora society composed of blacks, whites, and Indigenous Americans in which the black population is formed by those who self-identify as black or brown. According to the latest *National Household Survey of the Brazilian Institute of Geography and Statistics* (IBGE 2010), 49.4% of the population falls in the self-declared white color or race category,

7.4% black, 42.3% mulatto, and 0.8 %, in another color or race category. In our education system, this multiplicity of identities is not always proportionally represented in the classroom at each grade level or in every subject.

Despite advances in discussions about ethnicity and race, the enactment of Law No. 10.639 in 2003, which establishes the guidelines and basis for mandatory inclusion of "Afro-Brazilian History and Culture," and the incorporation of cultural manifestations as a legitimate part of Brazilian national culture, as well as this law's modification as Law No. 11.645 in 2008 to include the same protections for Indigenous cultures, folkloric groups and Afro-dance classes are still seen as "black things" and considered inferior. From an "insider's" perspective, I can say that the work of Afro-dance predates these laws. Even before the enactment of the law, public schools of Salvador had already had (and still have) important experiences with inclusion of black culture in public school curricula, experiences that have earned recognition and legitimation. For example, three schools created by black cultural communities and later taken over by the government had already incorporated this content: (1) the Eugenia Anna dos Santos Municipal School within the Terreiro Candomblé Ilê Axé Opô Afonjá; (2) the Literacy School Mother Hilda within the Terreiro Ilê Axé Jitolu; and (3) the Malê Debalê Municipal School, created by Carnival *blocos afro* Ilê Aiyê and Malê Debalê. In these schools, in addition to the content of traditional schools, students also learned the Yoruba language, African mythology, respect for nature, and the use of herbs. In addition to these schools, other music and dance professionals, including myself, Clyde Wesley Morgan, Master King, Carlos Moraes, and Emília Biancardi, also incorporated African and Indigenous principles into education and performance practices taught in other community spaces.

Although there have been some advances in Brazilian society, we, black people, are still exploited and Afro-Brazilian culture still faces hostility in schools and professional environments. Considered vulgar and exotic, African Brazilian culture is remembered only during Folklore Week, on the anniversary of the abolition of slavery (May 13), on the Day of the Student, and on November 20, National Day of Black Consciousness. The school and university environments, including all personnel, do not understand yet the critical importance of African Brazilian socio-historical roles, which cannot be erased or ignored. These roles point to the ways many people experience things together and begin to address inequality and oppression. The country still needs to mobilize its immense creative abilities and its political will to adopt procedures that, in time, will achieve the justice Afro-Brazilians have been and are fighting for. Education, as a right that guarantees access to other rights, has an important role to play.

It is with this goal that Law No. 11.645 in 2008 stipulates:

Art. 1º O Art. 26-A The study of African-Brazilian and Indigenous history and culture is obligatory in public and private primary and secondary schools.

§ 1 The content referred to in this article includes various aspects of history and culture that characterize the formation of the population from these two ethnic groups such as the study of the history of Africa and Africans, the struggle of blacks and indigenous peoples in Brazil, black and indigenous culture in Brazil, and the black and the Indian in the formation of the national society, recovering their contributions in social, economic, and political areas, relevant to the history of Brazil.

§ 2 Content related to Afro-Brazilian and Brazilian indigenous history and cultures will be taught across the entire school curriculum, especially in the areas of arts education and Brazilian literature and history [...].

Art. 2º This Act shall enter into force on the date of its publication [...] (Anon. 2008).

Today, education in Brazilian schools is guided by this law and the *National Curriculum Guidelines* (PCN), incorporating African values and references within the curriculum to ensure that, with respect for the cultural, regional, ethnic, religious, and political diversity of a multicultural, stratified, and complex society, education can act decisively in the process of building citizenship. Brazilian laws and curricula have as their objective the ideal of growing equal rights among citizens, based on democratic principles. In the area of the arts, the guidelines propose a model of "education that fosters the development of artistic thought, featuring a special way to give meaning to people's experiences" (Secretaria de Educação Fundamental 1997). With such guidelines and principles, the future Brazilian student who dances should understand the structure and functioning of the body and the elements that comprise movement; she/he/they will be interested in dance as a collective activity; and she/he/they will understand and appreciate the various dances of Brazil as cultural manifestations.

Although dance is not the only means of human communication, and its performance does not require an ethnic boundary, it stimulates diversity. It is an expression of time and space; it is the control and manipulation of movements and gestures in order to communicate and express emotions. It also provides collective work and creation. I want to emphasize also that Afro-dance becomes the best representative of Brazil's African-descendent ethnic and cultural traditions when it is performed in spaces that include those families and members of Candomblé and *blocos afros* in public squares, conventional stages, or Carnival parades. Whatever the situation, such community membership, space, and time provide the dancer and the viewer an understanding of the world that moves beyond rational entertainment. The dances performed and created jointly or as solos, with or without music, contribute to both continuity and sociocultural change.

But who teaches Afro-dance? Who learns? What is learned? And where does learning take place? We must be aware and careful as we answer these questions for a plural student body in the twenty-first century.

We are social actors working to the beat of the drums, which can bring us home to mother Africa. Africa is present in my life as an artist, educator, and social activist, and in the lives of other Brazilian women and men, in ways that build my and their African Brazilian identity. These attempts to create a plural education bring to mind a verse from another song, "Highlight," by our former Minister of Culture, Gilberto Gil (1979), in which he emphasizes our examples of struggle:

Don't worry!
What we can do, we can do.
What we cannot will explode.
It is brute force
and the source of force is neutral.
And suddenly, we can.

References

Anon. (2008), "Presidência da República Casa Civil," http://www.planalto.gov.br/ccivil_03/_ato2007-2010/2008/lei/l11645.htm. Accessed August 3, 2016.

Bachelard, Gaston (1991), *Land and Daydreams from Home* (trans. Paulo Neves da Silva), Sao Paulo: Martins Fontes.

Barenbein, Manoel (1969), *Canção Aquele Abraço*, Philips Records.

Chasteen, John (2004), *National Rhythms, African Roots*, Albuquerque: University of New Mexico, pp. 44–45.

Ferreira, A.B.H. (1986), *Novo dicionário da língua portuguesa*, 2nd ed., Rio de Janeiro: Nova Fronteira.

Gil, Gilberto (1979), *Álbum Realce*, Gravadora WEA, Rio de Janeiro: Produzido pela GG Produções Artísticas.

hooks, bell (1991) "Black women intellectuals," in bell hooks and Cornel West (eds), *Breaking Bread*, Boston: South End Press, pp. 147–65.

—— (2014), *Black Looks: Race and Representation*, New York: Routledge Press, pp. 1–20, 133–44.

Instituto Brasileiro de Geografia e Estatística (IBGE) (2010), "Censo Demográfico 2010," http://www.ibge.gov.br/home/estatistica/populacao/censo2010/default.shtm Accessed September 28, 2016.

Kaeppler, Adrienne (1991), "American approaches to the study of dance," *1991 Yearbook for Traditional Music*, 13, pp. 11–21.

Luz, Narcimária Correia do Patrocínio (2005), "*Pássaros Inaugurais*," *Jornal A Tarde*, 2, November, n.pag.

Nóbrega Oliveira, Nadir (1991), *Dança Afro: Sincretismo de movimentos*, Salvador: EDUFBA.

—— (2007), "Ago Alafiju, Odara! The presence of Clyde Wesley Morgan at UFBA Dance School from 1971 to 1978," Masters' thesis, Federal University of Bahia, Salvador.

Primus, Pearl (1969), "Life crises: From birth to death," *American Dance Therapy Association Fourth Annual Conference*, Philadelphia, pp. 1–13.

Secretaria de Educação Fundamental (1997), *Parâmetros Curriculares Nacionais: introdução aos Parâmetros Curriculares Nacionais*, Brasilia: MEC/SEF.

Silva, Ana Célia da (1989), *A Escola e a ideologia das aptidões*, Salvador: Official Diary of the State of Bahia.

Sodré, Muniz (2002), *O terreiro e a cidade: A forma social negro-brasileira* (*The Yard and the City: A Black-Brazilian Social Form*), Rio de Janeiro and Salvador: Imago and Cultural Foundation of the State of Bahia.

Thompson, Robert Farris (1974), *African Art in Motion*, California: University of California Press.

Welsh Asante, Kariamu (ed.) ([1994] 1998), *African Dance: An Artistic, Historical, and Philosophical Inquiry*, Trenton: Africa World Press.

Welsh Asante, Kariamu and Hanley, Elizabeth A. (eds) (2004), *African Dance: World of Dance*, New York City: Chelsea House Publishers.

Verger, Pierre (1987), *Fluxo e Refluxo do Tráfico de Escravos entre o Golfo de Benin e a Bahia de Todos os Santos dos Séculos XVII a XIX* (*Flux and Reflux of the Slave Traffic between the Benin Gulf and the Bay of All Saints Seventeenth to Nineteenth Centuries*) (trans. Tasso Gadzanis, from French original), Sao Paulo: Corrupio.

Notes

1   A traditional Bahian festival in homage to the Catholic saints, Cosmos and Damian, who are associated with children. "Caruru" also refers to a stew made with okra and palm oil, which is served with various other Bahian dishes.

2   A reference to the song "Aquele Abraço," by the composer, performer, and former Minister of Culture Gilberto Gil.

3   A reference to Afro-Brazilian religion.

4   Editors' note: The following authors are not published in Portuguese, so access is difficult in Brazil; see also Primus (1969), Kaeppler (1991), and Welsh Asante ([1994] 1998).

5   The *alfaia* is a musical instrument belonging to the family of membranofones, used in *maracatu* rhythms; the *xequerê* or *agbê* ("shekere" in English and "sekere" in Yoruba orthography) is a percussion instrument that consists of a dried gourd cut at one end and wrapped in a net with beads woven into it; the *agogô* is a gong or bell instrument made of one or several bells, which is characteristic of West African traditional music.

6   *Calunga* is a divinity of Congo/Angola origin, which in *maracatu* is represented by a black doll.

7   *Congada* is an Afro-Brazilian cultural and religious manifestation. It consists of a dramatic dance with instrumental music and song that recreates the coronation of a Congolese king (Ferreira 1986: 453). *Maculelê* is a dance form that simulates tribal battle using two staffs as weapons, called *grimas* (swords), with which the participants stab and pull back to the rhythm of the music. *Coco alagoano*, which has both African and Indigenous influences, is a circle dance accompanied by singing, danced in pairs, lines, or circles during popular festivals in coastal and backlands regions of northeastern Brazil. *Capoeira* is a martial art dance/game that is seminal to African Brazilian culture. *Frevo* is a Brazilian musical rhythm and dance that originated in the state of Pernambuco and which combines marching,

maxixe, (an early urban form of *samba*, originating in Rio among Bahian migrants at the end of the nineteenth century) and elements of *capoeira*.

8   See also: http://grupobrasil.files.wordpress.com/2008/06/maracatu.jpg. Accessed May 22, 2018.

9   Ballet styles of choreographers Victor Navarro, Luís Arrieta (modern); National ballets of Senegal and Angola.

10 See the works of bell hooks. Editors' note: hooks (2014: 1–20, 133–44) and (1991: 147–65).

Chapter 7

Dancing into the Politics of Race: From Bahia to Kingston

Deborah A. Thomas

Scene 1

I had applied for the Arnold Fellowship at the last minute, having only found out about it some days before the deadline from my professor, Anani Dzidzienyo. Anani got everyone interested in Bahia; he was (and still is) the center of things Brazilian at Brown University. My angle, given my own background in African American performance and popular theater, was that I wanted to know how contemporary dancers in Brazil were drawing from the movement structures and music of Afro-Brazilian Candomblé to inform their choreography and socio-political messages. During the late 1980s and early 1990s, the black arts movement was hopping in Salvador, and a number of modern dance companies were drawing from "folkloric" dance to put forward their ideas about African ancestry, diasporic connections, and Afro-Brazilian pride. This was being done as part of a more general political agenda, to expose "racial democracy" – the foundational tenet of Brazilian nationalism – as a myth, and to celebrate those aspects of Afro-Brazilian history and cultural practice that had been denigrated for so many hundreds of years. I didn't know how to write a research proposal, so I wrote an extended poem outlining what I then saw as an interesting paradox – that at the very moment when "multiculturalism" was becoming a policy buzzword in the United States (and when activists began to worry that this new focus would fracture community organizing efforts designed to highlight the long-term effects of segregation and white supremacy), Brazilians seemed interested in rejecting claims to "racial democracy" (their own brand of multiculturalism, in a way) and instead embraced a view of themselves as having emerged from a history of racial discrimination and violence, one that couldn't be papered over by appeals to a sort of nationalist color-blindness. I wrote about wanting to see how this was happening in the world of the performing arts, and specifically dance, and wanting to study it by dancing with people. When I found out I was to be interviewed for the fellowship, we were in the middle of intensive rehearsals for our spring dance concert, and I left the dance studio in sweaty dance clothes to interview in the dean's office. Needless to say, I was pleasantly surprised to find out I got the fellowship.

I graduated and moved to New York, having arranged to defer the Arnold for a year so I could dance in the city. Of course, what this meant was that I did every possible odd job I could find while performing with pick-up companies here and there. I ran sound for a theater in Chelsea during their production of *George Washington Slept Here*; I read scripts for a variety of theaters; I did a little freelance writing for the *Village Voice* and *Essence* magazine; and eventually I landed a part-time job as assistant dramaturg at Crossroads

Theater Company in New Brunswick, working with Sydné Mahone. And I took classes everywhere – ballet, modern, African, Afro-Caribbean, Afro-Brazilian, everything.

Toward the end of that first year in New York, I figured I'd better get my act together regarding Bahia. I started taking Portuguese lessons with Ligia Barreto out of her apartment in Park Slope. Ligia also taught Afro-Brazilian dance at Lezly Dance and Skate – the center of African dance at the time in New York. And eventually I called Anani again to ask him for contacts in Salvador. He gave me one number, that of Clyde Morgan who was teaching dance at State University of New York (SUNY)-Brockport. Clyde was a former dancer with the Limón Company who retooled, moved to Brazil for a time, and became central to the promotion and teaching of Afro-Brazilian dance at Brockport and beyond. He was finishing up the semester there when I called and spoke with his wife, Lais. I had purchased my ticket to Rio, but had made no other arrangements, and I think she was a little shocked that I was not worried about this. She told me they would be there at the time I planned to arrive, and suggested I stay with them when I got in, which was, of course, a godsend. I didn't reach Salvador until after midnight, and fell asleep immediately after the taxi dropped me off at their house.

This was June 1989, toward the end of the transitional period that followed the military dictatorship but before the first democratic elections since 1960, which would happen later that year.[1] To my eyes, Afro-Brazilian culture was everywhere and unavoidable: Bahianas lined Avenida Sete and every other public gathering place, selling *acarajé*, *abará*, and *cocadas*; people joked that Brazil was 80 per cent Catholic but 100 per cent Candomblé; and it seemed that *encontros* of issues *Afro-Brasileiros* were weekly events. Luckily for me, Clyde and Lais were also planning a performance for the following month. The day after my arrival, they took me along to a lunch they had scheduled with various friends and dance-theater bigwigs, like Mario Gusmão, who told Clyde my eyes were so big because I was trying to absorb everything all at once. I laughed to myself because jet lagged and linguistically inept, I thought if I opened my eyes wide enough I would understand what was going on around the table. Later that day, Lais took me to the Casa do Benin. This was a museum of sorts, an homage to a sister city across the seas, and at the time they also rented two rooms at the very top of the tower to visiting students, which Lais told them I was. She told me I could stay there until we found a suitable apartment, and as she got back in her car she instructed me to meet everyone the next afternoon at 5 p.m. in the UFBA (Universidade Federal da Bahia) dance studio for our first rehearsal. I carried my too-large duffel bag up what seemed like a million steps and decamped in a room with a tiny window far above the cobblestoned streets of the Pelourinho.

Scene 2

I can't remember when or where I got it, but in those first couple of days I bought a tiny *ocarina*, a clay flute of sorts, and taught myself how to play "Redemption Song" while staring out that tiny window at the people walking up the hill to the Casa Jorge Amado (originally, the auction site of the enslaved) and points beyond in the Terreiro de Jesus, or down in the other direction toward the Forte Sto. Antonio, where I would later find out a Rastafarian couple – Jorge and Kafuné – then active in the black arts scene, were living with a number of others who were involved with the *bloco afro* Ilê Aiyê. Working out that Marley melody was at once a way to honor my own roots as a "Jamerican" who spent my early childhood in Kingston, and the means by which I generated the courage to explore those streets and alleys on my own. This was, remember, before the expansion of Olodum's center that followed visits by Jimmy Cliff and Michael Jackson in the early 1990s, before the massive removal of community residents to pave way for the onslaught of tourist venues and restaurants quoting prices in US dollars, before, before, before…

On Tuesdays, all the churches in the *terreiro* opened their doors to the public. I remember standing in awe in the Igreja de São Francisco, picturing in my mind's eye all the enslaved Africans whose hands placed sheets of gold across those lofty ceilings, skillfully sneaking in Candomblé symbols here and there, confirmation that already by the late seventeenth century a robust religious duality had taken hold. These same Africans, however, were relegated to worshipping in the Igreja Nossa Senhora do Rosário dos Pretos, a church they built for themselves replete with imagery of black saints. In those days, only a few intrepid tourists ventured up to the *Pelo*, as Pelourinho District was affectionately called, and those who did were also greeted by incredible displays of *capoeira* and vendors selling dyed fabrics, instruments, and other "artisanal" fare. Tuesday nights the place to be was the Bar Reggae, a center of Rastafari solidarity and gathering spot for pan-Africanist visionaries. It was there that I met an itinerant black South African in Bahia to make political linkages; he did not know it then, but his activities were being monitored by undercover police, and after I talked with him so were mine, for a time anyway.

Eventually I found my way to the dance studio, where Clyde was getting ready to lead the warm-up. There, I met everyone who was anyone in the Salvador dance scene, many of whom were trained by Mestre King, the dance visionary who was the first to develop a movement vocabulary that fused modern and Afro-Brazilian dance traditions, one that was further elaborated by Rosângela Silvestre (who then taught company class for the Balé Folclórico da Bahia every Saturday), Isaura Oliveira (who, with Rosângela and a few other women, made up the company M'Bunda), and Armando Pekeno (whose own company presented an innovative synthesis of more abstract modern dance and *dança afro*), among others. On the first day of rehearsals, I also met DeAma Battle, who in the 1960s founded the traditional African dance company Art of Black Dance and Movement in Boston. She was traveling with one of her drummers (Jerry) and one of her dancers (Edir), himself Brazilian, and she too was interested in exploring the aesthetic and political dimensions of black dance in Bahia. Once we found out we traveled to Bahia with exactly the same books, we became bosom buddies, moving as one during our day-to-day for the month she stayed. Indeed, DeAma is responsible for the tattoo on my left ankle; waiting while she went under the needle, I flipped through the books she brought detailing various Akan symbols and their meanings and one stuck – "we should never fight because we have the same belly," a cross made of two crocodiles sharing one midsection. DeAma and I explored the Mercado Modelo together, discovering the basement tunnels where the enslaved disembarked from their middle passage journey; we went to Cachoeira, where we participated in the Festival de Boa Morte and met several of the sisters there; and we danced, laughed, and compared notes constantly.

For three weeks we all rehearsed almost every day. The performance was designed to showcase the luminaries of Afro-Brazilian dance and provide a forum for newer Afro-modern choreography, including Clyde's. I was happy to be in a number of pieces, and thrilled to become part of that social community of artists. As I tagged along with them to shows, to bars, to parties, my Portuguese soon became passable, and then fluent. As dancers and musicians, we were a crew – music was everywhere and we were making it, debating it, singing it, and dancing it. And of course, we went to the beach. We roasted in the sun, occasionally paying a young boy to sprinkle cold water over our feet for refreshment; we played paddleball; we danced and we sang together. Even in black arts scene in New York I had never experienced anything quite like the camaraderie we had with each other, and as someone from a mixed racial background who identified as black, I had never before felt less unusual.

Finally, the weekend of our performances at Teatro Castro Alves in Campo Grande arrived. Costumed and standing in the wings for the finale, I held onto Isaura's hand tightly, waiting for our entrance. After our final bows, one of the musicians – Cícero, a trumpeter from São Paulo who had moved to Bahia a decade before – introduced me to his girlfriend Tyrrah Young, an African American originally from Oakland who was living in Bahia teaching at the American School in Salvador. Herself a dancer (she had worked with the Kumbuka African Dance and Drum Collective in New Orleans for many years), we became fast friends. As the excitement of those weeks of rehearsals and performances wore off, and as Clyde and his family and DeAma and her company members prepared to go back to the States, Tyrrah became my touchstone. I spent many afternoons and evenings in the apartment she shared with Cícero in Rio Vermelho, borrowing her books and a small television (by then I had moved into a two-bedroom apartment owned by Lais's family in Barra).

There were many texts that had become central to my investigations, and that were critical for the explorations of the various choreographers with whom I was working at the time. These were Pierre Verger's *Fluxo e Refluxo do tráfico dos escravos entre o golfo do Benin e a Bahia do Todos os Santos*, Robert Farris Thompson's *Flash of the Spirit: African and Afro-American Art and Philosophy*, and Melville Herskovits's *Myth of the Negro Past*. All three of these classics gave us evidence for the continuities we were attempting to demonstrate, the continuities between Africa and the African Diaspora that served as the basis for the elaboration of both a new sense of ourselves and a new mode of political action. We were, of course, not the first to discover these authors, and we would not be the last. And while their work was critical to our projects – providing the basis for many an "ah ha!" moment – we could not completely shake a particular kind of discomfort. Why were the authors who were tracing the histories we felt were so important to our understanding of what we were doing all white? Was it that black scholars, and other scholars of color, were not interested in these connections, either because they didn't feel cultural practices could serve as the basis for a revolution or because they were ashamed? Was it because they weren't encouraged to study them? And if they weren't, who was preventing them from doing so?

It was through Tyrrah's library that I found some of the answers to these questions. There, I was introduced to George James's *Stolen Legacy*, Assata Shakur's autobiography, Ivan Van Sertima's *They Came Before Columbus*, and Cheikh Anta Diop's *The African Origin of Civilization*, among many others. Angela Davis's *Women, Race, and Class* so impressed me that I was (naively) moved to send her a long letter written in tiny print on airmail stationary via her editor at Vintage Press. I spent pages describing what I was discovering, thinking through how her arguments would work in a Brazilian context, encouraging her to come and see for herself, letting her know that she could stay with me since I had an extra bedroom. When I met her years later at an academic conference, long after I had stopped dancing with the Urban Bush Women and had received my Ph.D., I told her about the letter, assuming her editor had thought I was a nutcase and didn't pass it along. She laughed and said she remembered, and I was embarrassed. But in those days, when everything about Bahia was new to me, I couldn't contain my excitement.

Scene 3

After a couple of months I got into a routine. Isaura was working at CEAO, the Centro de Estudos Afro Orientais, and I would read there most mornings, learning about *quilombos* and the history of Afro-Brazilian expressive and political cultures. In the afternoons, I would attend dance classes, sometimes with Mestre King, sometimes with Rosângela, sometimes with Isaura or Armando Pekeno. We all moved together to the various conferences and performances that were occurring, and through one of the drummers I became close to Cici, a member of a Candomblé *terreiro* beyond the dunes past the airport in Laura de Freitas, Ilê Axé Opô Aganjú. Cici, a bus attendant by trade, taught me the ins and outs of what she thought was important to pass on. She washed my *elekes*, cared for me when I was sick, and became a sort of surrogate mother. I also had befriended a young Japanese woman whose family was among the thousands who relocated to Brazil beginning in the early twentieth century after the end of feudalism in Japan. Brazil, in fact, boasts the largest Japanese population outside of Japan, as immigration options elsewhere were closed during that period; the 1924 Immigration Act barred Asians from moving to the United States, and the whites-only immigration policy prevented settlement in Australia. Makiko had thus spent much of her childhood in Brazil, returning to Japan as a teenager, at which point she felt too different to fully assimilate. She returned as an adult to live in Bahia on a number of occasions, and she has now moved back permanently. Married to a *capoeirista*, she hosted us recently to screen our documentary film *Bad Friday* as part of their Festa Angola. Makiko was a beautiful singer, and was also an aficionado of *dança afro*.

One day, rushing to class, I ran into a dancer friend in the Pelo who told me he had met "another Jamaican" that day, a painter. He also said that this other Jamaican needed a place to stay and that since I had an extra bedroom he thought I should offer it to him. "But I don't even know this person," I protested. Never mind, he was coming to our rehearsal that evening. As it turned out, the "other Jamaican" was Bryan MacFarlane, now a very well-known artist who has exhibited his paintings – including those he was inspired to create while living in my apartment in Bahia – all over the world. In accordance with the funny twists of fate, Bryan also has a studio in the community where I lived and did my Ph.D. research in Jamaica. Last summer in Kingston I ran into him in a café. His mother had passed and he had returned from China to sort out the arrangements for her funeral. He looked disheveled and disoriented, and told me to come up to the studio. He wanted to paint me again. I say "again," here, because while he was living in my apartment there was a constant stream of people (mostly young and extraordinarily beautiful women) in and out of his room. Portraits, he said. I drove up the hill to his studio on the ridge overlooking Kingston and he came out of his back room with an easel and watercolors, surprised that I hadn't removed my clothing. I laughed. "You never painted me nude in Bahia!" He corrected me, reminding me of the day he asked fifteen or twenty of us dancers to stand in a clumped line, all in contorted positions, holding on to each other looking both forward and back – a representation of the middle passage, if I remember correctly.

Scene 4

The year I lived in Bahia was punctuated by several crucial world events. In November 1989, Rosângela, along with several dancers and drummers, traveled to Frankfurt and Berlin to present some workshops and perform. While they were there the Berlin Wall came down. I remember watching the images on my borrowed black and white television, wondering how the crew from Bahia – themselves about to participate in their first election ever – made sense of what was happening around them. When they returned I asked Rosângela what it was like to be there for that, but I'm not sure it was as monumental to her as it seemed to me at that moment. And in April, I had gone with Chester Higgins, Jr., the African American photographer who was in Salvador doing research for his book, *Songs of My People*, to the home of Terciliano, a wonderful and well-known painter who flirted with Chester's wife and me the whole day. As we were getting ready to leave, we heard on the radio that Sarah Vaughan had died, and we held an impromptu memorial for her, commemorating her with Terciliano's many jazz recordings.

Scene 5

I turned 23 in Bahia. As luck would have it, by then I was in rehearsals again, this time for a performance on my birthday in December with Bira Reis's experimental Afro-Brazilian jazz band Ilú Batá, a group of percussionists and singers who occasionally also enlisted dancers to perform with them. I wanted to host a traditional *caruru* (the feast for the gods at a Candomblé gathering) to celebrate after the performance, so my friend Dora and I spent the whole day before the show buying and preparing food – *acarajé, vatapá, caruru, xinxim da galinha, arroz, milho branco cozido, feijão fradinho com dendê, pipoca….* I left her in my kitchen to finish up while I went to the theater.

After the show, everyone took the bus back to my apartment. We ate, we drank, we sang and danced, and all those who didn't leave before midnight (no one did) were stuck in Barra until the buses began running again at 5 a.m. That's when the real fun began. Rosângela orchestrated an impromptu talent show, and everyone participated. Instruments materialized, new songs were written hastily, and skits were improvised. My neighbors, hearing all the noise, came over to join in. At daybreak people began packing up and started on their way home. Tyrrah stayed to help me clean and then, exhausted, we fell asleep until Cícero came to pick her up.

Scene 6

Throughout October 1989, we all attended political rallies. Election fever had taken control of everyone from 8 to 80, and every conversation on every corner, in every bar, and at every event at some point made its way around to the impending elections on November 15. For all of my friends, this was their first time voting, and they had the ebullient enthusiasm I and everyone else I knew, as jaded cynics about the political process, lacked. One could not help but get caught up, and we campaigned for Luiz Inácio Lula da Silva – or Lula, affectionately – whenever we could. Lula was the Worker's Party (Partido Trabalhador/PT) candidate, and the favorite among most poorer folk and left leaning middle class progressives in Salvador. As with most events in Bahia, political rallies resembled parties, or more specifically, *desfiles*, parades down the streets with people waving banners and singing "Lula, Lula, Lula…" to a tune resembling a Carnival chant. More than twenty candidates from an equally diverse set of parties took part in the first round of elections, after which the field was narrowed to Lula and Fernando Collor de Mello, the conservative capitalist and clear US preference given his emphasis on privatization, the promotion of free markets, and public debt reduction. Between November 15 and December 17, the date of the second round of voting, we handed out flyers and other pro-PT material, and generally prepared ourselves for what we thought would be a secure victory.

On December 17, Cícero and Tyrrah picked me up and we drove to Cícero's polling station so he could place his vote. We celebrated and took photographs the whole time – of him finding his name on the voting rolls, of him writing his ballot, of him folding the ballot and inserting it into the slot in the box. It seemed strange to us that so few people were there with us, but since we went at the earliest possible time, we thought maybe people just hadn't reached as yet. Then we went out on the road and we saw the first sign: "Give us a ride! They've taken the buses off the streets! The people want to vote!!!" Rumor had it that Collor's family was close with the owners of the transportation company that owned the public buses, and that the drivers had been barred from accessing their vehicles that morning. We spent the next several hours squeezing people into the car and taking them back and forth to their polling stations. Uncertainty and worry began to fall over us, and when the polls closed we went to our favorite spot at the beach for fish. There, we complained with others about this and all other injustices, and optimism about democracy seemed to vanish.

Collor won the elections, but wouldn't be inaugurated until March 15, 1990. During the interim months, the economy went crazy. People said all the time that whatever happened in Argentina always came to Brazil a few months later, and this seemed to be proven true as inflation levels reached more than 80 per cent per month. It was not unusual to be in a grocery store and see an employee changing prices on items toward the end of a row, thus being forced to rush to pay for those items at the lower price before the employee got to the end of the row. New currency amounts were being printed as *cruzados*, then *cruzados novos*, then *cruzeiros* seemed insufficient to meet people's basic needs. Then on inauguration day, a bank holiday, the other shoe dropped. During his inauguration speech, the new president announced the Plano Collor – a series of drastic measures designed to curb hyperinflation through, among many other things, freezing all bank accounts over 50,000 *cruzeiros* (at the time, approximately US$1300) for eighteen months. This money was then turned into government bonds and taken out of circulation, but was to be returned to citizens after the stated period. Of course, no one believed this would happen. Businesses closed and previously bustling restaurant and nightclub districts became ghostlike. People who had closed on house purchases but had not yet paid down their money were suddenly out of luck. Hotels and upscale restaurants were no longer accepting credit card payments because they didn't know what the exchange rate was going to be. There were many suicides. My parents arrived for a visit in the middle of all this. Needless to say, all the information I had given them about how much money to bring and what the exchange rates would be was completely useless, a condition I realized when, for the first time ever, I couldn't find my black market currency exchange man at the airport. They were worried, said it reminded them of Jamaica in the 1970s, and wanted to know if I was *sure* I wanted to stay another couple months. They couldn't figure out why everyone seemed to be taking it all in stride. I said it was just the Brazilian way. They weren't convinced.

Scene 7

By early 1990, my friendship with Kal dos Santos, a drummer and actor whose mother was a *mãe de santos*, had turned romantic, and when my lease for the apartment ran out after eight months, I moved to the small house he built at the top of a *morro* off Avenida Sete on the way to Rio Vermelho. In the mornings, Kal ran down the hill to buy fresh bread, then he made coffee for us to enjoy with his homemade yogurt. I was the incredulous beneficiary of this largesse, and I lapped it up gratefully. We spent our days pursuing the arts, in one way or another, and in the evenings, we talked and talked and talked....

As Carnival season rolled around, there were concerts in the outdoor amphitheater all the time. Everyone came through: Milton Nascimento, Caetano Veloso, Djavan (whose *Oceano* had dropped big earlier in the year); and closer to home, Margareth Menezes (who had recently returned from a big tour with David Byrne) and Lazzo Matumbi (whose "Me abraça e me beija" was one of my personal favorites). These concerts were actually more like sing-alongs with family. People talked about the artists like they were cousins, like they had a personal stake in their success or missteps, like they were merely giving voice to what everyone already felt anyway. And I got lifted, like everyone else, when we sang together. "*Amar é um deserto e seus temores, Vida que vain a sela dessas dores, Não sabe voltar, Me dá teu calor...*" ("To love is a desert and its fears. Life lived in the saddle of this pain does not know how to return. Give me your warmth") (Djavan 1989). Or, the more upbeat "*Ele, ele, elegibô....*" (Menezes 1989). Or, with Lazzo, "*Onda do mar me levou, me levou mas hoje estou aqui, Onda do mar me levou, e eu resisti...ooo...vem correndo me abraça e me beija*" ("The ocean wave swept me away, swept me away, but I'm here today. The waves tried to take me away but I resisted; oh, I'm still here, run, come hug and kiss me") (Matumbi and Cliff 1989).

Carnival came closer and closer, and Kal started making plans to leave Salvador. He wasn't a big fan of the constant *lavagems* that always seemed to leave the city dirtier, and didn't want to get caught up in the crowds. Having never been to Carnival, I, of course, wanted to stay. I went out with Tyrrah and Cícero in their *bloco*, and traipsed the streets for the first three nights, having planned to meet Kal in the country in the middle of things. I also wasn't sure how I would like being part of a human carpet, not being a huge fan of crowds myself, but I actually found it exhilarating. Experiencing such an intense freedom with other people all around was like nothing I had ever imagined, and certainly it wasn't like Carnival in Rio, which everyone says by that time was no longer a street festival. From the moment Kal saw my face as I was getting off the bus, he knew I wanted us to go back to the city for the last night of festivities. So we spent two days and nights in the country, cooking over open fire, strolling around the central plaza in the evenings alongside everyone else in the town, and sleeping when the sun went down. Then we headed back to Salvador to jump in the streets, ending up at Praça Castro Alves together, reveling in the sound clash that marks the beginning of Ash Wednesday.

Scene 8

By April 1990, I was getting ready to leave Salvador. So was everyone else. Having married DeAma's drummer Jerry, Rosângela was making her plans to migrate. She started out her US life in Boston, but left not too long after and moved without Jerry to New York. Armando Pekeno was on his way to London, where I saw him during one of my visits to my grandmother. He spent a Sunday afternoon with us, and my Jamaican family laughed at us speaking Portuguese the whole time. Kal was going to Paris, where he stayed for a time but then moved to Milan, where he still lives and runs an Afro-Brazilian music and dance group. Isaura Oliveira stayed in Salvador a number of years after I left, but later moved as well, first to Boston and finally to Oakland, California, where she now resides. It was a moment, a truly beautiful moment, and then the moment was over.

I returned to New York, and it took me months to dream in English again. There is a Portuguese word I have never been able to translate in a way that adequately conjures its meaning. *Saudade* means nostalgia, yes, an ache, a yearning even. But it's somehow also more than that. It's that feeling you get when everyone is singing "Mãe Menininha do Gantois," or "Aquarela do Brasil," or "Madalena..." – the simultaneous sense of perfect freedom and joy combined with the feeling that someone is reaching into your chest and ripping out your heart. *Saudade* is the force that compels you to kiss a complete stranger during Carnival, that drives you to offer a sacrifice to the sea for Iemanjá, that makes you move as one during the long dances of Candomblé. *Saudade* is that drive to return, that diasporic longing, but it is also what kept me from going back. In New York, people urged me to write about Brazil and things Brazilian. Friends at the *Voice* wondered why I was so reticent to review this new album or that performance. Fellow dancers in Urban Bush Women wondered why I listened to Brazilian music all the time, but didn't want to *sambar* on stage. And years later, as I began thinking about graduate school, advisors suggested I return to Bahia for more intensive and systematic research. But I couldn't. It was in Bahia that the seeds of many lifelong projects, many intellectual explorations, were planted. It was in Bahia that I felt the freest I have ever felt in life, as a woman, as a *morena*, as an artist. But I couldn't shake the *saudade* of knowing that while I loved living in *that* place at *that* time, and while friends often commented that I "became" one of them through living and laughing with them ("*ay Deborá, virou bahiana mesmo!*"), Salvador didn't belong to me and I did not belong to Salvador.

And so I do my research, my *vaivén* as Puerto Ricans would say, in Jamaica, where dancers were foundational to the anti-colonial movement, where the arts are windows onto questions of politics and history, and where I've been moved to archive various forms of violence, as well as the myriad innovative responses to these violences. My work in Jamaica is not uncomplicated by another sort of diasporic longing, but at least there I imagine that I have a legitimate claim to belong, to speak, to commiserate, to dream – to represent, in all senses of the word. Bahia taught me that. And it confirmed what I had hypothesized when I originally wrote my fellowship proposal, that the struggles of artists in Bahia might shed some light on my own, and those of other communities of black performers in the United States and elsewhere in the Americas, that I might be able to track some of the relationships between performance and politics, racial self-making and nation-building through dance and dancing. The *onda do mar me levou*, but I didn't resist and today I am here....[2]

References

Djavan (1989), "Oceano," *Djavan*, CBS Records.

Matumbi, Lazzo and Cliff, Jimmy (1989), "Me Abraca e Me Beija."

Menezes, Margareth (1989), "Uma Historia de Ifá," Mango.

Thomas, Deborah (2002), "Democratizing dance: Institutional transformation and hegemonic re-ordering in post-colonial Jamaica," *Cultural Anthropology*, 17:4, pp. 512–50.

——— (2004), *Modern Blackness: Nationalism, Globalization, and the Politics of Culture in Jamaica*, Durham: Duke University Press, 2004.

——— (2011), *Exceptional Violence: Embodied Citizenship in Transnational Jamaica*, Durham: Duke University Press.

Notes

1   The military dictatorship that began in 1964 officially ended in 1985 when the National Congress handed power to Tancredo Neves. Neves died before taking office and was replaced by José Sarney, who held power until democratic national elections were finally held in 1989.

2   Editors' reference for readers: Thomas (2001: 512–50, 2004, 2011).

Part IV

Defying Erasure through Dance

Chapter 8

Negotiations: Afro-Bahian Memory, Storytelling, and Dance

Lucía M. Suárez

Adaptations abound. Form follows function and vice versa. To traditional Africa, the world is a textured place with many focal points: the unity lies in the sensibility of the beholder making sense of the unruly reality.

(Sir Rex Nettleford)

Introduction

Bahia is a key site for Afro-Brazilian historical research and documentation. It is defined by narratives that create binding binaries from which, it would seem, no one can escape. On the one hand, it is touted as *"Bahia Terra da Beleza Negra"* ("Bahia, Land of Black Beauty"), *"Roma Negra"* ("Black Rome"), and *"A Terra da Felicidade"* ("Land of Happiness"). The beauty of blackness, the history of the African Diaspora, and an inherent cultural happiness are advertised in tourist brochures and on nightclub screens.[1]

Some international researchers spend lifetimes in Bahia, discovering Africa in the new world. African American roots tourism thrives in the Brazilian northeast, which has been established as a geography of the memory and translation of African religions and stories. On the other hand, the capital city, Salvador is conflated with alarming popular media coverage of drug-related crimes. Its large Afro-descendent population, which constitutes the poorest communities in the city, is often discursively dismissed as criminal, living in the margins of the law. Multiplying evangelical practitioners systematically deride African religious practices, rejecting the rich and important African heritage that permeates life in the city. In short, while Afro-Brazilian musical products feed a million-dollar culture industry, and Afro-Bahian dance classes are central to community programming, African-descendent/Afro-Brazilian lives are disproportionately linked to scenes of violence and an underworld of life lived cruelly in shadow spaces or defiantly in the fast lane.

Instances of life in the fast lane abound in the news. For example, the murder of Kelly Cyclone was on everyone's mind during one of my research trips, the summer of 2011.[2] Cover stories stated: "Brazilian Kelly Sales Silva aka Kelly Cyclone was the girlfriend of a famous drug-lord who got killed ... On July 18, 2011, she came back from a party and got killed by a rival gang in Lauro de Freitas" (a neighborhood close to the airport).[3] Illegal coverage included a video clip of the body at the morgue. Pictures of her dead body either scantily clothed or naked, with open eyes and shots to the abdomen were readily available online; blogs and chat rooms were humming about this homicide, which had turned into a viral community event.

Kelly Cyclone was, by her own admission, a party girl out to have fun. Video clips that she uploaded herself showed her off as a part of Brazil's infamous gang culture, defying the social norms and mores of upper-middle class Brazilian society. These were usually filmed on the beach or in a bedroom, and featured her dancing to Afro-Brazilian popular rhythms such as *samba*, *axé*, and *pagode* music.[4] Her body, as a sight of resistance to the Brazilian elite through the model of insurgent citizenship, presented a sobering warning.[5] She was a brown, sexualized, uncontained dancing body. The sensationalized media coverage of Kelly Cyclone's murder relayed the tragic tale of a dancing body as disposable excess. Through the violence enacted upon her body, she was reduced to the symbol of recklessness. The pictures of her dead body told the harrowing story of a life that could be discarded; her story readily affirms established Brazilian prejudices of black and brown bodies as hyper-sexual and disorderly.

Across the capital city, cover stories of recklessness define and label poor and indigent communities, which are disproportionately black, as sites of uncontrollable violence. I see these as disempowering narratives that provide Brazil's elite with a reason to continue constructing walled cities, blaming a large sector of the society, and finding reason in the continued derision of black lives. Afro-Bahians continue to be afflicted by distortion through the media and unofficial, but deeply embedded sociocultural segregation, despite the fact that Afro-Bahian traditions are marketed internationally as foundational narratives that promote multi-threaded understandings of Bahia's plural cultural history. Bahia, the city of African heritage, continues to be a place of extreme racism and classism by which antagonistic narratives of access and exclusion, citizenship and disenfranchisement, are blatantly played out.

In contrast to these disempowering narratives of crime and disposability, an even larger and more complex repertoire of stories merges traditional, African-origin and Afro-Bahian storytelling and dance, promoting cultural agency and human dignity. My combined experiences, as a cultural tourist enjoying Afro-Bahian stories (1999–2001), as a dancer, dance student, and researcher confronting violence (2006–14), add up to fifteen years of on-site and archival research and participant observation, emphasizing individual interviews. I have witnessed the challenges of sociocultural recuperation in a world that, despite propaganda of improved human rights and citizenship rhetoric, maintains traditional hierarchies of power firmly in place. In this context, I argue that African-origin and Afro-Bahian dance and storytelling are seminal sites of memory, resistance, and translation that play a pivotal role in community and socio-political consciousness building. While there are several African-origin religions that survive in Brazil, this study looks at Candomblé, specifically, because it has received so much attention in Bahia and because I worked within Candomblé communities during my field research.

In this essay, I focus on several stories, gathered and based on oral histories, survival parables, and Afro-Bahian dance collaborations, all of which expose the complex, interrelated narratives that play a pivotal role in the propagation of, and resistance to, racism and violence in Bahia. I feature the powerful interventions of Master Griot (storyteller) Dona Cici (Nancy de Souza e Silva), dancer Negrizú (the name he prefers to use, also known as Carlos Pereira dos Santos), the alliances facilitated by the Pierre Verger Foundation (PVF), and Afro-Bahian memories honored by Luiz Badaró and Linda Yudin within their dance company, Viver Brasil. Through such varied stories, I highlight the workings of human rescue within and against the current violence and anti-Afro-Bahian media madness that distresses the lives of Bahia's majority Afro-descendent population. Stories of African-origin *Orixás* (divine spirits) retain histories of the African Diaspora in Bahia. Storytelling and dance are frequently found together in African-based cultures and African-influenced communities, and as I argue here, in Bahia and beyond, they are political acts of memory and possibility in motion.[6]

Intertwined Lives and Storytelling

Born on November 2, 1939, in Rio de Janeiro, Dona Cici is a small 4'10" woman who walks with the aid of a cane. An initial impression of this 78-year-old woman might be that she is frail; but after speaking with her for five minutes, it is immediately evident that she is life force personified. Dona Cici is a member of Ilê Axé Opô Aganjú, an important African religious *terreiro* (temple or sacred space), led by *babalorixá* Balbino in the community of Lauro de Freitas. As per her Candomblé initiation, Dona Cici is a daughter of Obatalá, Oxum, and Ewa (names of three prominent *Orixás* or Candomblé divinities); thereby, she is one of the most prominent figures of her generation.[7] She is part of a coterie of Bahian women – storytellers, doll makers, dance teachers, performers, priestesses, *ebomis* (wise women, this is a title achieved after many years, through concerted devotion to the study and teaching of Yoruba-based religious traditions) – who, aware of the various tensions of representation, performance, and social action, adeptly operate within the local and the global, always grounded by a strong sense of African and Afro-Bahian heritage. In Candomblé, the most well-known practice is that of reading the cowry shells (*os búzios*/the cowry shells used for divination), and the role of those initiates who can give advice and read people's lives. Readings are advertised, easily accessed, and require little or no commitment, as opposed to attending a *xirê* (a Candomblé ceremony), or joining a *terreiro*, which take time and a lot of money. *Búzio* readings offer a primary means of making a connection to Afro-Brazilian religions and the energy of the *Orixás*.

The griot, who teaches through stories, song, and dance, offers a deeper and more complex connection to the African and Afro-Brazilian past. This is the role that the spirits bequeathed upon Dona Cici within the Candomblé.[8] Her work, as a storyteller, is a legacy she honors from her childhood as part of her family's house of worship. Her storytelling manifests itself in three critical ways: her personal life stories (a window into the serendipitous coalitions and experiences that have shaped her), her Candomblé stories and parables (evidence of the importance of her heritage), and the stories of her work as an educator (testimony to the challenges inherent in teaching African and Afro-Bahian histories in the Brazilian school system).

Throughout Dona Cici's life, all of the open passageways, and those she makes accessible for others, have occurred in triangles that link the African continent, Bahia, and the United States or Europe, constructing creative constellations of memory and activism among her family, her community, and foreigners. Dona Cici emphatically values the importance of the personal experiences that can be passed down only through ritual practice and family memories; and she honors the work of those who are dedicated to rescuing, archiving, and teaching a culture that has been historically dismissed in Brazil. She proudly recounts what she inherited from her biological father, a man who belonged to a long lineage of Yoruba practitioners and who personified the circuitous routes by which the myriad stories of the *Orixás* (both in religious practice and in mythic stories) have not been forgotten. Dona Cici also recounts that he was "negro, negro" ("black, black") and that her mother was very light-skinned. Interestingly, Dona Cici's mother (96 years old at the time of my interview in August 2011), who supports her daughter's African religious affiliation, was not religiously involved throughout her life, until she recently became a Protestant.

With pride also, Dona Cici recalls how her life was saved at least twice by the wisdom of the Candomblé *Orixás*. The first time, as a child, her uncle, also an initiate, came to her house because he had been told by his *Orixá* that his niece was in trouble. Dona Cici had been so ill she could not eat. Upon arrival, her uncle went into trance, incorporated his *Orixá*, and gave his brother, the young Cici's father, detailed instruction to get certain foods and herbs. She was cured within the week. Many years later, after her father's death in 1971, Dona Cici suffered from depression and what the doctors determined were hallucinations. This led to her hospitalization and continuous medication; however, conventional medical treatments were not working and, once again, she resorted to Candomblé. She was told that she was seeing her father's spirit; his *egun* (a dead spirit) would not leave her side. A series of rituals were immediately performed and Dona Cici was initiated during the first week of January 1972 in Bahia. She was then told that she had to move to Bahia and that her life was going to be fulfilled there after her hair had turned grey. This shocked her since she was still in her thirties and did not expect to have grey hair for a while, but she trusted her spiritual leaders, listened, and moved.

In Bahia, as her hair was turning grey, she started to work with Pierre Verger, the French photographer, ethnographer, and *babalawo* (Yoruba priest of Ifá, a divining system[9]). Verger had met Dona Cici when she was still quite young and living in Rio de Janeiro, when he had visited her family's *terreiro*; he learned much from both her uncle and her father, who were leaders, initiates, and practitioners at their house of worship. Verger and Dona Cici established an auspicious relationship based on shared stories, exchange of ancestral knowledge, devoted research of African and Afro-Bahian stories, and a relentless faith in the human spirit; their intertwining of lives, which is foundational to Dona Cici's personal story, became salient as she became Verger's spiritual daughter and daily assistant. She discovered

Figure 7: Dona Cici, Organizing Pierre Verger's Photographs. Photograph by Christian Cravo, Lucía M. Suárez archive.

more about her own heritage through Verger's photographs from the African continent. He shared with her his collected stories of the Candomblé *Orixás*, as he had experienced them himself throughout Africa and in Bahia over many years; he taught her new skills, such as how to use a lens and organize his photographs. She wrote the notes to over 1000 entries describing his photographs.

Verger's story merits attention at this moment because it underscores the myriad figures that learn from and contribute to the important valuation of African Diaspora histories. Verger is described as a "Frenchman by birth, Bahian by choice, and African by affinity." Mãe Senhora, his *mãe de santo* (counseling priestess in the Candomblé religion) consecrated his head to Xangô and confirmed him as an "emissary between Bahia and Africa." In 1953, Verger had been initiated in the town of Ketu as an Ifá priest and took on the name "Fatumbi" (Lühning 1999: 78–79). He became an initiate of important religious houses in both Benin and Bahia. His life was dedicated to collecting and honoring the stories of Africa throughout the Transatlantic Triangle (Lühning 1999: 82).[10]

In Bahia, he discovered the close linkages between Brazil and countries in West Africa, and the course of his life's investigations became rooted in "renewing and innovating, creating and recreating human contacts" between the two sides of the Atlantic (Lühning 1999: 82). His work, much to the chagrin of the well-regarded US anthropologist Melville Herskovits, who ultimately viewed Bahia as a static site of African traditions, underscored the active, changing, and inter-culturally informed stories of the *Orixás* specifically in Benin and Bahia. His twenty-year study, *Flux et Reflux de la Traite des Nègres entre le Golfe de Bénin et Bahia de Todos os Santos* (1968), traced, with fascinating details, the ebb and flow of lives, practices, and mechanisms of cultural and economic survival that peoples of different African nations had to navigate in what is now Nigeria and Benin and in Bahia.[11] His book, *African Legends of the Orishas*, with sketches by Carybé,[12] recounts the stories of the Yoruba deities/divinities. These stories serve as a testimonial to the rich tales he learned from the elders in Benin and Bahia, when he was training to become a *babalawo*.

Documenting the original Yoruba stories and tracing their translations are at the base of the work Verger did throughout his life. A modest man who chose to live in the working-class neighborhood of Vila América, teeming with Afro-descendent and slave histories, he considered all people worthy of dignity and recognition, regardless of race, class, or religions. He was focused on collecting knowledge and understanding the many versions of African Diaspora history and culture that were all equally valuable at different historical moments and in varying geographic places. Verger's investigations gave him the opportunity to study and understand the political and historical circumstances that shaped African and Afro-Bahian societies in the nineteenth and twentieth centuries. His extensive exchanges with French anthropologists (such as Alfred Métraux, Roger Bastide, and Gilbert Rouget), his close relations with Brazilian artists and intellectuals (such as Jorge Amado, Carybé, Mario Cravo Neto, Thales de Azevedo, Vivaldo da Costa Lima, Waldeloir Rego, and Odorico Tavares), and his active affiliation with historic Candomblé houses (such as Ilê Axé Opô Afonjá, Ilê Iyá Omin Axé Iyá Massê/Gantois, and Ilê Axé Opô Aganjú), made him a principal intellectual figure in the study of African and Afro-Bahian religious rituals. Even Lydia Cabrera, the renowned writer and literary activist for Afro-Cuban religions and author of *El monte* (detailing African religious practices in Cuba), spent time with Verger in his home. Thus, his home in Engenho Velho de Brotas (EVdB)/Vila América was an important place of research and intellectual exchange, generating a better understanding of Yoruba, Fon, and Ewê cultures on both sides of the Atlantic.

Verger/Fatumbi hoped to contribute to the creation of a positive image of African culture through his research and publications and help to overcome past injustices. He believed in the power of positive examples, and always said that an attitude emphasizing conflicts without offering solutions led to poorer results than one based on affirmation. While not denying existing problems and conflicts, he sought to leave a positive message of the power of culture and cultural identity. His profound integration within various African and Afro-Brazilian communities is still attested to by people visiting the places he lived on the African continent, and can be witnessed by the respect with which he is still remembered by those who knew him (Lühning 1999: 82).

Dona Cici's work with Verger, and others who surrounded him, revealed important stories for her life; she read avidly and was dedicated to the study and uplift of her people. She shared the story of a well-fated encounter regarding Angela Elisabeth Lühning (a German ethnomusicologist, then doctoral student) who coincidently went to the *terreiro* of Dona Cici's *Babalorixá/pai de santo* (counseling priest in Candomblé) for her research. Angela was told that Dona Cici was the only one who could be of help; however, Dona Cici told Angela to study with Pierre Verger. Angela finished her dissertation, became a professor herself, and decided to stay in Bahia. She worked endless hours with Verger, exchanged stories, and learned all she could, becoming a well-respected ethnomusicologist in Bahia. Presently, she is the secretary-director at the Pierre Verger Foundation (PVF) and professor of ethnomusicology at the Federal University of Bahia (UFBA) (Fundação Pierre Verger n.d.).

When I asked Dona Cici what she thought about Europeans and North Americans delving into her culture, she looked at me with a knowing smile, like she has been asked that question before. She told me that in Candomblé the spirit has no race. While it is a religion that is a fundamental source of guidance, community, healing, advice, and memory for African descendants, who are mainly the poor of Brazil, the spirits of the Candomblé have no race. She says that the practices do not belong to a certain ethnic group or a set population. It is a religion of the chosen, those called by the spirits. So, proselytizing is not practiced and race is not limited. The religion originated in Africa, but it is nonetheless, not limited to that continent. She asserts that this adaptability and openness will keep the memories of a time long gone, alive in a contemporary way. Thus, she welcomes the respectful study of and involvement in Candomblé with everyone.

For example, Dona Cici defended her Pai Fatumbi, through whom she had continued language acquisition (which she had learned from her paternal family members who were Candomblé practitioners, and which he had learned through his Ifá practice and travels through Nigeria and Benin). He was a respectful and respected journalist of a world that he had adopted as his own. Dona Cici also considered Angela Lühning a daughter and applauded Angela's dedication to Verger's work, his foundation, and the critical community programming for children of the surrounding neighborhoods. For another example, she spoke at length about her conversations with Africanist art historian Henry John Drewal, apparently admiring him and his interests in Bahia greatly.

Intertwining of lives is a central motif throughout all of the work of Dona Cici, Pierre Verger, and many of those dedicated to the cultures of the African Diaspora. Thus, knowledge is cultivated continuously through what I call "circles of collaboration." For example, Dona Cici's life trajectory highlights the complex interactions between foreigners and natives, which have led to a unique network of global culture and memory bearers within which she remains an active part. Ongoing dialogues between practitioners, researchers, teachers, and activists have led to deeper and shared knowledge of the ancestors and the plural manifestations of their customs on Bahian soil.

This is the key: Dona Cici believes that learning is ongoing, never-ending, and dynamic. For Dona Cici, her storytelling is activism, education, memory, and a gift that allows her to lead a meaningful life. Per her convictions, storytelling is an ancestral legacy that connects people and aims to cultivate a more humanistic existence, full of respect and dignity, in Bahia and beyond.

Figure 8: Dona Cici. Photograph by Christian Cravo, courtesy of Lucía M. Suárez archive.

Afro-Bahian Memory and Education

Storytelling, like dance, is a foundational educational tool, which honors and saves histories that would otherwise be lost to a fast-paced media mediated world. Dona Cici's work reveals and reflects a symbiotic relationship between the past and the present, between African history and the politics of its negation. Her work underscores a rich constellation of cultural preservation and daily adaptations. She has elaborated:

> *Bom, a dança a gente faz, a gente ensina algumas danças do Candomblé mas conta a história do gestual, por que que se dança assim. É como uma ópera, como o que vocês conhecem. Então eu passo, eu conto a história e digo "bem, era uma vez um príncipe chamado Oxossi, era um grande caçador. Então quando ele dança ele bota um arco e uma flecha e ele pisa no chão devagar para que as aves, para não assustar as caças.*

Well, the dance that we do, we teach some of the dances of the Candomblé, but we recount a history of the gestural, because that is how we dance. It's like an opera, which you know. Then I pass on, I recount a history, saying, "Well, there was once a Prince named Oxossi, who was a great Hunter." So when he dances, he throws up a bow and arrow, and he moves slowly on the ground so that the birds, his prey, are not frightened away (2010).[13]

By comparing dances, songs, and their explanations to the opera, Dona Cici secularizes and thus positions the dancing and singing of Afro-Brazilian traditions in a place that often seems to reject African religious practices (i.e., the dances and songs are "safe from the devil," as evangelists might argue). She thus imparts Afro-Bahian history and memory without imposing African-descendent religions. Dona Cici works with "a *história, com o ritmo e com a coreografia da história*" ("a history, with rhythms, and with the choreographies of those histories"). As such, her stories reflect history, but they are also always evolving. For example, *reggae* and African dance come into the picture seamlessly, as they are part and parcel of contemporary culture (television, parties, etc.) with which the children she teaches are familiar and most comfortable. As one of my interviews ended, Dona Cici somberly talked about the *jogo da cintura* or dancing/playing from the waist, so to speak.[14] She talked about the flexibility and spontaneous creativity that are necessary for any and all kinds of social or community work. A game or "play at the waist" suggests flexibility and adaptation in the moment. At issue is the hard labor of defying debasing cultural understandings with uplifting heritage stories. These provide memories and education through a positive historical and social narrative in the lives of Afro-Brazilian children.

As a storytelling educator, Dona Cici frames her efforts in terms of a *pedagogia da realidade*, pedagogy within the reality at hand. Afro-Bahian *realidade* is harsh and involves historical amnesia and daily violence in overcrowded neighborhoods. For example, the Pierre Verger Cultural Space (PVCS), where she works is presently one of the most populated neighborhoods of Bahia. Yet, in 1960, when Verger bought a little plot of land for a modest one-room home, the EVdB was a quiet neighborhood. It contained a rich history of African descendants, since it was built upon old colonial sugar mills and slave quarters (therefore the name "*engenho*," which means "sugar mill"). In literary history, the neighborhood is well regarded for having been the home of the nineteenth-century abolitionist poet, Antônio Frederico de Castro Alves (known as "*o poeta dos escravos*" ["the poet of the slaves"]). It bordered another neighborhood, Engenho Velho de Federação, which was the site of the first-documented, cleared land for a Candomblé *terreiro* in 1830. Albeit forgotten by today's inhabitants, EVdB has historical significance.

Pierre Verger had never thought of a center for the community. He had considered using the plot of land for raising medicinal plants, which he had studied extensively and written about. However, sometime between the late 1980s and the present, the population tripled, and the neighborhood became impoverished, afflicted by growing violence connected to drugs, such as crack cocaine. The locals had no idea who Verger was, nor did they understand the exciting cultural events with researchers and prominent members of society that took place in his home and in the name of the Foundation. They were completely disconnected. In response, Angela Lühning took it upon herself to found the PVCS, to connect the community to its history, and also to offer the neighborhood's children a safe space of possibility.[15] Lühning is a deeply committed cultural agent in her own right.

The Pierre Verger Foundation was established in 1988 by Verger and a group of friends that included Carybé, with the goal of making his extensive body of work available to generations of researchers. In response to the neighborhood's intense poverty and growing violence in 2005, Angela Lühning established the PVCS on the same property of his home and the foundation. The programming at the space honors Verger's life-long research, highlights Afro-Bahian culture, and gives the communities' children a safe place to belong. I have returned to PVCS numerous times to watch classes and witness, first-hand, the dedication of selfless teachers and the infectious energy of so many children thriving within the special programs offered. Yet, clashes between gangs afflict the neighborhood and the presence of an iron gate and many locked doors to keep the Center secure suggest imminent dangers.

PVCS is located on the border between two neighborhoods and antagonistic groups, who are in frequent rivalry. The bus route to get to the center necessarily traverses these two "territories" (belonging to different gangs). The summer of 2011, two young men from one side had made sexual advances to the girlfriend of a young man from the other side. When the boyfriend went to defend his girlfriend, he was stabbed to death. With heightened conflict in action, taking the bus on that route and getting off at the corner of the Center was dangerous. So the children on both sides stopped going to their classes.

The other incident that was occupying everyone's mind was much more theatrical, and equally devastating for the general morale of the Center and its children: the Kelly Cyclone tragedy, which I discussed in the introduction. On the day of her funeral, schools were closed and access to the cemetery had to be restricted because mobs were expected to create havoc. Scared parents kept their children at home all month, and teenagers were also keeping low profiles. The PVCS was experiencing difficulty with student attendance as a consequence of the uproar, which also incited increased violence throughout the city. The volunteer teachers and staff did not show up to work; a number of children stopped attending classes; and the ones that were there were over-stimulated, following their drug-traffic-related idols.

While the Kelly Cyclone murder did not occur anywhere near the PVCS, it was the spectacular news of the moment that echoed, in grand media style, the more immediate violence that was afflicting the children and teachers of the center.[16] A number of the adults I spoke with were deeply upset by the murder, the media spectacle that followed it, and the reaction of the neighborhood children.[17] According to one of the teachers, some children did not think much of the drama. Perhaps more troubling, though, is the more general lament that many young children from the area have become so accustomed to the violence, that it is more exciting than tragic. They followed the story with a certain degree of exhilaration. Dona Cici, whom the children call Vovó Cici (Grandmother Cici) because she provides them with food, games, and loving attention, was deeply saddened by this turn of events.

Kelly had lived a relatively long life. She had made it to 22, while most youngsters caught in the drug world began as children, and rarely made it past their fifteenth birthdays. The teachers I spoke with at PVCS affirmed that this was the reason community centers were so critical. The hard work lies in saving, if only one child from these high-risk conditions. It was clear to me that the simple, yet almost unattainable, goal of the teachers at the Center was to help the community trade fast-paced media-hyped drug culture for cultural memory, which might give the students a sense of self-worth outside the dominant violence that kept them addicted to brief moments of excitement. Relying on narratives of African and Afro-Bahian origin to give the children a sense of history and self-esteem requires making realistic connections between stories of the past and a present reality that obliterates history, heritage, and possibility. Most of the dominant narratives that occupy these children's daily lives are negative. In fact, in commercial culture, the co-optation of Afro-Bahian rhythms and symbols rarely equal inclusion of the poor into Brazil's middle class or any sort of fundamental life improvement. The dynamic played out by the culture industry is dual: visibility of Afro-Bahian culture should be empowering; unfortunately, the mass marketing of Afro-Bahian symbols has been co-opted by an affluent white and light-skinned elite, which still disparages Afro-descendent communities and their diverse, historic heritage.

The work of PVCS by devoted, patient cultural agents is to convince children that the future is actually viable for them, and that they have something to live for; however, teachers, dancers, and activists need spaces of possibilities in which to work. While they can and do take advantage of state, local government, and private support to do their civic work, they also know that they are often left to fend for themselves, as volunteers and leaders, when official structures fall through the cracks (as they often do). Even though these volunteer leaders are struggling themselves to make ends meet, their faith in, and commitment to, human potential drives their education interventions in a world of debilitating violence.

Dona Cici understands the inner workings of the children around her. Their life circumstances are precarious, as they are victims of daily violence and the negation of their African heritage. That heritage could, otherwise, serve as a source of historical pride, emotional mooring, and enlightening education. *Pedagogia da realidade* as a practice employs official, grass-roots, and historical materials in order to teach history; it emphasizes uplifting stories, and connects individuals from all sectors of society. *Pedagogia da realidade* asks Afro-Bahians to imagine an identity that would reject pervasive prejudice, internalized self-aggression, and the acute violence, exacerbated by a barrage of negative media stories, which Brazil's poor encounter regularly. Working with the realities at hand, Dona Cici adapts stories and collaborates with Protestants, politicians, and foreigners to open pathways of understanding Bahia's Afro-descendent population. Through storytelling, which leans heavily on dance, music, and cultural memory, Dona Cici re-inscribes African Diasporic history, and gives Bahian children a narrative through which they can see themselves as clever participants in the challenging world around them. Her life as a storyteller took on a new dimension as she collaborated with others at the PVCS in a government-funded Griot Project, under the auspices of Pontos de Cultura (Cultural Hot Spots).[18]

Cultivating and encouraging Afro-Bahian memory are not tasks for the weak. Memory is not only of African myths and dances, but also, and quite importantly, of local history and the diverse experiences of Afro-Bahian lives. The Law No. 10.639,[19] which specified the "obligatory teaching of Afro-Brazilian and African cultures and histories at all grade levels as a fundamental part of the national curriculum,"[20] and was meant to encourage African-descendent and Afro-Bahian cultural and historical memory, has not met with the kind of successes its supporters envisioned.

Three Schools and the Griot Storytelling Project, Ação Griô

Dona Cici's work for PVCS as a griot at three local schools was part of a laudable effort, called Ação Griô or the Griot Storytelling Project, that situates Candomblé stories within a contemporary, local context. In my early visits (2006–10), the immediate possibilities were encouraging and Dona Cici was largely enthusiastic. However, in later visits (2011 and 2012), the circumstances were more of "life as usual," i.e., funds for programming were redirected; new leaders did not value African-descendent histories; and one school was temporarily closed in response to uncontrollable violence. Once again, Dona Cici emphasized a *pedagogia da realidade*, meaning she had to continue teaching without important resources, but with whatever she had. Her labor as a teacher in varied settings gives a telescopic lens into the empowering narratives (defiance and resistance through arts, dance, and education), which challenge Brazil's cemented and disempowering narratives (continued structural racism and derision via mass media), which impede the realization of a truly democratic and inclusive social situation.

A Escola Municipal Maria Quitéria, Escola Municipal Martagão Gesteira, and Grupo Escolar João XXIII are the three, very different schools where Dona Cici taught. The first school, named after Brazil's famous heroine, Maria Quitéria de Jesus (c. 1792–1853), who valiantly fought in the war of independence from Portugal (1821–25), is a pilot school, comparable to a US charter school. This school boasts of having been the first in Brazil to raise the flag to African culture. Education there includes all that is African – the countries, the heritages, and the continued cultural representations of the present, including Afro-Bahian history and culture. The school entrance has pictures of important African and African-descendent figures. With a combination of pride and humility, Dona Cici told me that her picture is included on that honorary wall. Many of the teachers in the school are black social activists who are dedicated to the rescue of African culture and history. Thus, Escola Maria Quitéria enacts a groundbreaking educational vision, creating a curriculum that is attentive to issues and histories of race, and integrating "special needs children" into their system. Structurally, it has computers and musical instruments; philosophically, it has unparalleled models through teachers who were once like the children they serve. The teachers have become educators through hard work, political and cultural commitment, and by valuing their particular ethnic and racial histories. Dona Cici affirms how much she loves to bring her stories and dance to this space of human potentiality.

The second school, Martagão Gesteira, does not have the benefits of sufficient funding or a focus on the African continent or Afro-Brazilian heritage. Despite being a poor school in a poor neighborhood, however, most of the children are blessed with calm households and supportive families, and are therefore "innocent" and joyful. Dona Cici uses the term "innocent" here, referring to the fact that they have not been directly exposed to violence and drugs in their immediate environments. Their parents are poor, hard-working people who do their best, and the children are safer for this. As Dona Cici talks about this school, her body relaxes; she smiles; and she confesses how much she appreciates working with this group. She remembers how the children's eyes opened wide when she told them the stories of Oxum or Iemanjá. They would jump up to move to the stories and the rhythms that are associated with each one. She would gather them, "[v]*amos dançar agora, vamos ser o personagem da história!*" ("Let's dance now, let's play the characters in the story!") (Cici 2008). As she says this, Dona Cici enthusiastically moves her body, as if getting up, and sweeping the children into a dance.

The third school, João XXIII, is a very different kind of institution also. The majority of the children in this institution "*Vivem com o tráfico de drogas*" ("They live in the context of the drug trade")(Cici 2008). Often, Dona Cici is warned not to go to the school when there are problems. Other times, the school is closed because of violence. When she does go up the hill to teach, participation in the storytelling and dance classes is uneven. The children who are involved in the drug trade, dress differently with thick, gold or silver chain necklaces and often feel that the class is below them, infantile. Other children are evangelical Christians who are not allowed to participate in any kind of African class because of their parents' belief that the African religious perspective comes from the devil, denying the principles of One God and the sacredness of the Ten Commandments. Dona Cici laments that "[a]s *crianças protestantes não aceitam a cultura afro-brasileira*" ("Protestant children do not accept Afro-Brazilian culture") (2008). In this context, she is very careful about how she recounts her stories.

First, she tells the Yoruba stories about relationships between parents and children, about daily human suffering and difficulty, and about the nefariousness within some human conduct. Some of these stories involve violence, but Dona Cici re-tells the stories differently. She knows that she should not upset children, especially with any kind of insinuation that the stories of violence are about them. She is also careful not to alienate the Protestant children. "*Lá o trabalho social é um trabalho aberto*" ("There, the social work is an open work") (2008). She always makes sure that her stories do not present conflict at home for the children. She suggests that their beliefs are correct, and that these are other stories of past times in the neighborhood, or in another place in Brazil.

Nonetheless, many children will not come to class because they have been scared off. They are terrified that the class might be a big Candomblé ceremony, which they view as a low-level African ritual that channels devil worship. (Dona Cici put her hand on her head when she talked about this.) Instead of insisting on Yoruba culture and memory, she presents fables. In effect, introducing history, she notes that in the nineteenth century *contos de assombração* or stories about animals were very popular. Such stories recalled life in Africa where co-existence with nature, the plants and animals, was a daily reality. Thus, Dona Cici does not only recount the stories of the *Orixás*, but also, the stories that fascinated enslaved children throughout history, helping the neighborhood children make sense of the world the African children occupied, very far away from the African countries of their origins.

Originally, the *contos de assombração* were passed down to Dona Cici from the elders, who lived in her childhood home and community. These fables recalled a specific time in the lives of enslaved peoples in Brazil. Dona Cici remembers that the elders even used a different language to tell them, as accents and grammar had not been changed by a mass media. When Dona Cici shares fables with the children, she is giving them history, and not religious training. The history she recounts runs in contradistinction to television programs, advertising, and general pop culture that inform the community. Still, she repeats that she wants the children to learn new stories without causing any conflict in their home lives. In effect, Dona Cici is engaging in foundational education, inviting the children to self-identify according to their new knowledge, which includes many African-derived experiences, in addition to their present-day reality.

Here I share one of Dona Cici's favorite stories (told to tour groups, children in different settings, and myself thrice in interviews over the span of five years, 2007–12). The tale of "*O gato e a onça*" ("The cat and the jaguar"), which exposes how knowledge is a tool to negotiate survival.

A cat who had lived for a long time among humans, returned to the bush. He found a good tree where he set up his house and put up a sign that announced, "*Mestre Gato, Professor de Capoeira*" (Master Cat, *Capoeira* [Brazilian martial art/combat dance/game] professor). The other animals in the community, such as the monkey, the parrot, and the alligator, all went to meet this new community member and to ask about this sign. *Mestre Gato* told them that *capoeira* was a martial art form and that it was danced to the sounds of the *berimbau* (an African origin percussion instrument that defines *capoeira* games and is the main instrument of *capoeira* music; it is made of a gourd, a long stick, and a wire). He played the *berimbau*: dim, dim, dom/dim, dim, dom/dim, dim, dim, dim, dim, dim, dim, dom/dim, dim, dom (the sounds of the *berimbau*). The rhythm was catchy and the jungle animals started the movements, back and forth, back and forth, jump, back and forth, back and forth, kick, crouch, kick, back and forth, back and forth (the basic moves of *capoeira*, called *ginga*). Then *Mestre Gato* told them that the lesson was done for the day. They were curious, and without a doubt would return, but the next day, *Comadre Onça*, Mrs. Jaguar, came to get lessons for herself.

Mestre Gato, an intelligent businessman, did not turn her away. He told her to come back the next morning for her lesson. She agreed. Then the jungle animals, who had been watching this interaction from the safety of a good distance, came out. They asked *Mestre Gato* if he was crazy. "She will return hungrier tomorrow and surely will eat you," they said. *Mestre Gato* simply gave his students a new lesson in movement and music, and Dona Cici made the sound of the *berimbau*: dim, dim, dom,/dim, dim, dom, etc. Mestre Gato, she said, told his pupils to *ginga*, the back and forth, jump, back and forth, crouch *capoeira* movements.

The next day, *Comadre Onça* returned for her first lesson. She was keeping up appearances and seemed polite enough. *Mestre Gato* showed her some jumps and some side way movements with her feet, all kept closely to the ground. After a few minutes, he told her that the lesson was done. She was surprised, "But *Mestre Gato* we have only just begun and I am getting the hang of it." The teacher responded that they were finished for the day because she was such a good student and had learned and performed very quickly. Again, as soon as she departed, the jungle animals came out from their safe viewing stations to question their teacher. "For sure," they warned, "she will come back tomorrow ravaged, and will eat you up with one bite."

At this point, *Mestre Gato* observed that they had been good students also and that they could join in for the lesson the next day. He assigned each community member a position, playing the *berimbau*, clapping, moving forward, backward, sideways, sideways, forward, backward, jumping. Initially, they were quite nervous. They did not want to be seen or eaten by the jaguar. But *Mestre Gato* convinced them that as a group, they had nothing to worry about. He gave them positions they would occupy for the class. They assented and got ready. The next morning, they were there early and ready for class. *Comadre Onça* arrived quite hungry. She looked around at the class and thought, "Oh, I will have lunch AND dessert today for sure." *Mestre Gato* started the class: dim, dim, dom/ dim, dim, dom. And the animals all moved defensively and smoothly. *Comadre Onça* looked over and saw her chance. The monkey was not moving quickly. She jumped high and strong, but as she was landing over him, with her mouth wide open, he jumped sideways suddenly – out of the way. She bit into the hard dirt and broke all of her teeth. With a mouth full of dirt and missing teeth, she complained, "Mestre Gato you did not show me the sideways move!!" And at that moment, she died from the impact of her fall. The jungle animals cheered, since they would not be in danger any more.

Dona Cici prolonged her story by singing the *berimbau* rhythms, looking around to ensure she had everyone's attention, clapping the rhythm and pace of the story, moving her arms and body to the swaying movements she was describing, and whispering or shouting when needed. She took time to reproduce the call and response style of *capoeira* songs and brought the story to life because she is an extremely agile storyteller. At this point, she told her thrilled students, "[i]t is as important to know who your enemy is to keep yourselves safe, as it is to work together" (Cici 2008). She looked at me and asked what the moral of the story might be. "*Se você é treinado na vida você sabe vencer os problemas....Agora, esse treinamento não é só de berimbau, é estudar, aprender a trabalhar, aprender a se conciliar com as pessoas*" ("If you have a good education in life, you will know how to resolve many of your problems. That training is not just about the *berimbau*; it is about studying, learning to work, and also to reconcile with those around you") (2008). She reminded me how often the jungle animals did not get along, but through the mastery and practice of *capoeira*, they became a close-knit group, one that was able to protect itself from the jaguar, and make the community a safe place to live. As in all of the other socio-political instances we had been discussing, it was those who desired to educate that needed to be creative and flexible, so that many different circumstances could thus be tackled. The trick is not only to survive, but to thrive in an honest and responsible manner.

The education Dona Cici talks about is founded in alternative strategies for learning and teaching, which depend on *capoeira* and storytelling. The reality in which she teaches rarely relies on official backing. Her backing, and that of other such teachers, is in their own communities; they draw from their communal knowledge passed down as memories and stories, not from what they have been taught in schools or in their educational training. In fact, while the Law No. 11.645/2008 requires teaching African heritage and both Afro-Brazilian and Brazilian indigenous histories, it is applied only to K-12 pedagogy. The lack of an official curriculum for university levels means that there are so far, no officially trained professors to teach this required material. A veritable critique lies in the fact that the law requires inclusion of a history that is not taught in higher education, where the K-12 teachers receive their training.

In brief, although a school like Escola Maria Quitéria exists, teaching African heritage in the national school system at present is a real challenge. Dona Cici observes that, "...*é uma barreira muito forte no Brasil se falar de negro. E uma coisa que ninguém gosta, ninguém quer*" ("...there is a huge barrier to talking about blacks. Nobody likes to, nobody wants to") (2008). In 2011, Dona Cici lamented that the work at three schools that she had so enthusiastically talked about just a year earlier had been "suspended." In a new series of interviews, she focused on the shift in school ideology, which reflected changes in the political climate and could be felt even in the main Afro-Bahian tourist district, Pelourinho. She noted, "*Infelizmente, a escola pública tem problemas...[os] maiores são políticos. Quando muda a política, muda toda a estrutura*" ("Unfortunately, public schools have major problems that are political.... When the politics change, the entire structure changes") (2011).

At the time of my research, the mayor of Salvador, João Henrique Carneiro, like the new leadership within the elementary and secondary school system, was Protestant. Despite a national law insisting on the teachings of Afro-Bahian heritage, the new administration throughout the primary and secondary school system systematically withdrew Afro-Brazilian heritage and culture from the curriculum. This entailed replacing teachers that were teaching anything related to African and/or Afro-Bahian culture with others from the Protestant population. Dona Cici explained the absurdity of this situation, observing that everything in Bahia is syncretic in some way or another. She points out that even the Evangelical Church has African influences within its practices; some congregations include call and response singing, shouting and feeling the Holy Spirit in bodily movement, and instrumental accompaniment that accentuates rhythm and percussion over melody and harmony. She also mentioned Protestant Bishop Macedo, who borrowed from much of what is otherwise Candomblé practice, including an emphasis on symbolic colors and congregational singing, for his Christian services. While he focused on Jesus, his language and practice were not solely European, but rather African-inspired practices as well. Many in his congregation were practitioners of different Afro-Bahian religions and have consequently found a new home with familiar practices in his church.[21]

Nonetheless, all of the *mestres populares*, the local teachers, have lost their jobs. References to the history of Africans and their contributions, or to festivals honoring local popular culture were being systematically erased. For example, the Escola Maria Quitéria removed the picture exhibition that honored important Afro-Bahian figures (including Dona Cici) and dispersed the artisanal display of clay jugs from the Recôncavo (the rural outskirts of the city), which were believed to be the first earthenware objects made by enslaved Africans in Bahia. The removal of these honorary displays sent the tacit message that this history was once again being erased, or in the very least, that it did not deserve such a prominent place in the halls of that educational institution.

New budget cuts impacted the Griot Project, which was disbanded, forcing storytellers, dance professionals, percussionists, and social workers to volunteer their time, if their community work was to continue. The minimal funding Dona Cici received to help her travel to the schools was suspended. One of the other schools was closed for "*renovations*" (Cici 2011, original emphasis). Renovations were not the ones most people would expect, like painting or adding space. Instead, the administration was putting in gates and higher walls to protect buildings from vandalism. The state had created programs to feed children while in school, but the storage areas and the kitchens were being raided at night and over the weekends. Also, some children were bringing in weapons to steal from weaker children. The renovations meant that dollars for programs were being funneled into gates, walls, and surveillance systems to keep the school property safe, while the state program to feed the children so they could focus and study was being torn apart.

Dona Cici sighed after detailing the most recent turn of events, challenging the exciting projects that had barely begun to make a difference. She repeated, yet again, that to survive these circumstances "[w]e all have to know how to be clever, with creative flexibility." During an interview around that time, her focus was on surviving and thriving despite the recurrent impasses:

In Bahia, we all have to have a way or a knack for doing things; it is all about the *jogo de cintura*." You just improvise as needed, "from the waist," to stay afloat, not fall or fail. Life has to be imagined as a game because the harshness of the set-backs would otherwise depress anyone. And there is no time or place for depression (2011).

Historically in Bahia, social and educational programs get a certain amount of funding from the government that almost always dries up before real changes can be established. Having a place like the PVCS to belong to is life-saving. It serves as a consistent space of possibility and resilience, in which important work can continue, on both a volunteer and paid basis, within and outside of the registers of the state and cultural projects of the moment.

Dona Cici's ancestral gift as a storyteller and *Orixá* movement teacher allows her to cultivate Afro-Bahian memory, which has important consequences. Through the Candomblé dances, the *Orixá* stories, and the use of *ginga* from *capoeira* as a concept for survival and negotiation, she gives her students critical tools with which to survive as a community and thrive as individuals.

Dignity through Dance

While much has been written about the kinds of negotiations Dona Cici uses under the rubric of *pedagogia da realidade*, for example in theories of education, music, and theater (see Freire [1970] 2012; Boal 1985; hooks 1994; Giroux 2001; Sommer 2014), the socio-political work and history of Afro-Bahian dance, and the dancers that have cultivated it in Bahia, remain almost non-existent.[22] Besides pleasure and entertainment, dance in Bahia serves two critical politico-historical roles: (1) as resistance from oppression and historical erasure and (2) as a multipronged strategy for survival.

Anthropologist Ruth Landes' book *The City of Women* ([1947] 1994), exposed dance as a central tenet of respite and cultural survival in Bahia.[23] Her text underscored a situation that holds true today, 70 years later: African-related traditions and practices in Bahia continue to be fraught between remembrance and forgetting, honoring African heritage and assimilating to Brazil's larger visions of modernization, salvaging of memory by the elders and disparagement of this memory by local circumstances (repression from government and police, dramatized violence).

Succinctly and considerately, Landes related the lives of the stevedores, for example, who had been able to squeeze out a living and gain respect through the unions; then she explained how the repression of dictator/President Getulio Vargas's government dismantled the unions and Afro-Brazilian lives became more abject. Landes arrived in Brazil during a time that was especially challenging for a single woman doing research; it was at the brink of the Second World War. She experienced racism and sexism. At that time, women did not stay at a hotel alone unless they were the prostitutes of high officials. In addition, secret government agents, who suspected that Landes was a spy, kept her under watch. Despite these obstacles, she was able to connect to folklorist and journalist Edison Carneiro, who helped her enter important Candomblé communities.

Landes' book pointed to the negotiations the urban poor had to continuously engage, to dodge the hostility of the police and the state (which raided Candomblé houses/temples and closed down unions, etc.). She observed how poverty did not preclude dignity and how the Candomblé *terreiros* were sites of integrity, offering an alternative and safe space of memory and community for their members. She also noted that highly respected African-descendent elders (such as Mãe Meninha [child of enslaved grandparents, and *ialorixá*, head priestess at Gantois *terreiro*] and Martiniano [a Candomblé priest or *babalorixá*, who underwent training as an Ifá diviner in Lagos, Nigeria,]) "found it terrible that the new generations did not care much about cult practices, and that present-day standards for these practices were being lowered and weakened." (Cole in Landes [1947] 1994: 23). Additionally, Landes reported that at the time of her investigations, traditional rituals that kept sacred dances alive were being challenged by contemporary social dances such as the *foxtrot*.

Regardless of the genre or style, dance was an integral part of Afro-Bahian lives, offering the urban poor a respite from daily harshness and a venue for community and pleasure. Landes dedicated several chapters to her thoughts on dance, and quotes one of her informants as he described the importance of dance in Afro-Bahian society: "… hard labor keeps us strong, and hard fun keeps us young. In Bahia everything is glorious! … The splendor of Brazil lies in the path of the drum. So, let us dance!" (Cole in Landes [1947] 1994: 70). She also quoted her friend and lover, Edison Carneiro, when he declared the pivotal role of dance among African descendants:[24] "Their dancing is like living: it is their avenue of comprehension and response, it is their mode of thinking, their way of conversing" (Landes [1947] 1994: 201). She continued by describing how "each god dances a certain way, and a priestess must learn this or the god won't feel at home. Yoruba teaches it one way, Angola another, and Caboclo differently again. Of course, the woman's temperament can't help but coming through" (Landes [1947] 1994: 204). Her informants ensured that she understood that there are several African nations well represented and remembered in Bahia and each one has particular ways of worshipping; further, at the time, many were in some way linked to the Catholic Church.

Thus, Landes concluded that dance has a special place in Afro-Bahian lives; it represents survival in its basest form; dance amongst the urban poor was a venue for spiritual and cultural survival and it continues to be so. However, I argue that, in addition, dance represents education, paid work, and social mobility for those who learn to dance and cultivate dancing lives in Bahia (see Suárez 2013). The following are stories of danced dignity, which give us brief case studies of how a sense of genuine citizenship and inclusion occurs through the work of dance.

Negrizú

A brief case study of Negrizú (Carlos Pereira dos Santos), teacher and performer at PVCS, allows a view of citizenship and inclusion through dance. Born in 1959, Negrizú recounts his poor childhood in the neighborhood of Federação, which is similar to Engenho Velho de Brotas, where PVCS is today. He often repeats, "…*essa dança que me traz como autodidata, ela tinha ainda mais surpresas para mim*" ("…that dance that I learned myself, brought me many surprises") (Negrizú 2010). When I asked him if he danced the traditional dances of the *Orixás*, his response was not what I had expected. He said that he was influenced by pop music from the United States, such as James Brown, Michael Jackson, and Donna Summer. With solemn humility, he answered, "[e]*u sou dançarino, eu não sou filho de santo. A técnica, até certo ponto, é educacão que é democratizante*" ("I am a dancer and not the child/initiate of any saint. Technique, to a certain point, is education, which is democratizing") (2010). Negrizú danced because it made him feel that he had something that was his; because others applauded his energy and opened doors to him; because he was handsome, muscular, and very creative. Dancing gave him joy, a sense of self-worth and apparently, he had had no connection to a Candomblé house.

His story is one that connects him closely to the children he teaches at PVCS. Just like them, he did not grow up in a religious community. He does remember that, as a child and teenager, he would go to family parties and dance, which allowed him to forget his worries. He noticed that everyone loved to watch him dance and his passion for dance grew. This experience elevated his self-esteem. He tells his young students that doors were opened to him because of this passion and his passion for dance led him finally to discover the world of the *Orixás*.

In 1974, Negrizú turned his attention to issues of ancestrality through his participation in Ilê Aiyê, the revolutionary Carnival *bloco afro* of Bahia (a community of people connected by African-based dances, rhythms, and traditions, which celebrates African and African-descendent culture). He emphasized that it was not until 1979, when the group Afoxé Badauê was founded in Engenho Velho de Brotas, that he began to dedicate his energies to a memory/tradition of African heritage. It was neither memory nor tradition, but rather a personal quest for a better place in life that led Negrizú to embrace the politics of the 1970s, especially Brazilian soul power translated from the United States to Rio de Janeiro. This, in turn, led him to discover his ancestral history.

In 1983, he met Verger and they established a life-long friendship. He learned French and was able to read Verger's works both in French and Portuguese. Negrizú's eyes sparkled when he talked about the discovery of a history that to date is not taught in earnest in Brazilian schools or talked about in the media. He was able to make his dream of visiting Africa a reality when he accompanied his honored teacher, Verger, to Benin toward the end of his life. More recently, alongside his colleague, Dona Cici, he was one of the participants in the Griot Project or Ação Griô, which gathered storytellers, dancers, and musicians to teach African and Afro-Bahian culture.

Negrizú recognizes how he represented African-ness aesthetically throughout his career, and that he was at the right places at the right time. As anthropologist Patricia de Santana Pinho notes, "[t]he black body, weighted with an African-ness previously taken as negative, backwards, and associated with ugliness and filth, has been invested with an African-ness resignified to instill pride and beauty. This way, Africa is *reinscribed* onto the body" (de Santana Pinho 2010: 9, original emphasis). Negrizú's looks, his movements, and his hunger for work, travel, and possibility won him prominent, public roles in Rio de Janeiro and Bahia. For example, in the 1988 Carnival (which celebrated the centenary of the abolition of slavery in Brazil), he performed the character of Obá Dudú, an African king. Organized by Bahian poet Wally Salamão, Obá Dudú represented the *rei dos negros*, King of the blacks in homage to Africa.[25]

In an interview in the newspaper *O Globo*, Negrizú was featured as a dancer who promoted Afro-dancing (his own version of dance performance, which combines African, Afro-Bahian, and popular dance styles) in the flying circus.[26] The interview further underscored how he combines the dances of the *Orixás* with other movement vocabulary. Negrizú's conceptualization of identity is shaped by his looks, which affirm his genetic ancestry; but he makes it very clear that his connection to ancestral history occurred thanks to the social and political work of the *blocos afro*, and the Soul Power Movement in Rio. His commitment has

Figure 9: Negrizú. Photograph by Christian Cravo, courtesy of Lucía M. Suárez archive.

equally focused on the research, writing and dissemination of the writings of Pierre Verger. Negrizú's life trajectory makes his story a powerful example of citizenship through dance. That is, he is able to be an active member of civil society through dance performance and teaching, shifting his socio-economic status through African-descendent dance as valued cultural capital.

Notably also, Negrizú performed the role of Exú[27] in the 1990 miniseries *Mãe de Santo*.[28] While the series was severely criticized for its inaccurate representation of Candomblé and its *Orixás*, several activists saw the series in a socially positive light. Antônio Angelo Pereira, the president of the Society of São Jorge in Bahia, noted that while the Bahian Candomblé was not accurately represented per se, some of the rituals could be correct in other African-derived practices, such as Umbanda and Quimbanda in Rio de Janeiro. He defended the script's author, Paulo Cesar Coutinho, on the merit of at least representing African religion in the main stream. Ana Célia da Silva, a militant of the Black Movement in Bahia, who completed her master's thesis about stereotypes and prejudices of blacks in educational texts in the School of Education of UFBA, also commended the series because it was important for Afro-Brazilians. In particular, she was pleased to see main acting roles given to black actors; they were thus not relegated to the usual roles of domestic servants or criminals. She admitted not being a specialist of the Candomblé, but asserted that, "[c]omo militante do movimento negro, acho que a série é importante porque tenta resgatar a identidade e valoriza *a cultura negra*" ("As a militant of the black movement, I think that the series is important because it attempts to redeem and value black identity and culture").[29]

Still at issue was the question of how to value cultural programming, the representation of Afro-Bahian religious culture, and what this meant for the bodies that found visibility through this national venue. In the summer of 2010, I interviewed Negrizú about the sixteen episodes. He was proud to have portrayed this *Orixá* and lauded the series for its massive dissemination of religious information. He was not as concerned about the accuracy of the representation; instead he, like activist Ana Célia da Silva, commended the constructive space this series offered to black actors and dancers. In social terms, the series gave positive exposure to black performers. On a personal level, the series offered him a role, a job, even if it was because his looks satisfied a certain aesthetic expectation. His career benefited, and few actors would say no to work especially in a national production. Perhaps we can interpret that he felt that his representation of Exú was true to his vision, regardless of the larger representational concerns in the film. Exú is known for acting different parts; Negrizú, as a dancer and actor, like this significant *Orixá*, employed well his ability to wear many hats and thrive. Employment for actors and dancers is shaped by the possibilities at hand, and the negotiations they can craftily manage; Negrizú was able to negotiate between learning, representation, and employment. Embodying the character of Exú presented him with a new pathway to his own process of continuing discovery and agency. It is important to note that Negrizú did not stay stuck in a character role; he used that experience to advance his career as a choreographer and teacher inventing his own style, reframing, on his terms, the meaning of acrobatics, dance, and performance.

From my observations, Negrizú's classes at the PVCS are enthusiastically attended. This may have to do with the fact that Negrizú is a living example of the potential every child in that space has, and the successes they, too, can attain. In the dance classes, they may be rescued from the violence of the streets; and through movement and technical body demands, they are taught discipline, which they can apply to education and work in other areas. Most importantly, they are being asked to see themselves as valuable individuals in the world. Many Bahian dancers, teachers, and choreographers, whom I have interviewed, such as Rosângela Silvestre and Luiz Badaró, have come from very humble backgrounds, and have experienced poverty, even homelessness. In each case, they credit dance as a life-saving practice.

Luiz Badaró

Similarly to Negrizú's life experiences, Luiz Badaró has also danced his way into citizenship and cultural agency. Although he was orphaned at the age of thirteen, training in *capoeira*, folklore, and dance kept him engaged in art forms that have defined his life.

Badaró learned *capoeira*, the Afro-Brazilian dance/fight/game of bodily combat, as a child in his Garcia neighborhood within Mestre Bandu's backyard *capoeira* academy.[30] With this early and strong beginning, he excelled and was later able to teach the main combat dances of Brazil: *capoeira* and *maculelê*, the Afro-Brazilian stick-fighting dance from the agricultural part of Bahia State. Badaró was also introduced to a teacher at Colégio de São Jorge, professora Aldemira Conceição, who was connected to the Candomblé traditions. Badaró continues to thank her for his grand history lessons about Brazilian culture and for amplifying his folkloric knowledge to include more northeastern folk dances than his own from Bahia, such as *maracatu*. Eventually, Badaró taught *Orixá*/Candomblé dances, *capoeira*, and *maculelê* at the Colégio São Jorge. In addition, his uncle, Raimundo José Badaró, who had participated in SESC's dance group, O Grupo Balu, introduced Badaró to Mestre King (Raimundo Bispo dos Santos, the "father of Afro-Brazilian dance"). Badaró credits his career to these three formidable teachers, Mestre Bandu for his foundations in *capoeira*, professora Conceição who taught him history and culture, and Mestre King who taught him dance technique and the music and dances of the *Orixás*.

During the 1960s and 1970s, during Folklore Week in August, *Bahiatursa* sponsored student games (*os jogos estudantis*) where each school performed folkloric dances (combinations of African, Indigenous, and Portuguese community dances). The best school groups would compete in the National Student Games, representing their respective States in the national capital, Brasilia. Schools such as Colégio São Jorge and the Colégio Estadual Duque de Caxias became feeder schools for dancers that went on to having extensive performing careers locally (in dinner theaters, for example), nationally and internationally (in spectacles featuring Bahia as a site of Brazilian energy and uniqueness). Ironically, without giving poor people equity, the tourist boom that was cultivated from the 1960s to the 1980s, which depended heavily on folklore and dance spectacles, opened many doors to numerous young people from otherwise marginal and/or poor neighborhoods. While the shows themselves paid poorly, they were an ideal platform from which to gain professional experience.

When these performers traveled internationally, they were able to gain better wages. Through work in folklore shows, these energetic youngsters gained consumer agency (they could buy things for their families) and cultural capital (dependent on racially and ethnically marked bodies dancing "authentic" rhythms and traditions), and came to understand their own value in economic terms. Badaró and many others of his generation found work as performers and created their own folkloric companies. Consequently, they became cultural ambassadors and teachers in other countries, which welcomed their historical, cultural, and aesthetic knowledge. While the nation state was appropriating local culture, those inherently from the local culture, inadvertently, were becoming visible national and global citizens.

Badaró was employed dancing local specialties, while also fulfilling the tourist need for "performed authenticity."[31] He worked in numerous dinner theaters, such as Moenda, Tenda dos Milagres, and Restaurante Alto de Ondina, where the shows included dance performances by *mulatas* (women of mixed race), staged Candomblé dances, theatrical dance pieces depicting fishermen pushing/pulling their nets, and *cafezal*, a harvest festival dance recalling and honoring the hard labor endured in the harvesting of coffee.[32] The memory of local culture and its bearers during the height of tourism was a *bona fide* commercial enterprise. Travel agent owners (such as Claudio Maia, for example) also owned restaurants that featured these dances.

The same dances were taught at local schools and community centers. Badaró taught dance and *capoeira* at the Urban Community Center in Liberdade (Centro Social Urbano da Liberdade), which received limited state funding from diverse sources.[33] Since there was ample work available for this kind of representation, he formed his own company, Urban Group from Liberdade (Grupo Urbano da Liberdade). During a tour performance in São Paulo, Zezé Motta, Brazil's most important black actress, claimed that his company had *muito axé,* a lot of energy. Badaró immediately understood the appeal inherent in such an endorsement and he changed his company's name to Bahia Axé Bahia and performed lucratively for twenty years.[34]

Again, reminiscent of Dona Cici's focus on *pedagogia da realidade,* the disempowering, dominant discourse, which maintains that the mostly darker skinned and black peoples are less valuable, is defied by the artistry and sophisticated training presented by Negrizú and Badaró – just two of many Afro-Bahian cultural dance agents. In Bahia, dance is education, through community programming, collaborations with dancers, choreographers, dance anthropologists, cultural theorists, and via major performance venues. Yet, because of the strains of dance on the body, and the fact that it does not bring the kinds of mega profits that internationally acclaimed music (*samba, reggae*) does, it is also understood as an ephemeral pedagogical resource that has not been appreciated as much as it merits. From interstitial spaces (ritual, concert stage, and dance parties), dance allows individuals to belong to, and negotiate many spaces (international stages, community programming, roots tourism, Afro-Bahian dance groups, including dancers who return to teach their national and international experiences); these teaching and performing spaces involve both the local and global levels. Such negotiations exemplify *pedagogia da realidade,* i.e., whatever the circumstances, there is a will and a way to teach, and learn, about African and Afro-Bahian cultural legacies. As Jamaican scholar and choreographer, Sir Rex Nettleford has stated:

> The on-going study of African cultural heritage (as is here being done with dance – itself a powerful dimension of that heritage), is therefore a necessary and vital imperative for the continuing struggle for human dignity and cultural certitude of the millions across the globe who actually make up two-thirds of the world but who are otherwise known as people of the Third World.
>
> (1994: xvi)[35]

Resisting Racism

The struggle for inclusion of African cultural heritage and African-descendent peoples in Brazil is a long and arduous one. As theater and performance studies scholar Denise Corte sums up, "[t]he unique capacity of Brazilian society to combine political repression and co-optation with a culturally sophisticated denial of racial conflict has always made the development of black oppositional currents very difficult" (in Sommer 2006: 203). While full-fledged black

Figure 10: Dance class at *escola de dança*, FUNCEB. Photograph by Christian Cravo, courtesy of Lucía M. Suárez archive.

oppositional organization has not experienced huge success in Brazil, it is necessary to mention the groundbreaking work of the *blocos afro* in creating spaces of community and black inclusions into the national image; however, the denial of racial prejudice is evidenced by how Afro-Brazilian performance is celebrated while its people are regularly marginalized.[36]

Despite the visible work of dance cultural agents, leaning on dance as an alternative model for education, Afro-Bahian dance and its dancers have experienced a continued history of disparagement. For example, the dance department at UFBA did not officially include African and Afro-Bahian dance in the curriculum until recently because it viewed such dance as "primitive," undisciplined, and easy (as in something learned in the streets with no real value). Thanks to decades-long insistence of the Afro-Bahian dance community, this situation received redress in 2016, when official professorial positions were announced at UFBA. A national search was held to fill two positions with specialization in popular, Indigenous, and Afro-Brazilian dance (*Estudos do corpo com ênfase em danças populares, indígenas e Afro-Brasileiras*). In June, the winners of these posts were announced: first place, Marilza Oliveira da Silva, second place, Vania Silva Oliveira, third place, Fernando Marques Camargo Ferraz, and fourth place, Denilson Francisco das Neves. Vania Oliveira chose to stay at her home institution and an extra position was funded. Thus, UFBA's School of Dance has welcomed a stellar team of three new professors specializing in local, Indigenous, and Afro-Brazilian dance forms.

This critical shift rejects a long, ingrained history of racism. For example, artist and set designer J. Cunha (José Antônio), who traveled with Viva Bahia, recalls how, while on tour, the dancers were exempted from the elegant dinners and kept in separate sections from the audiences and the wealthy performance aficionados.[37] He underscored how their dances were seen as inferior to ballet; and he remembered how, on international tours, the dancers would be approached as exotic, sexual objects rather than well-trained, sophisticated artists.[38]

In fact, African and Afro-Brazilian dance arts engage strenuous training and ethical commitment. This is affirmed by the legacies of three early African-descendent representatives of African Diaspora dance traditions: Katherine Dunham, Mercedes Baptista, and Pearl Primus. It is further evidenced by the leading work of teachers, such as Mestre King, who, over the course of 40 years, trained many of Bahia's most successful dancers through a state sponsored program Social Service Center of Commerce (SESC, Serviço Social do Comércio). Additionally, the welcomed work of African American dancer, teacher, and choreographer, Clyde Alafiju Morgan also intervenes in this respect. He taught at the School of Dance in UFBA and directed its dance group, Grupo de Dança Contemporánea, from 1971 to 1978, combining José Limon technique and his research experience from travelling west to east on the African continent, exchanging traditional dances for modern dance technique (e.g., from Senegal and Liberia to Ghana and Nigeria, to Kenya and Uganda, etc.).[39] Specifically at UFBA, he featured Afro-Bahian performances of ritual dances (which are not actual rituals, but dance performances shaped respectfully by ritual origin movements), inviting men to be part of his celebrated performances.[40] Similarly, Walson Botelho, the director, and José Carlos Arandiba, the artistic director, of Balé Folclórico da Bahia ensure that their dancers have the best training, bringing both the energy of the streets they come from and the skills from rigorous dance classes they must master onto the stage.[41]

Dance technique, practice, and performance experiences can catapult an individual from isolation to a large, unified community. Dancers, dance teachers, activists and choreographers in Bahia (this includes Bahians and Bahian-connected foreigners who are dedicated to this art form and history) create critical networks of possibility, within the *pedagogia da realidade*, and foster Afro-Bahian knowledge and ancestral connections. The creative and flexible communities shaped by African Diaspora and Afro-Brazilian dance generate multiplying, active spaces of dialogue, connect multiple stories, honor memory, and further value black lives.

Afro-Bahian Traditions in Translation

As the most evident embodiment of African rhythms, staged performances of the dances of the *Orixás*, accompanied by drums and unmatched vocals, advertise Bahia as a haven of memory and tradition, and also of authenticity. Bahia is a geographic site that makes possible many circles of collaboration, of which I have already introduced a few in this essay. However, an obvious question haunts all quests for origins and memory in the New World context: how can a colonial space, based on exploitation and shaped by layers of national cultures and races, harbor authenticity? Which of many traditions survive? How are foundational stories and memories cultivated, translated, and re-formed? With respect to Candomblé, anthropologist J. Lorand Matory offers a useful, and logical, clarification to the expectations of authenticity that weigh on memory and studies of cultural continuity:

> Candomblé is a field site defined not by its closure or its internal homogeneity but by the diversity of its connections to classes and places that are often far away. At the root of this diversity is the universally human capacity of worshippers to imagine their belonging in multiple communities that crosscut any given community, encompass it, or even distinguish [it].... Candomblé and other similarly African-inspired African-American practices provide perhaps the best proof that broadly translocal and cosmopolitan fields of migration, commerce, and communication are the normal conditions of human culture and its reproduction.
>
> (Matory 2005: 267)

> *... it is less places than translocal dialogues that produce cultural self-representations, which, throughout history, have been occasions of collective self-making.*
>
> (Matory 2005: 268, emphasis added)

Matory convincingly makes the case that African-originated practices have actually "flourished in urban areas and among prosperous populations that, through travel, commerce, and literacy, were well exposed to cultural Others" (2005: 267). As an example, he shows how it is that many of the religion's leaders, priests, and priestesses, were well traveled, stating that for them religion "was as much commercial as it was spiritual." He quotes the work of Joseph Roach who also "cites numerous traditions in which Europeans, Africans, and Native Americans have mimed each other in theatrical performances and thus hybridized, reinvented, and clarified their own ethnic identities in a circum-Atlantic 'interculture'" (Matory 2005: 272). This dynamic of spiritual practices and commercial exchanges studied by Matory and Roach is applicable to the present day cultural survival of Afro-Bahian traditions.

Arguably, and historically, this dynamic re-invention, translation, and thus cultural survival was facilitated first by dance companies and touring troupes, such as Viva Bahia and Bahia Magia. Their performances had been sponsored by the Ministry of Tourism expressly to highlight Bahia's unique Afro-historical and ethnic cultures and attract tourists, i.e., to build the tourist economy with which we are familiar today. Director Emília Biancardi called the early performances "basic rice and beans shows" that featured folkloric staples such as *maculelê*, *capoeira*, the *puxada de rede* (a folkloric dance that honored the fishermen and their fishing nets), *samba de roda* (a popular, versatile Afro-Brazilian dance, usually danced in a circle and recognized as the origin version of many *samba* variations), and a *xirê* (a ceremonial series of Candomblé *Orixá* dances). Many other dance companies have followed suit, creating a veritable commerce of spectacular performances, based on translated African traditions. These international spectacles opened numerous pathways for relationships amongst choreographers, dancers, and musicians, who worked collaboratively through theater, dance companies, and educational programs.

The translocal dialogues that have ensued, I argue, are exemplarily engaged by the Los Angeles based, Bahia informed, multiracial and multicultural Viver Brasil Dance Company (Viver Brasil).[42] A perusal of their performance programs introduces a who's who of Bahia's dance agents, culture bearers, intellectuals, musicians, and activists from the Pierre Verger Foundation, Balé Folclórico da Bahia, the Dance Department of UFBA, and the State Dance School in Pelourinho, among others. These programs offer detailed legends, word descriptions, and interpersonal stories that render any Viver Brasil spectacle a cultural experience of recuperation and translation. For example, the program notes for the 2003 performance of *Legends of Brazil*, "honor the rich cultural fusion of the Brazilian people," including "Indígena" (Indigenous), "Portuguese," "Africa," and "Caboclo" (the Brazilian name, which refers to the fusion of Indigenous, African and Portuguese) (Ford Amphitheatre 2004). Founded in 1997 by Brazilian master dancer and choreographer Luiz Badaró, and Jewish-American dancer and ethnographer Linda Yudin, Viver Brasil performs "Bahian exuberance" and exposes the complexities and successes of collective self-making. Interviews with the co-directors further reveal that the Afro-Bahian memory they honor through choreography and performance is the result of human resilience and strategic negotiations about presenting blackness, as well as a sincere devotion to the knowledge of African, Northeastern Brazilian, Indigenous, and Afro-Bahian cultural heritage.

Work for dance troupes and companies might have been readily available in the 1970s and 1980s, but by the 1990s, a decline in Bahian tourism meant local employment shortages.

(There was new tourism competition from other countries such as Cuba.) When Luiz Badaró's Axé Bahia Axé performed in the Paris based *Circus Archaos* (1990–93), only four of the eighteen original company members returned to Bahia, choosing employment in Europe. A trans-Atlantic trade of dance and performance remains one of the strongest components of Afro-Bahian memory.

This "trade," so to speak, is at the center of new models of survival for Afro-Bahian culture. For example, after seeing a performance of the *Orixás* by Bahia Magia (marketed in the United States as Brasil Tropical) at the Hotel Meridien in Irvine, California, 1986, Linda Yudin decided that she had to discover this world. She was one of a handful of US Americans to study Afro-Bahian dance in Bahia. Not unlike Pierre Verger, the rest of her life has been devoted to studying, teaching, and connecting the stories and dances of the *Orixás* and Bahia's extensive black culture. For her first year in Bahia, she lived with hostesses Renilda Flores da Silva and Rita Cassia da Silva, who were the directors of Bahia Magia. Although she initially went to research and write her Master's theses on Filhos de Gandhy, the construction of an *afoxé*[43] group in *Carnaval* and how that was a microcosm of Afro-Brazilian life in Bahia, she eventually became a student of Mestre King and developed a new dance company rooted in Bahian dance traditions with Badaró (whom I introduced earlier).

Together, Badaró's and Yudin's artistic innovation within Viver Brasil honors and cultivates a legacy of stories, connections, and networks between Bahia and Los Angeles, therefore establishing a living bridge between these two cities. Yudin emphasizes that the work they create gives voice to both Bahian and US American choreographers and composers. These collaborations form the artistic basis of their work. The company's initial repertoire included folkloric choreographies created by Badaró. By 2003, Rosângela Silvestre began to train and choreograph for the company and in 2014, Vera Passos, a former principal dancer with the Balé Folclórico da Bahia and a protégé of Silvestre, began training the company. Viver Brasil's US company members: Dani Lunn, Katiana Pallais, and Shelby Williams-Gonzalez were the first company members to create choreography for the company. Through a series of enterprises that include concert dance, community engagement, arts education and an international cultural immersion program to Bahia, the connections and collaborations that they facilitate keep Bahia's traditions alive, even when everything in Bahia has changed dramatically.

In an interview in 2009, Badaró revealed that his favorite choreography was *Lagoa de Abaeté* ("Abaeté Lagoon"), and was based on a famous legend.[44] As a child, he heard stories of the "*lavadeiras*" ("washer-women") that worked all day at the Abaeté Lagoon. Through these accounts, he witnessed the rare magic that only occurs in Bahia, and in Jorge Amado's texts. In particular, there was the story of a fisherman who had fallen in love with a siren named Iara. This siren, it seems, fell in love with him too, as he was the only fisherman who would come back alive from a mass drowning in the lake. Numerous versions of this story have developed over the years, and the Abaeté Lagoon is both a tourist bus stop on the way to a turtle reserve at Praia do Forte and a well-known site for muggings for those who are not careful and romantically wander into the darker, wooded sections. According to Badaró's memory, the lake was huge and the community of washer-women was enchanting;

they had developed their own dances, which were rooted in African rhythms. While he explains that the legend is primarily of Indigenous origin from the Tupi and the Guarani, the washer-women's *samba de roda* was a unique non-commercial dance that included local flavor from interior regions and African movements. For a period of time in the 1980s, there was a dance group formed by some of the washer-women, known as the Lavadeiras que Sambavam ("*Samba* Dancing Washer-Women").

Badaró's staged choreography pays homage to these women, and to this space. He recalled the site as luscious, the lagoon as huge and deep, and scenes of many people fishing while the women washed. His choreography is rich in the color, costumes, and music of his memories. Oxum, the goddess of the rivers, dances seductively and morphs into Iara. The fishermen dance energetically as the stage is filled with *lavadeiras*, all working hard, and dancing enthusiastically. As I watched a filming of the performance, I recalled the observations of Edison Carneiro (the Brazilian ethnographer noted earlier) that dancing is like living, since the performance underscored the parallels between the hard work of washing and the ecstatic relief found in dance and myth.

After viewing the piece and talking at length about it in Los Angeles, Badaró met with me in 2011 in Bahia on a private tour of this spectacular site. It had been almost 40 years since he had last been there. The lake had receded, and the washer-women had been evacuated. The town officials deemed washing laundry there un-hygienic and the *sambas de roda* as dangerous and violent. The lake glimmered in the sun. The small shore-line exposed dead fish, and I couldn't imagine fishermen drowning there, as it seemed so shallow. There were two washer-women on the site, and Badaró asked them all kinds of questions. He was shocked; he had wanted to revisit the lagoon of his memories, not the landscape in view.

I found their stories fascinating as they seemed to want the attention and came up with stories that were even more spectacular than the original ones. Big strong men still drown in there, they swore, and the violence that now afflicts the area is just dreadful; they shook their heads. But yes, their mothers, and their mothers before them, had done their laundry there. It was a tradition that was no longer an option for them.

There were fences keeping the area separated from the museum next door. The women felt excluded, forgotten, and robbed of their communities. "Where had everyone gone?," Badaró asked. They shrugged, "[m]any people are dead now, and others are in the drug trade." One of the women lamented, "[t]hat is the only business left to us." The two women shared their stories of loss and violence. What remained were echoes of a life of survival through washing and dancing erased by the economics of the drug trade. Thus, the myth of the Abaeté Lake endures in history only through choreography.

Collaboratively, Viver Brasil's cultural enterprises facilitate a twenty-first century process of collective self-making, with communities rooted in African Diaspora and Afro-Bahian traditions and the arts, transcending national borders and linguistic limitations. Yudin observes that Viver Brasil thrives because it is founded on respectful relationships, honoring Bahians, extending their knowledge to other communities, cultivating the creative voices

Figure 11: *Lagoa de Abaeté* (lavadeiras/washer-women), Luiz Badaró. Photograph by and courtesy of Jorge Vismara.

of the American company members and bringing students of dance and culture to Bahia regularly. For example, José Ricardo from the Balé Folclórico da Bahia has composed music and toured with Viver Brasil, and both Rosângela Silvestre and Vera Passos teach dances of the *Orixás* as well as Silvestre technique to Viver Brasil's workshop participants. Dona Cici has traveled numerous times to Los Angeles to share her extensive knowledge with Viver Brasil dancers as a cultural associate and consultant. She recognizes that for Viver Brasil to re-member, honor and continue representing the *Orixás*, the performers must understand that Yoruba philosophy allows, even encourages, artists to recreate fluidly. Viver Brasil, Yudin repeats, does more than perform what can be considered, and even criticized as "exoticism," it "educates its audiences and honors the African ancestry that was so resiliently recreated in Bahia" (2008). Viver Brasil creates critical places of inclusion of African-descendent peoples, facilitating visibility through dance (especially in large performance venues), and courageously negotiating collaborations with socially conscious individuals based on memory and the ethics of human rights.

Veteran Viver Brasil dancer Shelby Williams-Gonzalez has taken Dona Cici's teachings to heart. Her choreography, *Revealed* (2016) inspired by conversations with Dona Cici and Linda Yudin, exposes a concern that Shelby, an African American performer, could not leave at home, off stage. Shelby noted that as she was going into the studio to choreograph and

Figure 12: Dona Cici and Linda Yudin, photograph by Christian Cravo, courtesy of Lucía M. Suárez archive.

rehearse a new piece centered on the stories of the *Orixás*, she could not stop thinking of, or feeling, the violence that was receiving nationwide attention at that time. She stated, "[w]'ve had these horrific incidents of violence in Louisiana, Missouri, and Texas. The media attention and the Black Lives Matter movement underscore a present-day fight for racial justice, which is taking hold across the country" (Williams-Gonzalez 2016).[44] At home she was reading about the systematic marginalization of black people in the United States, recalling how this was also true in Brazil. She brought this news information to company rehearsals.

The first day, they talked about the education and the achievement gap that state wide tests are showing: both African Americans and Latinos in the United States are scoring very low. Before the rehearsal on July 9, 2016, she had read that sixteen black people had been killed by police. By the third rehearsal, she was further disconcerted by the news of the police shooting in Dallas. The discussion-based choreographic process gave her and the dancers a sense of belonging actively in the world around them; the dance piece, she felt, needed to focus on bringing the *Orixás* to the present, in the United States. She needed to bring this reality into the dance. Before the first performance, Shelby asked all to dance the piece with the following intention: "Think about what we are taking away from this experience. What will happen tomorrow, for the black women in the group, for all of us? How can we be responsible to our communities?" (Yudin 2016).

Revealed was presented in the Moves After Dark program of the Los Angeles Music Center, which brings contemporary dance to unconventional spaces in Los Angeles. Linda Yudin and Shelby Williams-Gonzalez chose to perform the site-specific piece on the grand staircase inside The Music Center's Dorothy Chandler Pavilion. They were inspired by the 1960s opulent setting and felt that the stately space would enliven the intended choreography. Yudin and Shelby discussed their desire to find a way to blend and retell the stories of the Three Wives of Xangô (Oxum, Iansã, and Obá), not as women vying for their one husband's attentions, but as women and mothers being supportive of each other.[45]

> Iansã, warrior goddess of the winds and ancestral world who possesses the ability to sever the life line; Oxum, queen of the sweet waters, protector of children, beauty and the essence of self-love; and Obá, robust hunter goddess of the earth, symbol of renewal and independence – remove their crowns and test their powers as mothers and activists responding to the very real human demands in the face of current racially charged violence, the senseless dying of black and brown youth (Dorothy Chandler Pavilion 2016).

Through the choreography, the female divinities are "revealed" both as *Orixás*, who are powerful forces of nature, and as hurt and distressed women, losing their children. Because they (like the choreographer, director, and dancers) are witnessing the social inequity occurring in the United States, where black and brown bodies are still dying in extraordinary numbers, they come to offer sympathy and healing. The dance is accompanied by live musicians and a script that is read in English and Portuguese, connecting the two national communities through language and a shared concern for black and brown lives.

This performance piece, set in an opulent 1960s decorated theater, recalls the lavish spaces for dance audiences' eyes that folkloric dance performances occupied in Bahia during that decade. In contrast, however, these dancers are neither hidden nor defined by the folkloric stories that render invisible their personal lives. In this new context, the dancers have an interactive presence. As the *Orixás* remove their luxurious costumes on stage, they are transformed into ordinary women. As women, they have a new narrative to tell, shifting the staged folklore of the past into a political response to a racially charged reality in the present that afflicts both Brazil and the United States. The *Los Angeles Times* reviewed the piece positively, noting:

> Four Brazilian goddesses, danced by Gonzalez, Laila Abdullah, Rachel Hernandez and Nagodè Simpson, twirled in sequined hoopskirts with exuberance and joy, while four women in black hoodies brooded over something far more serious. With names like "Trayvon," "Michael" and "Tamir" emblazoned on the backs of their jackets, the dancers alluded to the Black Lives Matter movement – but the dancing itself made an even more powerful political statement. A glowing Abdullah emanated elegance, grace and power with every sweep of her dress, every wave of her arm, every bend of her back, embodying the strength and resilience needed to mend broken ties, heal fractured bodies and reconcile fraught relationships (Campodonico 2016).

Figure 13: *Revealed*, Shelby Williams-Gonzalez. Photograph by and courtesy of Ivan Kashinsky.

In Candomblé tradition, the color black is rarely used in dressing the *Orixás*; however, in this choreography, dancers who represent the dead are dressed in black to underscore racial inequity as a visible impasse that blocks people, negates citizenship, and jeopardizes civil and human rights. The *Orixás* intervene on earth as women, as mothers, mourning their murdered children, protecting and caring for those who suffer; thus, the pantheon of stories about women enlarges. For Yudin, *Revealed* represents a "giant leap for the company of stepping beyond the archetype, reinterpreting this ancient wisdom as it relates to our very urgent contemporary reality" (2016).

Afro-Bahian ritual memory, staged as a commercial enterprise in conversation with contemporary issues, is a spectacle that potentially reaches large audiences and creates spaces of dialogue. Through this creative, performative, and defiant process, different bodies can negotiate their place in the world, gain cultural agency, understand their worth in the world, and demand respect for their lives. Consequently, negative news that over-sensationalize cases as the norm, like Kelly Cyclone and neighborhood violence, are actively countered by multilayered stories of tradition, honor, and resilience. Choreography tells new stories of empowerment and resilience; dance practitioners refocus our attention to what is possible and what can change.

Conclusion

Bahia has been narrated as a place of origins. This performative label makes possible the valuation of Afro-Bahian, Indigenous, Portuguese, and syncretic practices, through the vital labor of dance practitioners, cultivating education and civil rights through dance. Other examples, such as Fundação Cultural do Estado da Bahia (FUNCEB), The Dance School of the Cultural Foundation of the State of Bahia, and independent movements, such as the Dançando Nossas Matrizes Group (Dancing our Matrix, also translated as Dancing Our Roots), all confirm an artistically sophisticated and politically active community of dance culture in Bahia, which is critical precisely because of the local social work and the global connections Bahian dancers and choreographers create through performance and education.

The washer-women's stories of Bahia have underscored a dominant, disempowering narrative: longstanding subjugation at the hands of the typically light-skinned, middle and upper classes continues to deprecate a dark-skinned, middle and lower class. Inclusion remains a long and slow process. While people from different African nations, who practice their own religions, such as Candomblé (Ketu from the Yoruba practice of the *Orixá*, Jeje primarily from Vodoun or Vodun in Benin, and Angola mostly from Angolan and Congolese areas focused on *Nkisis*), are fundamental groups in Bahia, their actual presence in the Brazilian imaginary is still not fully recognized. At the same time that the dances of the *Orixás* are a mainstay of Bahia's economy, the practitioners of the real religions remain excluded from the national census.

For the last 70 years, staged *Orixá* dances and stories have provided a platform of creativity and flexibility for cultural survival and for healing from the violence of exclusion and negation. These dance translations, from the space of ritual to the proscenium of performance, are full of *axé* and positive vibrations, but do not reproduce ritual ceremony. Instead, the *Orixá* dances and stories, culled from Yoruba philosophy, affirm the value of ancient wisdom, inform contemporary life, and provide a source of emotional, psychological, and political strength to continue in the presence of non-stop violence and injustice.

Dona Cici reminds her students that they have permission to be dance and music artists, concerned about the world in which they live and create. The *pedagogia da realidade* that she regularly refers to is applicable to local community centers and national and international stages. This means that choreographers, dancers, and teachers can, and perhaps should, be arts social activists. For example, the *Revealed* choreography in Viver Brasil's performances re-narrates the stories of the *Orixás*, highlighting women as a foundational support system, offering their understanding and compassion, as well as underscoring their fierce presence.

This essay has described the work of storytelling and dance, cultivating Afro-Bahian memory as one of expansive humanistic efforts. African origin storytelling and Afro-Brazilian dance, I reiterate, are political acts of major importance in the education and survival of African-descendent cultural memory and also in the education and survival of black lives in Bahia and beyond. Historically contextualized, the commercial drive for tourism has propelled Afro-Bahian bodies, images, and beliefs onto the international stage, offering African-descendent rhythms, rituals, and symbols a place in Brazil's national imaginary. Yet, this presence in the national imagery has not meant equality or inclusion in the national body politic. Expressed in Bahian performances, the stories of the *Orixás* produce a fertile ground for African Diaspora legacies that enforce the inclusion of black and brown bodies. The lives in these bodies are otherwise debased and marginalized by harsh reality stories of violence, which are over-represented and sensationalized by the mass media. Through the possibilities that are facilitated by performance, individuals like Negrizú have discovered their personal heritages, sought knowledge, and reaffirmed a cultural and socio-political history of great importance. Original choreographies such as *Revealed* strategically use performance as a venue that resists a historically and nationally, degrading, and dominant discourse against African-descendent culture and thus negotiates constructive ways of viewing and valuing black lives.

Circles of collaboration, generated by memory bearers and cultural dance agents such as Dona Cici, Pierre Verger, Negrizú, Luiz Badaró, and Linda Yudin, attest to the critical place of African-origin and Afro-Bahian memory, and dance movement arts in the processes of cultural and socio-political inclusion. Accordingly, Afro-Brazilian storytelling and the hard work of dance function as effective platforms from which to advocate for healing, connections, and respect of black and brown lives. While real life tragedies like the Kelly Cyclone story dominate fast sound-bite media profiles, many more uplifting stories of survival, resistance, and success exist. True stories, such as the ones in this essay of creative collaborations, refocus our attention to community coalition building and human rescue. As a result, within a larger socio-political framework, the fight for equality and human rights is shared, and does not fall only on the shoulders of black and brown people.

References

Albuquerque, Severino and Bishop-Sanchez, Kathryn (eds) (2015), *Performing Brazil: Essays on Culture, Identity, and the Performing Arts*, Madison: University of Wisconsin Press.

Alexander, Simone A. James (2014), *African Diasporic Women's Narratives: Politics of Resistance, Survival, and Citizenship*, Gainesville: University Press of Florida.

Asante, Kariamu Welsh (1994), *African Dance: An Artistic Historical and Philosophical Inquiry*, New Jersey and Eritrea: Africa World Press, Inc.

Avelar, Idelbar and Dunn, Christopher (eds) (2011), *Brazilian Popular Music and Citizenship*, Durham and London: Duke University Press.

Boal, Augusto (1985), *Theatre of the Oppressed*, New York: Theatre Communications Group.

Browning, Barbara (1995), *Samba: Resistance in Motion*, Bloomington: Indiana University Press.

Butler, Kim (2000), *Freedoms Given, Freedoms Won: Afro-Brazilians in Post-Abolition São Paulo and Salvador*, New Brunswick and London: Rutgers University Press.

Campodonico, Christina (2016), "Review: Moves After Dark dancers turn the Grand Park fountain (and more) into a splashy stage," *Los Angeles Times*, 9 August, http://www.latimes.com/entertainment/arts/la-et-cm-moves-after-dark-review-20160808-snap-story.html. Accessed January 19, 2018.

Carneiro, Edison (1948), *Candomblés da Bahia*, Salvador: Editora do Museu do Estado da Bahia.

—— ([1936] 1963), *Religiões Negras*, Rio de Janeiro: Editora Civilização Brasileira.

Cici, Dona (2008), interview with Lucía M. Suárez, Bahia, July.

—— (2010), interview with Lucía M. Suárez, Los Angeles, March.

—— (2011), interview with Lucía M. Suárez, Bahia, July and August.

Daniel, Yvonne (1996), "Dance performance in tourist settings: Authenticity and creativity," *Annals of Tourism Research*, 23:4, pp. 780–97.

—— (2005), *Dancing Wisdom: Embodied Knowledge in Haitian Vodou, Cuban Yoruba, and Bahian Candomblé*, Urbana and Chicago: University of Illinois Press.

D'Houbler, Margaret ([1940] 1985), *Dance: A Creative Art Experience*, Madison: University of Wisconsin Foundation.

Dixon Gottschild, Brenda ([2003] 2005), *The Black Dancing Body: A Geography from Coon to Cool*, New York: Palgrave Macmillan.

Dorothy Chandler Pavilion (2016), *Revealed*, Moves After Dark Series, program notes, Los Angeles Music Center, Los Angeles, Summer.

Ford Amphitheatre (2004), *Legends of Brazil*, program notes in *Discover Hollywood*, Los Angeles County Arts Commission, Los Angeles, Summer.

Freire, Paulo ([1970] 2012), *Pedagogy of the Oppressed*, New York and London: Continuum.

Fundação Pierre Verger (n.d.), "Homepageen," http://www.pierreverger.org/en/homepageen-2.html. Accessed April 4, 2016.

Giroux, Henry A. (2001), *Theory and Resistance in Education: Towards a Pedagogy for the Opposition*, Westport and London: Bergin and Garvey.

Guerreiro, Goli (2000), *A Trama dos Tambores: A Música Afro-Pop de Salvador*, São Paulo: Editora 34.

Handler, Richard and Saxton, William (1988), "Dissimulation: Reflexivity, narration, and the quest for authenticity in 'Living History'," *Cultural Anthropology*, 3, pp. 242–60.

Höffling, Ana Paula (2015), "Staging Capoeira, Samba, *Maculelê*, and *Candomblé*: Viva Bahia's choreographies of Afro-Brazilian folklore for the global stage," in Severino Albuquerque and Kathryn Bishop-Sanchez (eds), *Performing Brazil: Essays on Culture, Identity, and the Performing Arts*, Madison: University of Wisconsin Press, pp. 98–125.

Holston, James (2009), *Insurgent Citizenship: Disjunctions of Democracy and Modernity in Brazil (In-Formation)*, Princeton, NJ: Princeton University Press.

hooks, bell (1994), *Teaching to Transgress: Education as the Practice of Freedom*, New York and London: Routledge.

Ickes, Scott (2013), *African-Brazilian Culture and Regional Identity in Bahia, Brazil*, Gainesville: University Press of Florida.

Johnson, Paul Christopher (2002), *Secrets, Gossip, and Gods: The Transformation of Brazilian Candomblé*, Oxford: Oxford University Press.

Kaeppler, Adrienne (1973), "Polynesian dance as 'airplane art'," *Dance Research Journal*, 8, pp. 71–85.

Kraay, Hendrik (1998), *Afro-Brazilian Culture and Politics: Bahia, 1790s to 1990s*, Armonk and London: M.E. Sharpe.

Landes, Ruth ([1947] 1994), *The City of Women*, Albuquerque: University of New Mexico Press.

Lühning, Angela (1999), "Pierre Fatumbi Verger: A view from Bahia," *Cahiers du Brésil Contemporain*, 38/39, pp. 75–95.

Martins, Suzana (2008), *A Dança de Yemanjá Ogunté: Sob a Perspectiva Estética do Corpo*, Bahia: Governo da Bahia, Fomento à Cultura.

Matory, J. Lorand (2005), *Black Atlantic Religion: Tradition, Transnationalism, and Matriarchy in the Afro-Brazilian Candomblé*, Princeton and Oxford: Princeton University Press.

Maxwell, Richard (ed.) (2001), *Culture Works: The Political Economy of Culture*, Minneapolis and London: University of Minnesota Press.

Militão, Wilson and Passos Pereira, Manoel (2007), *Povo de Santo*, Brazil Núcleo Omi-Dudu and Fundação Cultural Palmares do Ministério da Cultura.

Murphy, Ann (2012), "The DNA of dance," *Mills Quarterly*, XCX: 4, pp. 10–13.

Negrizú (2010), interview with Lucía M. Suárez, Bahia, July.

Nettleford, Rex (1994), "Foreword," in *African Dance: An Artistic Historical and Philosophical Inquiry*, Trenton and Asmara: Africa World Press, Inc.

Reiter, Bernd and Simmons, Kimberly Eison (eds) (2012), *Afro-Descendants, Identity, and the Struggle for Development in the Americas*, East Lansing: Michigan State University Press.

Robatto, Lia and Macarenhas, Lúcia (2002), *Passos da Dança Bahia*, Bahia: Governo da Bahia.

Romo, Anadelia A. (2010), *Brazil's Living Museum: Race, Reform, and Tradition in Bahia*, Chapel Hill: The University of North Carolina Press.

Rosa, Cristina F. (2015), *Brazilian Bodies and Their Choreographies of Identification: Swing Nation*, London: Palgrave Macmillan UK.

de Santana Pinho, Patricia (2010), *Mama Africa: Reinventing Blackness in Bahia*, Durham and London: Duke University Press.

Scott, James C. (1990), *Domination and the Arts of Resistance: Hidden Transcripts*, New Haven and London: Yale University Press.

Secretariat of Tourism of the State of Bahia (2009), *African Heritage Tourism in Bahia*, Salvador: Fundação Pedro Calmon.

Siqueira, Maria de Lourdes (2006), *Imagens Negras: Ancestralidade, diversidade, e educação*, Belo Horizonte: Mazza Edições Ltda.

Sommer, Doris (ed.) (2006), *Cultural Agency in the Americas*, Durham and London: Duke University Press.

——— (2014), *The Work of Art in the World: Civic Agency and Public Humanities*, Durham: Duke University Press.

Soulages, François and de Carvalho Olivieri, Alberto Freire, Barreto Biriba, Ricardo, Silva, Ariadne Moraes (eds) (2010), *O sensível contemporâneo*, Salvador: Federal University of Bahia.

Suárez. Lucía M. (2013), "Inclusion in motion: Cultural agency through dance in Bahia, Brazil," *Transforming Anthropology*, 21:2, pp. 152–68.

Taylor, Diana (2003), *The Archive and the Repertoire: Performing Cultural Memory in the Americas*, Durham and London: Duke University Press.

Thompson, Robert Farris (1974), *African Art in Motion: Icon and Act*, Berkeley and Los Angeles: University of California Press.

Verger, Pierre (1968), *Flux et Reflux de la Traite des Nègres entre le Golfe de Bénin et Bahia de Todos os Santos du XVIIe au XIXe Siècle*, Paris: Mouton & Co and École Pratique des Hautes Études.

——— (2006), *African Legends of the Orishas*, English ed., Bahia: Corrupio.

Williams-Gonzalez, Shelby (2016), phone interview with Lucía M. Suárez, Amherst/LA, August.

Yudin, Linda (2008), interview with Lucía M. Suárez, Bahia, August.

——— (2016), conversation with Lucía M. Suárez, Amherst/LA, August.

Notes

1 See historian Anadelia A. Romo's study, *Brazil's Living Museum: Race, Reform, and Tradition in Bahia*, which argues that Bahia has been culturally crafted throughout the twentieth century and is, therefore, not a static cultural preserve, but a "living museum" of constant historical and traditional development and transitions.

2 News coverage reported that Kelly Cyclone had taken another name in honor of one of her lovers, Bombado Doçura, a percussionist for Saiddy Bamba, and was called Kelly Doçura, "Kelly Sweetness" because cocaine is supposed to be sweet. See massive exposure on YouTube and Facebook about Kelly's life and death.

3 See, LiveLeak.com, last accessed, July 2016.

4 *Axé* is a popular music genre started in Salvador da Bahia in the 1980s. It fuses Afro-Caribbean and Brazilian music styles. *Pagode* is another popular Brazilian music style, which originated in Rio de Janeiro as a sub-genre of *samba*.

5 See anthropologist James Holston's theory of insurgent citizenship by which defiance and violence are a way of being seen as part of a social body politic from which many have been excluded (2009).

6 Robert Farris Thompson's seminal study, *African Art in Motion*, has generated many such "in motion" titles.

7 In the interviews, Dona Cici talks about Obatalá. She explains that the family of Obatalá includes 152 *Orixá* personalities, but many of the names have been lost over time. Obatalá is the elder in this lineage. He is considered to be very wise and compassionate. His children, i.e., those dedicated to him, are "godchildren," and would have the same traits. Dona Cici would have these presumably male attributes and she would also have traits of Oxum and Ewa, two divinities who are identified with a strong sense of womanliness and sensuality (for Oxum) and a fierce, proud, and principled female warrior (for Ewa). As their godchild also, Dona Cici would have a strong sense of womanly power and principled fighting characteristics as well.

8 She also holds the title of *Otun Iyá Ilê Fun* (one who paints the sacred designs in the initiation ceremonies).

9   Ifá is one of several African divining systems; it comes from Yoruba heritage and *babalawos* are the priests who perform the complex divining procedures that govern the lives of *iyalorixás, babalorixás*, (mothers and fathers of the saints or divinities), plus other initiates who participate jointly as extended families in *terreiro* households, compounds, and communities.

10   Verger published in the London *Daily Mirror* (1935–36), *Argentina Libre, El Mundo Argentino* (1941–42, while he lived there), and in the Brazilian magazines *O Cruzeiro* (1946–51) and *O Cruzeiro Internacional* (1954–57) (Lühning 1999: 77).

11   After 20 years of extensive research and writing, Verger defended his dissertation, "Flux et Reflux du Traffic des Esclaves entre le Golf du Bénin et la Baie de Tous les Saints," in 1966 at la Sorbonne, thus becoming a doctor of African studies (Lühning 1999: 75). The consequent 1968 book, *Flux et Reflux de la Traite des Nègres entre le Golfe de Bénin et Bahia de Todos os Santos* was translated into English in 1976, and eventually into Portuguese and published by Corrupio in Bahia, Brazil in 1987 (Pierre Verger Foundation Web Page: 3, accessed, September 26, 2013).

12   Carybé, aka Héctor Julio Páride Bernabó, was born in Argentina. His family moved to Brazil when he was 8 years old, and he became a Brazilian national (officially naturalized). He is often referred to as the most Bahian of all Brazilians. The connections and far reach of Afro-Bahian art and culture are evinced by the purchase of his artwork by Miami Dade Community College in Miami, Florida, to represent plural cultures in motion, connected, and thriving.

13   All translations are the author's unless otherwise noted. They are loose translations meant to best capture the meaning of what was said.

14   Interview with the author, Bahia, July 2010.

15   Personal conversation with Angela Lühning, Bahia, July 2011.

16   See https://www.youtube.com/watch?v=OBKdp79WIbc. Accessed April 1, 2018.

17   Conversations with the author, August 2011, Bahia. Informants have asked to remain anonymous and many may no longer be at the Center.

18   Pontos de Cultura were introduced by the Lula government in 2003, by noted musician and political activist Gilberto Gil. A native of Bahia, and founder of the *Tropicalia* Movement, Gil was the Minister of Culture from 2003 to 2008. He brought international attention and respect to all aspects of popular culture and national politics. One of his most important moves was to integrate the Pontos de Cultura initiative into federal sponsorship. Placed within the Ministry of Culture's Cultura Viva Program, Pontos aimed to contribute "to the creation of a grass-root digital ecosystem, promoting culture, education, and citizenship" (See http://studytourbrazil.wordpress.com/rio-de-janeiro).

19   In 2003, President Luiz Inácio da Silva (Lula) and the Brazilian legislation officially altered the 1996 Law No. 9.394 (the initial law, which "asked for" inclusion of Afro-Brazilian history in public curricula). It was expected that steps would be taken to implement the law so it would not remain a good intention stifled by a historically corrupt system. On March 17 of the same year, UNESCO representative in Brazil – Vincent Defourny – and the dean of Universidade Federal de San Carlos – Targino Araújo Filho – signed an agreement consciously implementing Law No. 10.639. The agreement confirmed a commitment

to the education of African history in Brazil. It also intended guarantees of political and educational action through a web of socio-political, national, and international education actors that include: UNESCO, UFScar, NGO Acción Educativa, the Centro de Estudios de las Relaciones de Trabajo y Desigualdades, the Education Programme for Racial and Gender Equality of the Center for East African Studies, and Save the Children UK, among others. The March meeting and its resulting memorandum concretely identified ways in which to implement the law, with both financial funding and cultural collaborations.

20 https://opendata.unesco.org/. Accessed April 1, 2018.

21 Interview with author, Bahia, summer, 2011.

22 Several books on dance and education exist in Brazil, in Portuguese. These include Martins (2008) and Robatto and Lúcia (2002), and Siqueira (2006). Translations are needed to make such studies accessible to larger international audiences. In English, Margaret H'Doubler spearheaded dance in education with the first degree-granting program at the University of Wisconsin in 1926 and writing her seminal theories in 1940. For one example of dance department development at the college and university level in the United States, see dance historian Ann Murphy's brief summary of Mills College, another pioneering dance department in the United States (2012: 10–13).

23 This was an ethnographic study initially sold as travel literature. Landes shares observations and lived experiences from her year of fieldwork in Bahia, Brazil (1938–39). At the time of her research, there were two major interpretative frameworks through which to study African American culture in the United States: "One measures the degree of assimilation into white American society, … and [the other] … look[s] to Africa to explain cultural differences between African Americans and whites" (Sally Cole, in Landes [1947] 1994: xxii). Raimundo Nina Rodrigues's school of ethnologists in Brazil also studied the differences, which incited numerous controversies around inclusion and exclusion of representation, voice, and authenticity. Landes's work was groundbreaking in that it presented a third framework for the study of Afro-Brazilian customs. She "believed that she was studying a new living Brazilian religion, and she wanted to portray Candomblé as fully integrated in the way of life of the urban poor of Bahia" (Cole in Landes [1947] 1994: xxii).

24 Edison Carneiro is renowned for his work detailing and honoring Afro-Bahian religious culture and Candomblé communities. He wrote over eleven books, which include *Religiões Negras* (Editora Civilização Brasileira, [1936] 1963) and *Candomblés da Bahia* (Editora do Museu do Estado da Bahia, 1948).

25 "Obá Dudu quer festa com harmonia," *Jornal da Bahia*, February 13, 1988.

26 Fittipaldi, Maristela (1992), "No compasso dos orixás," July 28.

27 According to legend, "Eshu [Exú] is the subtlest and cleverest of all the orishas" (Verger 2006: 11). He is considered the trickster because he likes to play tricks on people. If homage is duly paid to him, he is also generous and fair; however, if he is dishonored or lied to, then he can be very, very cruel.

28 Produced in 1990, *Mãe de Santo* ("Priestess" in the Afro-Brazilian religions) was a television miniseries in sixteen episodes about the *Orixás*. *Mae de Santo* was not favorably received by the Bahian public because it was considered bad and inauthentic programming. In the

local newspaper, *A Tarde, Caderno 2* (Friday, October 19, 1990), journalist Hamilton Vieira gave an explicit description of the situation through a series of interviews. For example, Waldeloir Rego, ethnologist and ogan (a type of ritual specialist) at the Ilê Axé Opô Afonjá (one of the most respected Candomblé temples in Bahia), complained emphatically that the text was weak and replete with interpretative errors in Candomblé rituals. He complained that the deity Iansã was erroneously represented as hyper-sexual and immoral. He denounced the series and suggested that official institutions such as The Center for the Study of African-Oriental Studies at UFBA and the Bahian Federation of Afro-Brazilian Cults should protest against the performance airing. Ildásio Tavares, professor of African literature at the university, also an *ogan* at the Ilê Axé Opô Afonjá, criticized the script's language, claiming that it was antiquated, unlike the contemporary way of speaking and interrelating in today's temples. His judgment was so piercing that he called the series a profanation of the religion of the *Orixás* that rendered a false image of life in Bahia.

Despite its brief run of one month, *Mãe de Santo* made a notable impact, creating a space for discussions about the differences among the numerous African religious settings, and debate about who the actors, interpreters, and representatives of this important part of Brazilian culture should be.

29 Vieira, Hamilton (1990), "Mãe de Santo: Série provoca polêmica nos terreiros," *A Tarde Caderno*, sexta feira, October 19.

30 Bandu is the well-regarded *capoeira* master of Bahia's Garcia neighborhood, a noted home of *capoeiristas*.

31 I have coined this term to underline the staging of something as native and original, when, in fact, this kind of representation conforms to the needs and expectations of a tourist industry that wants to experience a certain kind of other. See also Handler (1988), Daniel (1996), Kaeppler (1973).

32 See performance program, "Bahia Land of Magic" in *Discover Hollywood*, Los Angeles: Ford Amphitheatre, Los Angeles County Arts Commission, insert, Summer 2003.

33 Phone interview with author, Amherst/LA, August 2016.

34 Phone interview with author, Amherst/LA, August 2016.

35 Sir Nettleford (February 3, 1933–February 2, 2010) was also a social critic and vice-chancellor emeritus of the University of the West Indies (UWI).

36 These, however, do not exist without further representative and ideological divisions. For example, Ilê Aiyê gets criticized for being exclusionary based on phenotype.

37 For an informative history of (founding director) Emília Biancardi's Viva Bahia and its early stagings, see Höffling (2015: 98–125).

38 Interview with author, Bahia, July 2010.

39 Clyde Morgan interview with the author, Amherst, Massachusetts, May 11, 2013.

40 Continued stigma against dance for upper and middle class men in Brazil meant that Morgan had to seek dancers, or trainable young men, outside of the university setting. Most were poor from the countryside and marginal neighborhoods. Interview with author, Amherst, September 2010.

41 In June 2007, during a company rehearsal in Bahia as dancers were practicing a *capoeira* sequence, Botelho insisted that they bring the energy of their neighborhoods to the stage.

42 It is impossible here to give complete recognition to the many dance companies and artistic directors that are pivotal to dance in Brazil; my next project attends to that challenge in book form. For now, another award-winning company that must be mentioned is Dance Brazil, directed by Jelon Vieira.

43 *Afoxés* are, like *blocos afro*, Carnival music and dance organizations; *afoxés* use mainly Candomblé percussion instruments; while *blocos afro* mainly use *samba* and non-ritual instrumentation.

44 Interview with author, Bahia, August 2011.

45 The referenced movement was born in 2013 after a Florida jury acquitted George Zimmerman of second-degree murder in the shooting death of African-American teenager Trayvon Martin. National outcries reacting to the un-punished murders of African Americans by police brutality initiated what many today see as a second civil rights movement called "Black Lives Matter."

Notes on Contributors

Amélia Conrado (Amélia Vitória de Souza Conrado) received her post-doctorate in arts from the University of Paris (2011), a Ph.D. in education from the Federal University of Bahia (UFBA 2007) and is currently professor at the Federal University of Bahia's School of Dance. She is also a researcher at the International Group Recherches sur Esthétiques & Théorétiques Nouvelles Images & Anciennes (RETINA) of Latin America and with Grupo de Pesquisa em Culturas Indígenas, Repertórios Afro-brasileiros e populares (GIRA) (Research Group in Indigenous Cultures, Afro-Brazilian, and Popular Repertoires) in Brazil. Her choreography is regularly performed by the internationally renowned dance company, Balé Folclórico da Bahia, and she has presented extensively on the ground breaking work of *bloco afro,* Ilê Aiyê.

Yvonne Payne Daniel is professor emerita of dance and Afro-American studies from Smith College. She is a specialist in dance performance and Caribbean and Afro-Latin societies. After earning her Ph.D. in anthropology, she published three paradigm shifting studies: *Rumba: Dance and Social Change in Contemporary Cuba* (1995); *Dancing Wisdom: Embodied Knowledge in Haitian Vodou, Cuban Yoruba, and Bahian Candomblé* (2005); and *Caribbean and Atlantic Diaspora Dance: Igniting Citizenship* (2011). She has produced four documentary videos on Caribbean dance and African Diaspora religions and is credited with over 40 articles, encyclopedia entries, and chapters. Her book on sacred performance won the de la Torre Bueno prize from the Society of Dance History Scholars for best dance research of 2006. She is a Ford fellow, a Rockefeller fellow, and has been a visiting scholar at Mills College and the Smithsonian Institution. In 2018, she received the life achievement award for research on Black dance from the International Association of Black Dance (IABD). Dr. Daniel continues to publish and gives presentations in both academic and community settings.

Pilar Echeverry Zambrano received her Ph.D. from the School of Education at the Federal University of Bahia (Universidade Federal da Bahia). She is an anthropologist who also trained in dance. As a researcher, she focuses on the study of the body and dance in contemporary contexts and alternative education in Latin America. She has been awarded a fellowship from the National Council for Scientific and Technologic Development (Conselho Nacional de Desenvolvimento Científico e Tecnológico or CNPq).

Nadir Nóbrega Oliveira received her Masters and Ph.D. in performing arts from the graduate program in performing arts of the Federal University of Bahia (Universidade Federal da Bahia or UFBA). She is adjunct professor of dance studies and general director of the Museu Théo Brandão de Antropologia e Folclore da UFAL (Théo Brandão Museum of Anthropology and Folklore at the Federal University of Alagoas, UFAL). Her publications include: *Sou Negona, Sim Senhora! Um olhar nas práticas espetaculares dos blocos afro Ilê Aiyê, Olodum, Malê Debalê e Bankoma no carnaval soteropolitano* (2017), *Agô Alafiju, Odara! A presença de Clyde Wesley Morgan na Escola de Dança da UFBA, 1971–1978* (2007), and *Dança Afro: Sincretismo do Movimentos* (1992).

Jeff Packman received his Ph.D. in ethnomusicology at the University of California, Berkeley. He is now an assistant professor in the divisions of performance and history/ Culture at the University of Toronto's Faculty of Music. With support from the Fulbright Program and Canada's Social Sciences and Humanities Research Council, he has conducted extensive fieldwork in Bahia, Brazil since 2002. His research on professional music making, cultural politics, and discourses of race and socio-economic class in Bahia's capital, Salvador, has appeared in several journals, including *Ethnomusicology*, *Black Music Research Journal*, and *Latin American Music Review*.

Danielle Robinson received her Ph.D. in dance history and theory at the University of California, Riverside. She is an associate professor of dance at York University in Toronto, Canada, where she is cross-appointed with the graduate programs in theatre studies and Communication/Culture. She is the author of *Modern Moves: Blackness and American Ragtime Dancing* (Oxford University Press, 2015). Her scholarly work on the intercultural movement of African Diasporic popular dance has been published in *Dance Theatre Journal* (UK), *Dance Research Journal* (USA), *Dance Chronicle* (USA), *Dance Research* (UK), and *Research in Dance Education* (UK). From 2011 to 2012 she was a Leverhulme Trust visiting fellow at the University of Chichester (UK).

Lucía M. Suárez received her Ph.D. in cultural studies from the program in literature at Duke University. She is currently associate professor of Spanish and Latinx studies and director of the Latino/a studies program in the Department of World Languages and Cultures at Iowa State University. Her research on dance in Brazil is featured in "Bodies, Brazil, and dance: An overview" (2002) in *Speaking of Dance*; "Dance and citizenship in urban Brazil: *Grupo Corpo*, a case study" (2010) in *Rhythms of the Afro-Atlantic World: Rituals and Remembrances*; and "Inclusion in motion: Cultural agency through dance in Bahia, Brazil" (2013) in *Transforming Anthropology*. She is the author of *The Tears of Hispaniola: Haitian and Dominican Diaspora Memory* (University Press of Florida, 2006) and the co-editor of *The Portable Island: Cubans at Home in the World* (with Ruth Behar, Palgrave Macmillan, 2008). In 2011, she was a Peggy Rockefeller visiting scholar at The David Rockefeller Center for Latin American Studies (DRCLAS), Harvard University.

Deborah A. Thomas received her Ph.D. in anthropology from New York University. She is R. Jean Brownlee term professor of anthropology and Africana studies at the University of Pennsylvania. She is the author of *Exceptional Violence: Embodied Citizenship in Transnational Jamaica* (2011) and *Modern Blackness: Nationalism, Globalization, and The Politics of Culture in Jamaica* (2004), and is co-editor of the volume *Globalization and Race: Transformations in the Cultural Production of Blackness* (2006). She also directed and produced the documentary film *Bad Friday: Rastafari after Coral Gardens* (2011).

Piedade Lino Videira received her doctorate in Brazilian education in the *Stricto Sensu* post-graduate program within the Department of Education at the Federal University of Ceará (2010). She is an adjunct professor of pedagogy at the Federal University of Amapá (UNIFAP). Dr. Videira works with an emphasis on identity and ethno-cultural diversity in education, arts education, *Quilombo* education, education research, and ethno-racial culture in Brazil. Her published works include *Marabaixo, Dança Afrodescendente: Significando a Identidade Étnica do Negro Amapaense* (2009), and *Batuques, Folias e Ladainhas: A Cultura do Quilombo do Cria-ú em Macapá e sua Educação* (2012).

Index

authenticity, 129–130, 197–198
Axé music, 3–4, 128
Azevedo, Thales de, 176

B
Bacnaré (Black Culture Ballet of Recife), 29–30
Badaró, Luiz, 173, 192–194, 198–200
Badaró, Raimundo José, 193
Badauê, 57
Bahia
  Afro-Bahian knowledge and, 5–6
  as key site for Afro-Brazilian research, 3–4, 171, 197–198, 205
  map of, *21*
  racism in, 172–173
Bahia Magia, 198, 199
Bakhtin, Mikhail, 80–81
Balé de Cultura Negra do Recife – Bacnaré (Pernambuco), 19
Balé Folclórico da Bahia
  Passos and, 199
  Ricardo and, 201
  role and importance of, 3, 19, 30
  Silvestre and, 157
  training and ethical commitment in, 196–197
  Viver Brasil and, 198
Balé Folclórico Mercedes Baptista (Mercedes Baptista Folkloric Ballet), 28
Balé Popular do Recife (Popular Ballet of Recife), 29
Balé Teatro Castro Alves, 46
bamboulas, 8
Bandu, Mestre, 192–193
Baptista, Mercedes, 27–28, 30, 67n17, 84, 105, 196
Barbosa, Guilherme Santos, 142–143
Barleaus, Gaspar, 20–22
Barreto, Ligia, 156
Bastide, Roger, 176
Battle, DeAma, 157–158
batuque, 100

Biancardi, Emília, 30, 142–143, 147, 198
Bigenho, Michelle, 129
Bispo, Tânia, 59
black activism in Brazil, 5–6, 12, 27–32, 53–60. *See also* Black Lives Matter movement; Law No. 10.639 (2003)
black Catholicism, 100, 108–111
Black Lives Matter movement, 202
"blackness" and "black body"
  African matrix dance and, 79–85, 89–90, 91–92, 100–103
  Creole forms and, 7
  Kelly Cyclone and, 172
  in popular culture, 141
bloco de índios Apache, 57
blocos afros (African blocks)
  African matrix dance and, 85
  black activism and, 52–53, 55, 57–60
  children and, 122
  history and characteristics of, 128
  racism and, 194–196
  role and importance of, 3, 46
  See also Ilê Aiyê
body. *See* "blackness" and "black body"
Botelho, Walson, 30, 196–197
Brasil Tropical, 142
Brazil, *16*, 20, 141, 146–147
Brazilian Institute of Geography and Statistics (Instituto Brasileiro de Geografia e Estatística, IBGE), 97
Brown, James, 51, 189
Buarque de Hollanda, Chico, 46, 54
bumba meu boi, 19
bundas, 50
búzio readings, 173

C
Caboclo, 46–47, 48, 49, 51
Cabrera, Lydia, 176
cacumbis (*cucumbis*), 25, 26
calindas djoubas, 8
Candomblé
  authenticity and, 197–198